HARLEY-DAVIDSON
THE COMPLETE HISTORY

HARLEY-DAVIDSON
THE COMPLETE HISTORY

Edited by
Patrick Hook

PRC

Produced 2002 by
PRC Publishing Ltd,
64 Brewery Road, London N7 9NT

A member of **Chrysalis** Books plc

This edition published 2002
Distributed in the U.S. and Canada by:
Sterling Publishing Co., Inc.
387 Park Avenue South
New York, NY 10016

ISBN 1 85648 656-7

Printed and bound in Taiwan

In his seminal book *Hell's Angels: A Strange and Terrible Saga* about the Angels of the sixties Hunter Thompson points out that for many of the later arrivals in California it "was just another hard dollar" but that the coming of World War II meant that the migrants found work in a suddenly booming labor market. He wrote: "It is easy enough to trace the Hell's Angels mystique—and even their name and emblems—back to the Second World War and Hollywood. But their genes and real history go back a lot farther. The Second World War was not the original California boom but the rebirth of a thing that began in the thirties and was already tapering off when the war economy made California a new Valhalla."

Referring to the work of Nelson Algren entitled *A Walk on the Wild Side* he comments on how Algren's migrant "Linkhorns," for whom drifting was a habit, eventually drifted into California and into well-paid war-economy jobs. His "white trash" were Californians by the time the war ended as a result of either time in the service or laboring in the cities. "When the war ended, California was full of veterans looking for ways to spend their separation bonuses. Many decided to stay on the coast, and while their new radios played hillbilly music they went out and bought big motorcycles—not knowing exactly why, but in the booming, rootless atmosphere of the times, it

ABOVE: A 1936/1937 side-valve UL.

ABOVE LEFT: A single-cylinder machine from the late twenties.

LEFT: A 1935 VLD, which had a side-valve engine of 74cu in (1,200cc).

OVERLEAF: 1936 45cu in (740cc) side-valve WL.

seemed the thing to do." From here it was but a short step from "white trash" to "scooter trash." As Brock Yates wrote in *Outlaw Machine*, "the hard riding, grease stained independent rabble . . . would in a subtly perverse way, ultimately define the image of America's greatest motorcycle."

The first chapter of the Hell's Angels was formed in 1948 in Berdoo —San Bernardino, California. Ralph Hubert "Sonny" Barger, a confirmed descendant of the migrant workforce, was a founder member of the Oakland Chapter soon after. Other clubs followed quickly, and while Barger's club may have ridden east through Oklahoma, the other two major One Percenter clubs are the ones that have charters in Oklahoma City—the Bandidos MC and the Outlaws MC. The Bandidos MC was formed in Texas during 1966 and although strongest in the southern states of the

LEFT: A 1938 80 cu in (1,310cc) side-valve ULH.

ABOVE: A 1939 EL Knucklehead.

US, it has chapters worldwide. The Oklahoma City Chapter of the Outlaws MC is the westernmost chapter of an organization that traces its roots back to thirties' Chicago and currently stretches from Detroit and Chicago to Europe and Australia. Whether the members of these clubs are just hardcore Harley-riding bikers or full-time criminals depends on who is to be believed. Yves Lavigne paints a particularly grim picture in his rancorous books, while others view the bikers more generously.

Writing in the 1991 novel *Against the Wind*, J. F. Freedman sums up the bikers' appeal: "Straight society can't handle the truth they lay on the world so they've got to cut them down, categorize them, call them outlaws. Anyway so what if they are outlaws, that's the American way." Of such outlaws but particularly referring to Charles "Pretty Boy" Floyd and Jesse James, Arlo Guthrie said: "No wonder folks likes to hear songs about the Outlaws—they're wrong all right, but not half as dirty and sneakin' as some of our so-called 'higher-ups.' " So it is

with outlaw bikers; a theme that has echoed down the years. References to bikers abound in both rock and country songs, offering vignettes of a life on the road. Billy Joe Shaver's *Highway of Life* is typical:

"Oh the outlaws they ride
on their two-wheeled monsters
Like a big giant serpent
they glide through the night
Just shakin' their chains
like a diamond back rattler"

Brock Yates writing about the Depression era commented: "From this raw underside of life the [Harley-Davidson] motorcycle emerged as a 'real man's' machine."

The history of the Harley-Davidson marque is both long and proud and begins even before the days of the dustbowl migrations in the first years of the twentieth century.

The beginnings of the now mighty company were distinctly humble. Two of the Davidson brothers, Arthur and Walter, and William S. Harley built a single-cylinder motorcycle that

displaced approximately 10cu in (160cc) in their spare time in 1903. It worked well but lacked hill-climbing ability and so the group built two improved motorcycles in 1904 with the idea of selling them. The Davidson brothers' Aunt Janet pinstriped the finished machines prior to their sale.

So it happened that the surnames of two families, Harley and Davidson, European immigrants to the United States, combined to form one of the most recognized brands of motorcycle in the world. The famous brand Harley-Davidson is now much more than just a motorcycle, it is an American icon, the embodiment of America on two wheels.

The attentions of Hollywood moviemakers has no doubt helped the Harley-Davidson achieve such status. The most prominent are classic movies such as *Easy Rider*, *Electraglide in Blue*, *Mask*, and *The Loveless* among a host of others. These tales of latter-day outlaws and heroes are fascinating and vintage Harley-Davidsons can offer their owners tangible links to those turbulent times of the twentieth century.

ABOVE: A 1970s Shovelhead-engined FLH Electra-Glide.

RIGHT: A late 1970s 74 cu in (1,200 cc) FLH Electra-Glide full dresser.

Riding a Harley-Davidson, made in 1942 and displacing only 45cu in (740cc), is the culmination for the author of a long cherished dream. It combines a fascination with social history, military vehicles, old motorcycles in general, and Harley-Davidsons in particular. After switching the gas tap on, selecting neutral with the hand gear stick, engaging the clutch with the foot-operated lever, adding a touch of choke, twisting the throttle twice, switching the ignition on, and kicking down on the bicycle-type starter pedal with only a 4.75:1 compression ratio the old motorcycle rarely fails to go first kick. By the time the rider has pulled on helmet and gloves, the engine has settled down into the uneven but rhythmic beat that characterizes a 45-degree V-twin.

This type of Harley-Davidson is a WLC, one of approximately 88,000 Harleys made for the Allies in World War II. The designation means it is a military WL produced for the Canadian Army to a standard specification that varied slightly from the American Army's WLA (the C suffix indicates

Canada: the A suffix indicates Army). Suffixes and specifications may be as dry as a school on a summer afternoon, but as the owner of one of these bikes it is more than simply one of 88,000. Who originally rode the bike in those troubled days? Did some grim-faced Canadian despatcher escort the ambulances away from the docks when survivors struggled back into English ports after the debacle at Dieppe? Did some young man from Winnipeg name it after the girlfriend he'd left thousands of miles away? Or did someone ride it daydreaming of a canoe and the cool clear waters of the Algonquin? No-one will ever know but it doesn't stop the present owner from wondering.

Those of us fascinated with the detail of World War II military Harleys will be familiar with the photograph of a Canadian sergeant riding a WLC through a ford "somewhere in England" on a training exercise. The first time I saw the 45 that was to become mine I was strongly reminded of this photograph. The former owner arrived at a vintage rally one Sunday morning on the original looking

machine. Restored but not overdone, it had almost all the requisite genuine parts including the additional toolbox on top of the front mudguard that instantly identifies it as a Canadian-specification machine. Both front and rear stands were fitted, as were Canadian pattern lights, and wedged under the seat was a "For Sale" sign. I just had to have it. Monday morning I arranged some finance, the words "Harley-Davidson" did it, and the finance company, no doubt assuming I was considerably richer than I actually was, sent me away with a cheque.

Once the bike was unloaded from the hire van I learned to ride it on the lane that runs away from my house. The hand-shift and foot clutch arrangement is easier than it looks because the foot pedal for the clutch can be left in the disengaged position allowing the left foot to be put down at intersections. The low seat height helps too, and before too long I was piloting the machine along the back lanes between drystone walls, pogoing gently on the sprung saddle. The acid test of ability was my home town's

small but busy roads; hand signals, hand gear shifts, the ignition advance and retard left twistgrip, and rubber-necking motorists all had to be coped with. I really wasn't prepared for the level of interest in an old green Harley.

The vintage flathead elicits a variety of reactions. Some can't believe it can be ridden, while others look at it more nostalgically. At a vintage rally an elderly guy recounted how he'd bought one war surplus in the late forties. His friend had bought a 741 Indian and apparently there soon developed great rivalry between them. I couldn't help but smile as I imagined the two friends roaring around their local back roads unknowingly acting out the old factory rivalry. Through the thirties and forties it was the Harley v Indian competition that made motorcycle racing on

the dirt tracks the length and breadth of America, the spectacle it most certainly was. The bikes weren't that far removed from their khaki cousins either; the 45cu in (740cc) Harley-Davidson WLDR and Indian Sport Scout were the bikes on which Bert "Campy" Campanale and "Ironman" Ed Kretz slid sideways into the sand turns at Daytona, as Europe slid inex-orably toward war.

Sometime later I bought an Evolution Sportster, which is very convenient; just switch it on and ride it away. It is nimble, reliable, and fun, but I miss the clatter and vintageness of the flathead. Over the years other bikes have come and gone—Triumphs and similar, even a Kawasaki-engined chopper—but the WLC is here to stay.

Remembering 1944 and the

Normandy landings each June, proud old men with medal ribbons on their jackets wander among the restored military vehicles that were once so familiar. Their eyes fix on one that brings back memories and, hand trem-bling, they touch the matt green paint. Harley-Davidson is the freedom machine indeed.

John Carroll

ABOVE: An early 1980s Bay Area Lowrider.

Glossary & Abbreviations

There is a huge amount of jargon associated with Harley-Davidsons, so for those new to the marque here are a few pointers:

aiv Automatic inlet valve

bhp Brake horsepower; the power delivered by the engine to the output shaft as opposed to shaft horsepower, which measures the power transmitted by the output shaft.

bobbed Originally bobtailed, the term means cropping the front and rear fenders.

cu in/cc Cubic inch/cubic centimeter both have been used regularly to identify engine sizes and are used, untranslated, where appropriate.

Evo The V2 Evolution engine was first built in 1984 and continues to this day in various displacements.

Flatheads They were built between 1909 and 1973 in various capacities including 45cu in, 55cu in, 74cu in, and 80cu in (740cc, 900cc, 1,200cc, and 1,310cc) displacements.

ioe Inlet-over-exhaust, also known as pocket-valve. This produced the classic F-head single with a side exhaust valve below the overhead aiv

Knuckleheads Overhead valve engines; they were built 1936 to 1947 in 61cu in and 74cu in (1,000cc and 1,200cc) displacements.

ohv Overhead valve

Panheads Updated overhead valve engines, they were built between 1948

ABOVE: A fuel-injected twin-cam Softail known as a "Deuce."

and 1965 in 61cu in and 74cu in (1,000cc and 1,200cc) sizes.

rpm Revolutions per minute

Shovelheads There were two types of Shovelhead—Alternator Shovelheads were manufactured from 1970 to 1983 in 74cu in and 80cu in (1,200cc and 1,310cc) displacements. Generator Shovelheads were built in 74cu in (1,200cc) displacement only between 1966 and 1969.

Sportsters Made from 1957 to date in 55cu in, 61cu in, and 74cu in (900cc, 1,000cc, and 1,200cc) displacements.

sv Single valve

Harley-Davidson Models in Chronological Order

Year	Model	Description
1903		First machine
1903–05		25cu in single
1906–08		27cu in single, "The Silent Gray Fellow"
1909–12		30cu in single, 1912 new frame
1911–12		50cu in twin
1912		60cu in twin
1913–18	5–35	35cu in single, mechanical inlet valve
1913		61cu in twin, 2 speed rear hub
1915–29		61cu in twin, 3 speed gearbox, oil pump
1916–21	16R	8-valve racing twin
1916–21	16S	4-valve racing single
1919–23	WA	35 Sport, flat twin engine
1921–29	F series	74cu in twin with magneto
1921–29	J series	74cu in twin with generator
1921–22	CD	37cu in single
1926–29	A/B	21cu in sv single
1926–29	AA/BA	21cu in ohv single
1926–36		21cu in ohv racer, Peashooter
1929–31	D series	45cu in sv twin
1930–34	C	30-50 sv single
1930–36	V series	74cu in sv twin
1932–34	A/B	21cu in sv single
1932–36	R series	45cu in sv twin
1932–74	G	45cu in sv Servicar
1935–36	V series	80cu in sv twin
1936–41	E series	61cu in ohv Knucklehead twin
1937–41	W series	45cu in sv twin
1937–41	U series	74cu in sv twin
1937–41	U series	80cu in sv twin
1941	F	74cu in ohv Knucklehead twin
1941	XA	45cu in flat twin engine, as BMW
1942–45	WLA	45cu in military sv twin
1942–45	WLC	45cu in military sv twin
1945–47	61E series	61cu in ohv Knucklehead twin
1945–47	74F series	74cu in ohv Knucklehead twin
1945–48	U series	74cu in sv twin
1945–51	W series	45cu in sv twin
1947–59	S	125cc Hummer two-stroke
1948	61EL	61cu in ohv Panhead twin
1948	74FL	74cu in ohv Panhead twin
1949–52	61EL	61cu in ohv Hydra-Glide Panhead twin
1949–57	74FL	74cu in ohv Hydra-Glide Panhead twin
1952–53	K	45cu in sv twin
1952–69	KR	45cu in sv racing model in various forms
1953–59	ST	165cc Hummer two-stroke
1954–56	KH	55cu in sv twin
1957–59	XL	55cu in ohv Sportster
1958–64	74FL	74cu in Duo-Glide ohv Panhead twin
1958–71	XLH	55cu in ohv Sportster
1958–71	XLCH	55cu in ohv Sportster
1960–61		165cc Super 10 two-stroke
1960–65		Topper 165cc two–stroke scooter
1961–67		250cc Aermacchi Sprint single
1962		165cc Ranger two-stroke
1962–65		175cc Scat two-stroke
1962–65		175cc Pacer two-stroke
1965	74FL	74cu in Electra Glide ohv Panhead twin
1965–66		50cc Aermacchi Leggero two-stroke
1966		175cc Bobcat two-stroke
1966–69	74FL	74cu in Electra Glide ohv Shovelhead twin
1967–71		65cc Aermacchi Leggero two-stroke
1968–72		125cc Aermacchi Rapido two-stroke
1969–74		350cc ohv Aermacchi Sprint single
1970–72		100cc Aermacchi Baja two-stroke
1970–80	74FLH	74cu in ohv Electra Glide Alternator Shovel
1971–78	FX	74cu in ohv Super Glide
1972–85	XLH	61cu in ohv Sportster
1972–79	XLCH	61cu in ohv Sportster
1973–74		90cc X90 and Z90 Aermacchi two strokes
1973–77		125cc Aermacchi SS and SX two-strokes
1974–77		175cc Aermacchi SS and SX two-strokes
1974–81	FXE	74cu in ohv Super Glide
1975–77		250cc Aermacchi SS and SX two-strokes
1977–78	XLT	61cu in ohv Tourer
1977–78	XLCR	61cu in Cafe Racer
1977–79	FXS	74cu in Low Rider
1978–84	FLH80	80cu in Electra Glide
1979	FXEF	74cu in Fat Bob
1979–82	FXEF	80cu in Fat Bob
1979–82	FLHC80	80cu in Electra Glide Classic
1979–82	FXS	80cu in Low Rider
1979–85	XLS	61cu in Roadster
1980–82	FXB	80cu in Sturgis

1980–84	FXWG	80cu in Wide Glide
1980–83	FLTC80	80cu in Tour Glide Classic
1980–83	FLT80	80cu in Tour Glide
1980–85	XLH	61cu in Hugger
1981–84	FXE	80cu in Super Glide
1982–83	FXR	80cu in Super Glide II
1982-83	FXRS	80cu in Super Glide II De Luxe
1983	FXRT	80cu in Sport Glide
1983	FLHTC	80cu in Electra Glide Classic
1983–84	FXSB	80cu in Low Rider (belt)
1983–84	XR1000	61cu in Cafe Racer
1983–85	XLX-61	61cu in Sportster
1984	FLHT	80cu in Electra Glide
1984	FLHX	80cu in Electra Glide
1984	FLHS	80cu in Electra Glide
1984	FXRDG	80cu in Disc Glide
1984–85	FXRS	80cu in Low Glide
1984–90	FXST	80cu in Softail
1984–91	FLTC	80cu in Tour Glide Classic
1984–92	FXRT	80cu in Sport Glide
1984–98	FLHTC	80cu in Electra Glide Classic
1985	FXSB	80cu in Low Rider (belt)
1985	FXEF	80cu in Fat Bob
1985	FXRC	80cu in Low Glide Custom
1985–86	FXWG	80cu in Wide Glide
1985–87	FLHT	80cu in Electra Glide
1986	FXRD	80cu in Sport Glide Tourer
1986–87	XLH1100	1100 Sportster
1986–92	FXRS	80cu in Low Rider
1986–93	FXRS-SP	80cu in Low Rider Sport
1986–94	FXR	80cu in Super Glide
1986–95	XLH883	883 Sportster De Luxe
1986–98	FXSTC	80cu in Softail Custom
1986–2002	XLH883	883 Evo Sportster
1987–90	FLST	80cu in Heritage Softail
1987–94	FXLR	80cu in Low Rider Custom
1988–93	FLHS	80cu in Electra Glide Sport
1988–99	XLH1200	1200 Sportster
1988–99	FXSTS	80cu in Springer Softail
1988–99	FLSTC	80cu in Heritage Softail Classic
1988–2002	XLH883	883 Hugger
1989–93	FLTC	80cu in Ultra Classic Tour Glide
1989–93	FXRS-CN	80cu in Low Rider Convertible
1989–94	FLHTC	80cu in Ultra Classic Electra Glide
1990–99	FLSTF	80cu in Fat Boy
1991	FXDB	80cu in Dyna Glide Sturgis
1992	FXDB	80cu in Dyna Glide Daytona
1992	FXDC	80cu in Dyna Glide Custom
1993	FLSTN	80cu in Heritage Softail Nostalgia

1993–98	FXDWG	80cu in Dyna Wide Glide
1993–98	FXDL	80cu in Dyna Low Rider
1994–96	FLSTN	80cu in Heritage Softail Special
1994–98	FLHR	80cu in Electra Glide Road King
1994–98	FXDS-CN	80cu in Dyna Low Rider Convertible
1995	FLHTCI	80cu in Ultra Classic Electra Glide Anniversary
1995	FLTCU	80cu in Ultra Classic Tour Glide
1995–96	FXSTSB	80cu in Bad Boy
1995–96	FLHTCU	80cu in Ultra Classic Electra Glide
1995–98	FXD	80cu in Dyna Super Glide
1995–98	FLHT	80cu in Electra Glide Standard
1996–97	FLHRI	80cu in Electra Glide Road King (injection)
1996–98	FLHTCI	80cu in Electra Glide Classic (injection)
1996–98	FLHTCUI	80cu in Ultra Classic Electra Glide (injection)
1996–2002	XL1200C	1200 Sportster Custom
1996–2002	XL1200S	1200 Sportster Sport
1997–99	FLSTS	80cu in Heritage Springer
1998	FLHRCI	80cu in Electra Glide Road King Classic (injection)
1998–99	FXSTB	80cu in Night Train
1998–2002	XL53C	883 Sportster Custom 53
1999	FXST	80cu in Softail Standard
1999–2001	FLTRI	88cu in Road Glide (injection)
1999–2002	FXDX	88cu in Dyna Super Glide Sport
1999–2002	FXDWG	88cu in Dyna Wide Glide
1999–2002	FXDL	88cu in Dyna Low Rider
1999–2002	FXD	88cu in Dyna Super Glide
1999–2002	FLHR	88cu in Road King
1999–2002	FLHRCI	88cu in Road King Classic (injection)
1999–2002	FLHT	88cu in Electra Glide Standard
1999–2002	FLHTCUI	88cu in Ultra Classic Electra Glide (injection)
2000–02	FXST	88cu in Standard
2000–02	FXSTB	88cu in Night Train
2000–02	FXSTS	88cu in Springer Softail
2000–02	FLSTF	88cu in Fat Boy
2000–02	FLSTC	88cu in Heritage Softail Classic
2000–02	FLSTS	88cu in Heritage Springer
2000–02	FXSTD	88cu in Softail Deuce
2001–02	FLSTFI	88cu in Fat Boy (injection)
2001–02	FXDXT	88cu in Dyna Super Glide T-Sport
2001–02	FXSTDI	88cu in Softail Deuce (injection)
2001–02	FLSTCI	88cu in Heritage Softail Classic (injection)
2002	XL 883R	883 Sportster
2002	FLHTC	88cu in Electra Glide Classic
2002	VRSCA	1131cc, dohc, V-Rod

Harley-Davidson Models by Group

SINGLES

1903		First machine
1903–05		25cu in single
1906–08		27cu in single, The Silent Gray Fellow
1909–12		30cu in single, 1912 new frame
1913–18	5-35	35cu in single, mechanical inlet valve
1921–22	CD	37cu in single
1926–29	A/B	21cu in sv single
1926–29	AA/BA	21cu in ohv single
1930–34	C	30–50 sv single
1932–34	A/B	21cu in sv single

F-HEAD TWINS (ioe)

1911–12		50cu in twin
1912		60cu in twin
1913		61cu in twin, 2-speed hub
1915–29		61cu in twin, 3-speed gearbox, oil pump
1921–29	F series	74cu in twin with magneto
1921–29	J series	74cu in twin with generator

FLAT HEAD TWINS (sv)

1919–23	WA	35 Sport, flat twin engine
1929–31	D series	45cu in sv twin
1930–36	V series	74cu in sv twin
1932–36	R series	45cu in sv twin
1932–74	G	45cu in sv Servicar
1935–36	V series	80cu in sv twin
1937–41	W series	45cu in sv twin
1937–41	U series	74cu in sv twin
1937–41	U series	80cu in sv twin
1941	XA	45cu in sv, boxer twin
1945–48	U series	74cu in sv twin
1945–51	W series	45cu in sv twin
1952–53	K	45cu in twin
1954–56	KH	55cu in sv twin

OVERHEAD-VALVE TWINS

1936–41	E series	61cu in ohv Knucklehead twin
1941	F	74cu in ohv Knucklehead twin
1945–47	61E series	61cu in ohv Knucklehead twin
1945–47	74F series	74cu in ohv Knucklehead twin
1948	61EL	61cu in ohv Panhead twin
1948	74FL	74cu in ohv Panhead twin
1949–52	61EL	61cu in Hydra-Glide Panhead twin
1949–57	74FL	74cu in Hydra-Glide Panhead twin
1958–64	74FL	74cu in Duo-Glide Panhead twin
1965	74FL	74cu in Electra Glide Panhead twin

SPORTSTER

1957–59	XL	55cu in Sportster
1958–71	XLH	55cu in Sportster
1958–71	XLCH	55cu in Sportster
1972–85	XLH	61cu in Sportster
1972–79	XLCH	61cu in Sportster
1977–78	XLT	61cu in Tourer
1977–78	XLCR	61cu in Café Racer
1979–85	XLS	61cu in Roadster
1980–85	XLH	61cu in Hugger
1983–84	XR1000	61cu in Café Racer
1983–85	XLX-61	61cu in Sportster

SHOVELHEAD TOURERS

1966–69	74FL	74cu in Electra Glide Shovelhead
1970–80	74FLH	74cu in Electra Glide Alternator Shovelhead
1978–84	FLH80	80cu in Electra Glide
1979–82	FLHC80	80cu in Electra Glide Classic
1980–83	FLTC80	80cu in Tour Glide Classic
1980–83	FLT80	80cu in Tour Glide
1983	FLHTC	80cu in Electra Glide Classic
1984	FLHT	80cu in Electra Glide
1984	FLHX	80cu in Electra Glide
1984	FLHS	80cu in Electra Glide

SUPER GLIDES

1971–78	FX	74cu in Super Glide
1974–81	FXE	74cu in Super Glide
1977–79	FXS	74cu in Low Rider
1979	FXEF	74cu in Fat Bob
1979–82	FXS	80cu in Low Rider
1979–82	FXEF	80cu in Fat Bob
1980–82	FXB	80cu in Sturgis
1980–84	FXWG	80cu in Wide Glide
1981–84	FXE	80cu in Super Glide
1983–84	FXSB	80cu in Low Rider (belt)
1985	FXSB	80cu in Low Rider (belt) (V2 engine)
1985	FXEF	80cu in Fat Bob (V2 engine)
1985–86	FXWG	80cu in Wide Glide (V2 engine)

FXR TWINS OF 80cu in

1982–83	FXR	Super Glide II
1982–83	FXRS	Super Glide II De Luxe
1983	FXRT	Sport Glide
1984	FXRDG	Disc Glide (V2 engine)
1984–85	FXRS	Low Glide (V2 engine)
1984–92	FXRT	Sport Glide (V2 engine)
1985	FXRC	Low Glide Custom (V2 engine)
1986	FXRD	Sport Glide Tourer (V2 engine)
1986–92	FXRS	Low Rider (V2 engine)

1986–93	FXRS-SP	Low Rider Sport (V2 engine)
1986–94	FXR	Super Glide (V2 engine)
1987–94	FXLR	Low Rider Custom (V2 engine)
1989–93	FXRS-CN	Low Rider Convertible (V2 engine)

SOFTAIL OF 80cu in

1984–90	FXST	Softail
1986–98	FXSTC	Softail Custom
1987–90	FLST	Heritage Softail
1988–99	FXSTS	Springer Softail
1988–99	FLSTC	Heritage Softail Classic
1990–99	FLSTF	Fat Boy
1993	FLSTN	Heritage Softail Nostalgia
1994–96	FLSTN	Heritage Softail Special
1995–96	FXSTSB	Bad Boy
1997–99	FLSTS	Heritage Springer
1998–99	FXSTB	Night Train
1999	FXST	Softail Standard

SOFTAIL OF 88cu in

2000–02	FXST	Softail Standard
2000–02	FXSTB	Night Train
2000–02	FXSTS	Springer Softail
2000–02	FLSTF	Fat Boy
2000–02	FLSTC	Heritage Softail Classic
2000–02	FLSTS	Heritage Springer
2000–02	FXSTD	Softail Deuce
2001–02	FXSTDI	Softail Deuce (injection)
2001–02	FLSTFI	Fat Boy (injection)
2001–02	FLSTCI	Heritage Softail Classic (injection)

V2 EVOLUTION TOURERS OF 80cu in

1984–91	FLTC	Tour Glide Classic
1984–98	FLHTC	Electra Glide Classic
1985–87	FLHT	Electra Glide
1988–93	FLHS	Electra Glide Sport
1989–93	FLTC	Ultra Classic Tour Glide
1989–94	FLHTC	Ultra Classic Electra Glide
1994–98	FLHR	Electra Glide Road King

1995	FLHTCI	Ultra Classic Electra Glide Anniversary
1995	FLTCU	Ultra Classic Tour Glide
1995–96	FLHTCU	Ultra Classic Electra Glide
1995–98	FLHT	Electra Glide Standard
1996–97	FLHRI	Electra Glide Road King (injection)
1996–98	FLHTCI	Electra Glide Classic (injection)
1996–98	FLHTCUI	Ultra Classic Electra Glide (injection)
1998	FLHRCI	Electra Glide Road King Classic (injection)

V2 EVOLUTION TOURERS OF 88cu in

1999–02	FLHT	Electra Glide Standard
1999–02	FLHR	Road King
1999–02	FLHRCI	Road King Classic (injection)
1999–01	FLTRI	Road Glide (injection)
1999–02	FLHTCUI	Ultra Classic Electra Glide (injection)
2002	FLHTC	Electra Glide Classic

EVO SPORTSTER

1986–87	XLH1100	1100 Sportster
1986–95	XLH883	Sportster De Luxe
1986–2002	XLH883	Evo Sportster
1988–2002	XLH883	Hugger
1988–2002	XLH1200	1200 Sportster
1996–2002	XL1200C	1200 Sportster Custom
1996–2002	XL1200S	1200 Sportster Sport
1998–2002	XL53C	Sportster Custom 53
2002	XL 883R	Evo Sportster

DYNA GLIDE OF 80cu in

1991	FXDB	Dyna Glide Sturgis
1992	FXDB	Dyna Glide Daytona
1992	FXDC	Dyna Glide Custom
1993–98	FXDWG	Dyna Wide Glide
1993–98	FXDL	Dyna Low Rider
1994–98	FXDS-CN	Dyna Low Rider Convertible
1995–98	FXD	Dyna Super Glide

DYNA GLIDE OF 88cu in

1999–2002	FXDWG	Dyna Wide Glide
1999–2002	FXDL	Dyna Low Rider
1999–2002	FXD	Dyna Super Glide
1999–2002	FXDX	Dyna Super Glide Sport
2001–2002	FXDXT	Dyna Super Glide T-Sport

REVOLUTION SERIES

| 2002 | V-ROD | VRSCA |

TWO-STROKES

1947–59	S	125cc Hummer two-stroke
1953–59	ST	165cc Hummer two-stroke
1960–61		165cc Super 10 two-stroke
1960–65		Topper 165cc two-stroke scooter
1962		165cc Ranger two-stroke
1962–65		175cc Scat two-stroke
1962–65		175cc Pacer two-stroke
1966		175cc Bobcat two-stroke

IMPORTS FROM AERMACCHI

1961–67	250cc Sprint
1965–66	50cc Leggero
1967–71	65cc Leggero
1968–72	125cc Rapido
1969–74	350cc Sprint
1970–72	100cc Baja
1973–74	90cc X90 and Z90 models
1973–77	125cc SS and SX models
1974–77	175cc SS and SX models
1975–77	250cc SS and SX models

1903–1919
Early Riding Days

On January 10, 1901, a major breakthrough took place in Texas that was to put the internal combustion engine ahead over horses, steam, and electricity as the primary source of power for vehicles. The huge Spindletop oilfield produced crude oil for the first time and from the liquid black gold came kerosene, paraffin, naphtha, and later, crucially, gasoline. Around this time the US population numbered approximately 76 million people, the majority living in rural locations. Roads existed but only 150,000 miles of them could be described as "improved" at the time. This did not mean surfaced—only 150 miles of the "improved" total were actually hard surfaced.

The first boom in motorcycle manufacture occurred in the years immediately after the turn of the twentieth century as the motorcycle changed from being a complex novelty into a practical proposition. Many of the earliest motorcycles were bicycles with an internal combustion engine added, and many of the earliest manufacturers of motorcycles were established bicycle makers who saw the internal combustion simply as another component to be bolted on to a bicycle. Harley-Davidson's major domestic competitor, the Indian marque, started a couple of years before the Milwaukee concern as a result of the collaboration of George Hendee and Oscar Hedstrom and their interests in pedal cycles. Bicycle racing was a major sport around the turn of the

ABOVE: The start of it all—the first Harley-Davidson motorcycle was produced in 1903; it had a single cylinder engine with belt drive.

LEFT: This immaculate machine is a faithful replica of the first Harley-Davidson ever produced.

RIGHT: Beautifully restored, Harley-Davidson serial number 1 is on display in a glass case as part of an exhibition entitled "Birth of a Legend."

century in both America and Europe. Races were often held on specially constructed tracks known as Velodromes. The dangerous technique of slipstreaming became established to allow solo cyclists to reach higher speeds. They were slipstreamed by a tandem until the development of pacing machines powered by the internal combustion engine. These machines originated in France and usually used De Dion Bouton engines. Inevitably some of these pacing machines were imported into the United States and the machines were employed at New York's Madison Square Garden Velodrome in 1899. For the 1900 season Oscar Hedstrom constructed an American-made pacing machine.

George Hendee had become involved in bicycling manufacture in the Springfield, Massachusetts area and subsequently involved in cycle race promotion. This venture brought

RIGHT: The elaborate belt and tensioning mechanisms acted as both the clutch and the main drive.

BELOW RIGHT: The huge crankcase castings indicate that inside this engine there are some big flywheels.

BELOW: The first Harley-Davidsons had rigid forks, whereas this 1905 machine features rudimentary front suspension.

him into contact with Hedstrom and the result was the Indian motorcycle. Around the same time, late 1903, the Federation of American Motorcyclists (FAM) was founded. In time this organisation would go on to become the American Motorcyclist Association (AMA) and the governing body of sports motorcycling.

From the earliest days, because of the vast numbers of motorcycle

manufacturers—the total would eventually exceed more than 250 different companies—there was fierce competition to offer the most reliable, fastest, best, or cheapest machine. This competition spilled over into racetrack-type competition as manufacturers realized that the spectacle of speed and noise drew crowds eager to see thrills and spills. Many of the onlookers also became motorcyclists and, therefore, prospective customers themselves.

Specilized lubrication systems, starting mechanisms, ignition systems, and controls were quickly refined. Gradually the accepted formula for motorcycles became the hand throttle, foot clutch, and hand gear change. The final drive was either leather belt or chain, and both were perceived as having advantages and disadvantages. However, the advent of the functional clutch mechanism ultimately led to the chain final drive as the favorite for

approximately 80 years. Controls were variously mounted on the handlebars and in brackets on the sides of the gas tanks. Two engine configurations soon became dominant—singles and V-twins—although the US motorcycle industry persevered with in-line air cooled four-cylinder machines right up to the outbreak of Word War II.

As early as 1906 spring forks, purpose-designed frames, and magneto

ABOVE: Hard decisions have to be taken when restoring a motorcycle such as this 1907 Harley. Which parts should be left in their original state, and which renovated?

LEFT: Two glorious examples of early Harley engineering awaiting attention.

OVERLEAF: Early Harley-Davidsons had no kick-start lever, instead their engines were started using a pedal and chain.

ignition were in use, but were far from universal. However, by then, the motorcycle was beginning to catch on as an invention and companies created adventurous and exciting names and products, such as Flying Merkel, Peerless, and Cyclone. Advertising copy writers glorified the new form of transport: Iver Johnson's motorcycles were "Exquisite Mechanisms." Indian used the slogan "Hit the Indian to trail

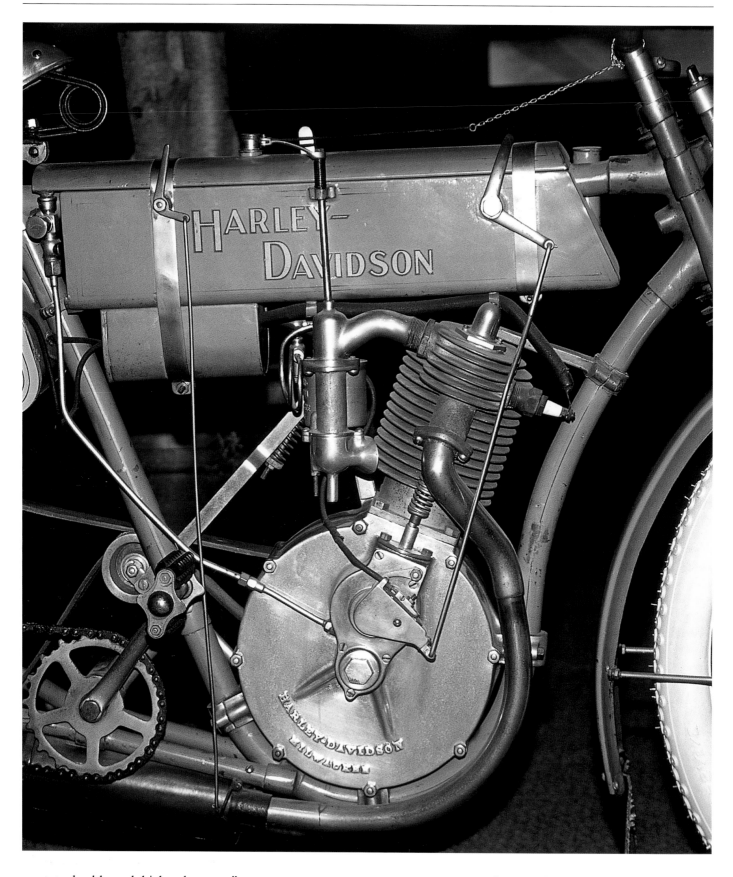

. . . to health and high adventure," "No limit to speed but the law," boasted Reading Standard and, "This motorcycle does the work of two horses," claimed Harley-Davidson.

The first motorcycle built by Harley-Davidson was the 10cu in,

ABOVE: Machines like this were tricky to ride; such things as ignition timing, engine lubrication, and throttle opening were all controlled by various levers.

four-stroke single of 1903. It worked well, but only produced 2bhp—hardly enough power to get up hills without pedaling! It was quickly replaced by a 24cu in engine developing 3bhp and two improved production motorcycles were built for sale in 1904. From then

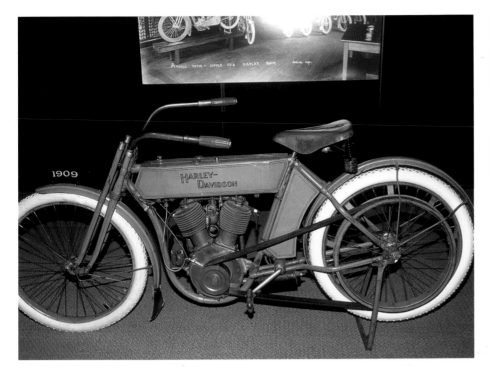

ABOVE: Magneto ignition and more advanced carburation helped establish Harley-Davidson's reputation for reliability.

LEFT: This 1909 machine features one of the hallmark V-twin engines for which Harley-Davidson would become so famous.

on the company expanded and production grew exponentially; in 1905 eight motorcycles, in 1906 50, 150 in 1907, and over 400 in 1908.

The first factory was a shed built by the Davidsons' father, and it took a loan from a rich uncle to allow the expansion of workspace needed to accommodate the extra production—the site chosen would become the Juneau Avenue factory. More management ability was necessary so another

Davidson brother—the eldest, William—joined the fledgling company as works manager. Harley-Davidson filed its incorporation papers in 1907 and it would stay under the control of the Harley and Davidson families until 1969 when AMF (American Machine and Foundry) bought it.

The 1905 Harley-Davidson motorcycles were F-head singles of 25cu in displacement in a bicycle-type diamond-style frame with a belt drive

and no brakes. Although the motorcycles were capable of 40mph, the rider pedaled backwards to slow down—fine on long flat roads but hardly ideal. The machines were finished in black and featured numerous bicycle-type components including the sprung saddle.

The most famous Harley motorcycle of the period was the Silent Gray Fellow of 1906—so named because of its quiet running, as a result of its muffler and the Renault gray paint scheme. The single-cylinder, four-stroke inlet-over-exhaust (ioe) engine was mounted in a single-loop steel frame and its displacement was sequentially increased from 25cu in when introduced to 30cu in in 1909 and then to 35cu in in 1913. Other changes made in the duration of the production run were to the design of the cylinder head cooling fins and a reshaping of the front downtube of the frame. The gas tank was redesigned in 1912 and 1916, while the belt drive was discontinued in 1914.

The 1912 Silent Gray Fellow was powered by an ioe single-cylinder, 30cu in engine that produced 6.5bhp at 2,700rpm and made the motorcycle capable of 45mph. It featured leading

Model	Single
Years	1903–05
No. cylinders	1
Valves	aiv, ioe
Bore/stroke inch	3 × 3½
Capacity cu in	25
Capacity cc	405
Ignition	coil
No of gears	1
Drive system	direct belt
Suspension	rigid
Wheel type	wire
Rear brake	coaster
Wheelbase inch	51

Model	Single—the Silent Gray Fellow
Years	1906–08
No. cylinders	1
Valves	aiv, ioe
Bore/stroke inch	3⅛ × 3½
Capacity cu in	27
Capacity cc	440
Ignition	coil
No of gears	1
Drive system	direct belt
Front suspension	rigid, 1907 leading-link
Rear suspension	rigid
Wheel type	wire
Rear brake	coaster
Wheelbase inch	51

link forks and weighed 195lb. The production of all singles ended in 1918; the trend was towards V-twins by American manufacturers.

V-twins increased the power of a motorcycle engine cheaply and the design fitted the shape of the existing frames. The ioe belt-drive V-twin engine was first catalogued by Harley-Davidson in 1909, although an experimental one had been exhibited in 1907. The Harley-Davidson V-twin was not catalogued for 1910 but returned for 1911 as the Model 7 V-twin. This displaced 50cu in and featured mechanical inlet valves.

The Harley-Davidson company is most famous for the production of V-twin-engined motorcycles and this was the first successful one that the company made. It was soon followed by the 8E, a 45-degree 61cu in V-twin of 1912. The chain final drive and a rear hub clutch were first introduced in

Model	Single
Years	1909–12
No. cylinders	1
Valves	aiv, ioe
Bore/stroke inch	3⁵⁄₁₆ x 3½
Capacity cu in	30
Capacity cc	490
Ignition	coil, magneto option
No of gears	1
Drive system	direct belt
Front suspension	leading link
Rear suspension	rigid
Wheel type	wire
Rear brake	coaster

Model	Single
Code	5–35
Years	1913–18
No. cylinders	1
Valves	ioe
Bore/stroke inch	3⁵⁄₁₆ x 4
Capacity cu in	35
Capacity cc	570
Ignition	magneto
No of gears	1, 1914–2, 1915–3
Drive system	chain
Front suspension	leading link
Rear suspension	rigid
Wheel type	wire
Rear brake	drum

RIGHT: The belt tension is controlled by this lever—when the rider wanted to move off, he would tighten the belt in much the same way that a modern rider releases a clutch lever.

BELOW: Single-cylinder machines such as this 1910 model continued in production long after the V-twin engine was first introduced.

Pre-WWI Motoring

Accounts of the Federation of American Motorcyclists (FAM) Convention in 1913 give an indication of what motorcycling was like in those early days. The first time such an event had been run west of the Mississippi River, the convention was hosted by the Colorado Motorcycle Club who had premises at the intersection of Colfax Avenue and 14th Street.

Motorcyclists began arriving in Denver on July 21, 1913, after a group of 40 riders from Chicago, Milwaukee, and the Dakotas covered 125 miles from Stirling, Colorado that day. Another group of 133 arrived the next day from Kansas and the southern states; they had been accompanied from Colorado Springs by members of the Colorado Motorcycle Club. Among this group was the FAM President Dr E J

RIGHT: The case on the right side of the engine covers the drive to the magneto, which provides the ignition spark.

FAR RIGHT: There are few early motorcycles left which have been left unmolested by over-zealous restorers. This 1912 machine needs no further polish to exude class.

BELOW: Here a 1910 Harley-Davidson shares a display space with a four-cylinder Henderson.

Patterson, who had ridden from his home in Pratt, Kansas, and six women riders. One of these riders was EJ's daughter, 17-year-old Inez Patterson, who had already made two motorcycle trips with her father from Kansas to New York City. On July 23, a Wednesday, another group of riders arrived but, due to the condition of the roads in the Midwest as a result of heavy rain, they had come by train with their bikes. Those riders already in Denver rode to the station to meet them and it

is estimated that in total 400 motorcycles paraded back to the clubhouse. The column of motorcycles was escorted by members of the Denver Police Department and needless to say was extensively reported in *The Denver Post*.

The story of two stragglers, who also arrived on July 23, gives an indication of how tough biking could get in America's vast open spaces. Harry Williams had ridden from Detroit to Hutchinson, Kansas, where he had rendezvoused with the Kansas party and ridden with them to Cannon City, Colorado. Here another rider, Charles Pierce, had broken down and Harry stayed behind to help fix the disabled machine. Both riders left for Denver 24 hours behind the main group. Intent on making up the lost time, they rode through a severe thunderstorm, but both crashed when a bolt of lightning struck the road immediately ahead of them. The bikes were damaged but rideable and the pair continued until the road became impassable. To complete their journey,

they resorted to riding between the rails of the Santa Fe railroad.

Another motorcyclist at the convention with experience of riding in adverse conditions, Billy Teubner, had been heralded as a hero in the Dayton, Ohio flood of spring 1913. He rode his motorcycle around the outlying areas warning residents of the rising waters and raising the alarm. His actions allowed thousands to escape the rising waters. He made Denver from Indianapolis in 14 days. Jesse Campbell, the Ohio commissioner for the FAM, had covered

1,700 miles in ten days, which was a respectable daily average given the condition of the roads.

What of the convention itself? It too was fiery. Dr J P Thornley, Chairman of the National Competitions Committee was accused of siding with board track race promoters by T J Sullivan, the editor of *Motorcycling Magazine,* during a debate on board track racing. Violence was only avoided by President Patterson's firm control. Later in the evening the two accidentally met in the nearby Albany Hotel and started to

fight. The other delegates present had to separate them. Despite this, the evening's dance at the Colorado Motorcycle Club was generally acknowledged to have been a great success! After four days of racing and sightseeing the successful convention drew to a close—and the delegates had to negotiate their long way home.

ABOVE: This beautifully restored machine is a 4hp 30cu in (490cc) 1912 Harley-Davidson Model X8A. At this stage, single cylinder bikes still vastly outsold the twins.

LEFT: The Silent Gray Fellow became one of the most famous Harley-Davidson models ever.

ABOVE RIGHT: The rear stand, as seen here on this glorious 1912 machine, was used when starting the engine—it was then folded out of the way before riding off.

RIGHT: Fortunately for the rest of us, many owners are proud enough of their machines to display them to the world!

1912 and then 61cu in displacement V-twins were first offered in 1913.

In the year that followed, sales of Harley-Davidsons reached a high of 12,904 and the company looked to export markets for the first time. Englishman Duncan Watson was engaged to arrange imports and sales in the UK and Europe. However, the outbreak of World War I caused the cessation of exports to Europe less than a year later; they were not resumed until 1919.

By the time of the outbreak of World War I, motoring had become a major part of the national economy and altogether an estimated $700 million worth of vehicles had already been built. Roads too were improving. The Federal Aid Road Act encouraged the establishment of state highway

departments by offering individual states matching Federal Funds for the creation of better roads. The military had also seen the benefits of using the internal combustion engine and Harley-Davidson supplied a number of its motorcycles to the US Army for war service.

Harley-Davidson introduced the innovative Model F in 1915. This featured a three-speed gearbox, a mechanical oil pump, and optional electric lights for nighttime riding. The Model F retailed at $275 and was capable of 60mph thanks to its 61cu in displacement, 11bhp ioe V-twin engine.

The V-twin for a 1915 motorcycle was surprisingly modern. It displaced 60cu in and was bolted to a three-speed transmission with a clutch and primary cover pretty much the same as that on a

modern Harley-Davidson. The layout was not dissimilar, although the shape of

Model	Twin
Years	1911–12
No. cylinders	V-twin
Valves	ioe
Bore/stroke inch	3 × 3½
Capacity cu in	50
Capacity cc	810
Ignition	magneto
Drive system	belt
No of gears	1
Drive system	belt
Front suspension	leading link
Rear suspension	rigid
Wheel type	wire
Wheel size inch	22
Rear brake	drum
Wheelbase inch	59.5

ABOVE: This 1913 Model 9-B illustrates the fact that the rough roads of the era required the qualities of reliability and solidity above all other considerations.

LEFT: This close-up shows the Bosch magneto and the chaincase for the starter mechanism.

ABOVE RIGHT: The combination of rough roads and a complete lack of rear suspension meant that sprung saddles were a vital fitment for long range comfort.

ABOVE FAR RIGHT: This 1913 model had one carburetor feeding both cylinders and separate exhausts, just like most Harley-Davidson V-twins built since then.

RIGHT: Radially disposed cylinder head finning is evocative of the era, giving the engine its distinctive look.

each component has evolved almost beyond recognition over the years.

The flat-sided tank—rounded tanks would come in the next year, 1916—was divided into parts and on its top had both fuel caps and the oil filler cap. The oil pump was built into the tank, as the engine at that time still relied on total loss lubrication.

The rider checked how much oil he had before riding off. Then, as his journey continued, at regular intervals he would give a few pumps to put some more oil into the engine, the interval varying depending on speed. Braking capability on the motorbike was minimal and there was only a back brake fitted. There was, however, a silencer bypass fitted to increase performance when the rider was outside of any built up areas.

The frame and forks had the same basic shape that Harley-Davidson have long sought to keep right up to

the present day. Softail models are somewhere between a triangle and a diamond, while the springers are merely more slender versions of the type that were history until the Evolution-powered Heritage Nostalgia was

wheeled out of Harley-Davidson's design department. The other difference sported by the bikes of 1916 were the pedals: bicycle pedals were dispensed with and a kick start was introduced instead.

ABOVE: The top of the forks reveal the springs hidden inside the front tubes—these provided the compliance for the front suspension.

ABOVE RIGHT: This engine features an overhead intake valve and a side exhaust valve, as can be seen by the location of the pushrods and rocker gear.

OPPOSITE ABOVE: The rakish lines mark this out as a performance oriented bike.

OPPOSITE BELOW: This gorgeous motorcycle is a H-D 1914 Model 10C Sport, with inlet-over-exhaust valves and sports-style handlebars.

Model	Twin
Years	1912–20
No. cylinders	V-twin
Valves	ioe
Bore/stroke inch	3⁵⁄₁₆ x 3½
Capacity cu in	60
Capacity cc	980
Ignition	magneto
No of gears	1, 1913–2, 1915–3
Drive system	chain
Front suspension	leading link
Rear suspension	rigid
Wheel type	wire
Wheel size inch	22
Rear brake	drum
Wheelbase inch	59.5

PREVIOUS PAGE, LEFT: The wide handlebars of these early machines gave the rider much more control than the narrow 'bars of most modern motorcycles. It was sports bikes such as this that started Harley-Davidson out on the successful road of producing high performance motorcycles.

PREVIOUS PAGE, RIGHT: The location of the inlet pushrod shows that the camshaft is situated within the magneto drive case.

LEFT: A 1914 single cylinder engine Harley-Davidson.

BELOW: The production of single cylinder engines ceased in 1918 due to the popularity of V-twins.

RIGHT: The Silent Gray Fellow was a model favored by both civilians and police forces alike.

BELOW RIGHT: This is a 1914 Harley-Davidson Silent Gray Fellow. Note that it has the optional chain rear drive, at a time when many motorcycles still had belt drive.

The F was acknowledged as one of the motorcycles that consolidated Harley-Davidson's position as an American motorcycle maker. As 1915 was also a good year for Harley's racing team so the company could look to the future with confidence. The range for the year included the $240 11E model, the $275 11F model, and the $250 racing K model, which didn't have lights or any other road equipment fitted.

The company concentrated on twins from now on, with only the occasional single—such as the four-valve 16S racing single of 1916. That year also saw the introduction of the eight-valve 16R racing twin.

The Model J of 1918 was intended as a sidecar motorcycle and was also powered by a 61cu in displacement ioe V-twin engine. By 1919 the Harley-Davidson 61cu in displacement V-twins featured a three-speed chain-drive transmission with a foot operated clutch pedal and a hand

continued on page 49

ABOVE: The large seat and swept-back handlebars indicate that this 1914 V-twin Harley-Davidson was intended for long-distance riding and not for performance use.

ABOVE RIGHT & BELOW RIGHT: The striking colors of this bike must have been particularly impressive when it was new. The elegance of the first Harley-Davidson V-twin engines sets them apart from later models.

BELOW: The outbreak of World War 1 stopped all exports of Harley-Davidsons such as this until 1919.

ABOVE LEFT: This 1915 machine has a wicker-work chair attached, a form of sidecar that was very popular at the time, mostly due to their light weight and low cost.

BELOW LEFT: The Silent Gray Fellow could manage 45mph—a very respectable turn of speed for the time.

ABOVE: This exquisite machine is a 1916 Board Track Racer, from a time when the men who raced such bikes were very, very tough.

LEFT: A close-up of this racing engine reveals superb detailing of all the mechanical components.

RIGHT: This priceless machine is the only known example of a complete pre-1916 bike with the "M" race motor.

Board Track Racing

Motorsport is an expensive business and the canny businessmen that ran Harley-Davidson were very cautious about entering. But by 1909 board-track racing was flourishing and tracks were opening all round the country. That year a construction engineer, Jack Prince, who had built Velodromes, started construction of a larger track for use by motorcycles in Los Angeles, California. It was named the Coliseum. Soon there was a board track in Springfield, also built by Prince but partially financed by Hendee to ensure a competition venue on Indian's home ground.

The age of motorcycle racing as a mass spectator sport had arrived. Newspaper coverage was high and racing journalism filled with superlatives. It was a ruthless, dangerous sport for the participants, and top riders such as Jake De Rosier were badly injured or killed during the races. He had campaigned for improvements to the sport including the introduction of rules requiring helmets and goggles for racers, rules to keep novices and intoxicated riders off the tracks, and higher fences although he would not live to see such things implemented. Rosier died on February 25, 1913, from complications during surgery while recovering from a racing accident. His death shocked the American motorcycling world, as did the horrific deaths of six spectators and two riders at a race in Newark, New Jersey in September 1912.

Nevertheless successes for privately ridden Harleys saw a factory team started—the famous "Wrecking Crew". By the end of 1914 the crew had won a national championship at Birmingham, Alabama. The 1915 Dodge City 300-mile "Cactus Classic" saw a Harley walkover with Otto Walker (1st), Harry Crandall (2nd), Joe Wolters (4th) Leslie "Red" Parkhurst (5th), Spencer Stratton (6th), and Ralph Cooper (7th) placing in a field of 29 entrants watched by around 15,000 spectators. So began the domination of the sport by Harley bikes—and it was a story that would continue into the golden age of board racing, the twenties.

A Harley-Davidson KT board racer of 1915 was powered by a 61cu in displacement, 15bhp ioe V-twin engine. The KT was capable of up to 80mph on the dangerous board track circuits and some races covered 100 miles around such a track. The KR was a roadgoing version of the KT and featured a similar engine, but was more equipped for road use incorporating fenders, chainguards, and a sprung saddle. See pages 64–65 for the story of board track racing in the twenties.

operated gear shift, a configuration that remained standard for many years. This type of Harley also featured sprung forks, a type albeit upgraded and strengthened, that endured until 1948. The 61 cu in displacement V-twin engine produced between 7–9hp and many were used for pulling sidecars.

The postwar motorcycle market flourished and Harley-Davidson was well-placed to take advantage of the boom. It had contributed some 7,000 bikes for the military—considerably less than half the number produced by Indian who patriotically cut its profit margins to help the war effort, and created for itself commercial difficulties because of it.

Harley, producing around 13,000 bikes a year at the start of the war saw its small European sales disappear but other large commissions came in from US organisations such as the US Mail that ran 5,000 of the company's

machines. New models in the period included an unusually configured twin—the flat twin Model W of 1919 (see the flat-twin engine on pages 56–57). This was not a commercial success and the company soon took the concept of the 45-degree V-twin as its core brand product—and stuck to this choice.

And so the second decade of the twentieth century ended. In 1901 there had been 150 miles of "improved" road-ways; in 1919 the total of road miles was now approximately three million and there were a lot more planned—in the

OPPOSITE & ABOVE: These bikes were built to last! This is an original condition 1915 Harley-Davidson V-twin. The close-up of the inlet-over-exhaust V-twin engine (OPPOSITE BELOW) reveals that it could probably go on for another 75 years or so! The rear rack frame could be used to carry a passenger, or alternatively a surprisingly large amount of luggage could be strapped on.

same year Washington State allocated $65 million for road construction

Model	35 Sport
Code	WA
Years	1919–23
No. cylinders	flat twin
Construction	unit
Valves	sv
Bore/stroke inch	2¾ x 3
Capacity cu in	35
Capacity cc	570
Ignition	magneto
Primary drive	gear
Final drive	chain
No of gears	3
Front suspension	trailing link
Rear suspension	rigid
Wheel type	wire
Wheel size inch	20
Rear brake	drum
Wheelbase inch	57
Seat height inch	29

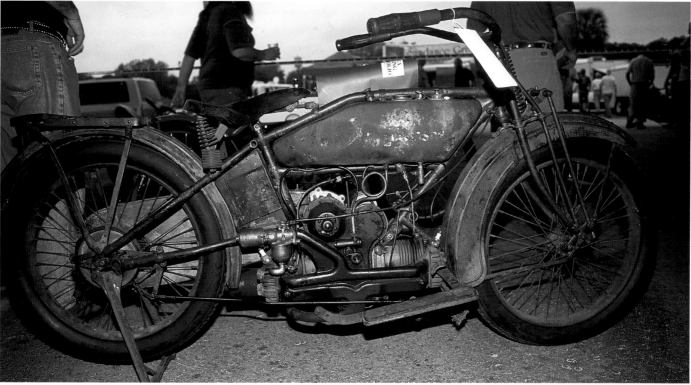

across the United States. The immediate postwar years had seen other, less palatable, developments. In 1919, the State of Oregon was the first to introduce a state gasoline tax. One cent tax was added to the price of every gallon sold.

Harley-Davidson was now a market leader waiting to meet the new decade with excellent prospects. It had consolidated its position in the market as the world's biggest motorcycle maker with

LEFT & TOP: Another original condition machine—this time a 1915 H-D Model 11F. The extreme scarcity of such original condition bikes makes them very sought after.

ABOVE: A rare Harley-Davidson—an untouched 1919 Sport model with a horizontally-opposed fore and aft flat-twin engine.

the Juneau Avenue factory turning out a staggering 23,000 bikes and 16,000

sidecars in 1919—so many that the workforce had had to be increased in the last years of the decade to over 1,500—some jump from the company's modest beginnings.

The company was producing motorcycles with a worldwide appeal. Arthur Davidson had set up a network of dealers and the racing team—the envy of all others—had proved the durabilty and reliability of its machines.

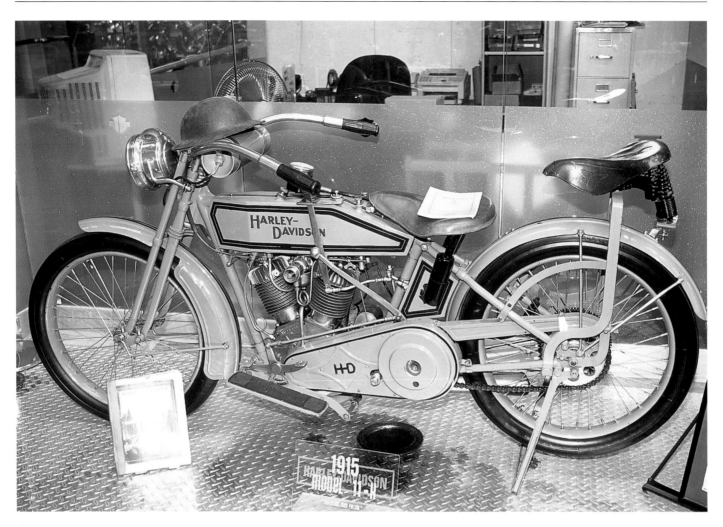

ABOVE: This 1916 Harley-Davidson Model JE featured a kickstart lever and chain drive—its general concept formed the basis of the design of most Harley-Davidsons from that point on.

LEFT: This is a 1916 Harley-Davidson Model 16F, which had chain drive and magneto ignition.

OPPOSITE ABOVE: Harley-Davidson's came in all sorts of shapes, sizes, and colors. This beauty is a 1915 Model 11H.

OPPOSITE BELOW: Sidecars also varied enormously in size and shape. This luxurious leather-lined example is attached to a 1915 61cu in Model 11F.

ABOVE: The strange position of the fully enclosed chaincase reveals that the gearbox is mounted above the crankshaft in this unusual engine design.

LEFT: A close-up of the horizontally-opposed flat-twin engine of the 1919 Sport model shows that it is radically different from the V-twin format.

OPPOSITE ABOVE & BELOW: This is another 1919 Sport model which has undergone extensive, but carefully judged restoration. Note the understated Harley branding.

LEFT: This is a 1919 Model J with an outrigger ski bolted to the side.

RIGHT: This close-up shows the Bosch magneto and external flywheel case on the flat-twin engine. These magnetos were outsourced from a factory in New York City.

Outsourcing

From the earliest days motorcycle manufacturers bought in parts to complete their motorcycles. Carburetors are one obvious example of this and specialist mahine companies such as Heitger, Schebler, and Linkert all made carburetors for numerous makes of motorcycle including Harley-Davidson. Many other parts were bought in from specialist manufacturers. Bosch magnetos were made in a 206 West 46th Street factory in New York City. Stewart Speedometers were made at 1910 Diversey Boulevard, Chicago, and numerous companies offered cyclemotor engines that could be used to upgrade pedal cycles into small capacity motorcycles.

Parts that wore out, such as drive chains, were supplied by a variety of companies including: Coventry Chains by Herbert F L Funke at 112 Broad Street New York, H R Chains by Peter A Frasse Inc at 419 Canal Street, New York, and Duckworth Chains by the Duckworth Chain and Manufacturing Co of Springfield, Massachusetts. Benton spark plugs were made in Vergennes, Vermont, while Champion plugs were made in Toledo, Ohio.

Tires are another important consumable and companies including Goodyear, Federal, US Tires, and Diamond were among those competing for motorcyclist business. "Watch the list grow" prophesied their advert.

For 1912 the Eclipse Machine Co of Elmira New York offered clutch assemblies on which they had a patent and supplied units to Merkel, Emblem, and Yale as standard equipment. Wagner, Pierce, M&M, Haverord, Pope, Detroit, and Marvel offered them as optional equipment.

Angsten-Kock of 4068 Princeton Avenue Chicago offered motorcycle locks as a fledgling part of what has become a large aftermarket industry. MECO—Motorcycle Equipment Company—of Hammondsport, New York, had an accessories catalog as early as 1913 that offered 1,216 items. By this time they had been in business for nine years and had also established a Pacific Coast branch in Los Angeles. Another company in a similar line of business was the American Thermoware Company Inc who had offices at 16–18 Warren Street, New York, and 143 N. Wabash Avenue, Chicago. Among its lines were goggles, horns, sirens, mirrors, and lamps.

Clothing specifically designed for motorcyclists became available and had novel tradenames such as Kant Leak suits and Koverauls. The latter were supplied by Nathan Novelty Manufacturing Co of New York City.

Electric lights were an accessory many wanted and were marketed by companies such as the Remy Electric Company of Indiana and Prest-O-Lite Co from the same state.

The sidecar was a popular addition for many motorcyclists at the time, especially the family men. Several manufacturers, including Harley-Davidson and Indian, supplied their own brand sidecars, but specialist manufacturers such as The Flexible Side Car Co (so named because it leaned with the motorcycle during cornering), Rogers, Pullman, and Goulding prospered. Harley-Davidson's own sidecars were actually made by Rogers until 1925. Also available were commercial three-wheelers, sidecars with van bodies, and forecars, which are trikes with two wheels at the front.

Later Harley-Davidson and Indian three-wheelers—the Servicar and Dispatch-Tow respectively—were introduced within a year of each other at the beginning of the thirties.

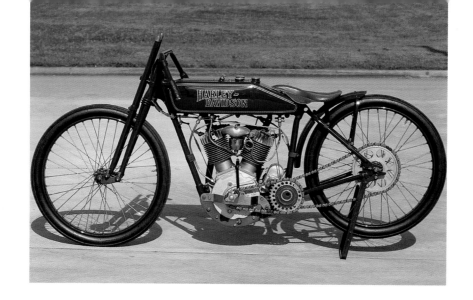

The Twenties

The twenties dawned to the Prohibition Era—the unpopular 18th Amendment to the Constitution in January 1920 prevented the sale and production of alcohol. It made little difference to Harley, who as we have seen entered the twenties as the world's leading manufacturer of motorcycles. Some 28,189 Harleys were sold in 1920, a staggering number, but by then the motor vehicle

ABOVE: Harley-Davidson's racing models have always had a style that no other marque ever matched. This stunning machine is a 1922 74cu in (1,200cc) Model JD Board Track Racer.

BELOW: Ahead of its time, this gorgeous board track racer had an eight-valve racing engine.

RIGHT: Board track races were fearsome and sometimes fatal events. This eight-valve racer is being prepared for a more gentle outing.

business was the largest industry in the United States—and the American road network continued to be developed and organized to cater for the rising tide of vehicles. The twenties saw the start of systematized referencing for roads—those going from north to south were given odd number designations, while east to west ones were given even numbers. Warren G. Harding became the first President to

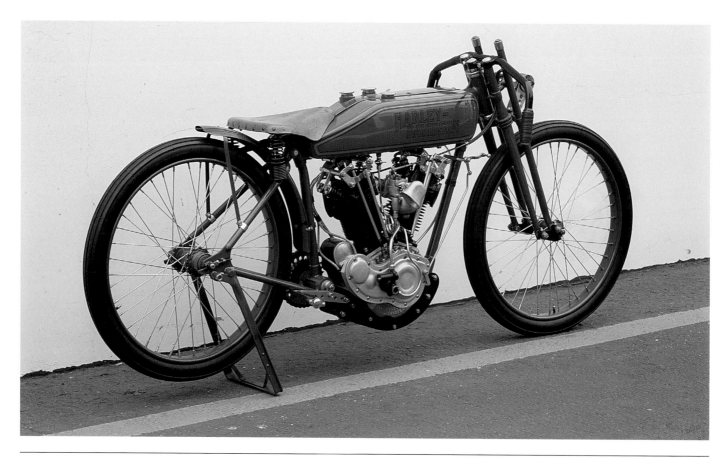

travel by car to his inauguration, when he rode in a Packard on March 4, 1921.

It looked like boom, but the decade was destined to be a bust for motorcycle manufacturing. After a bumper 1920, 1922 was the worst year for motorcycle sales to date. The success of the cheap mass-produced automobile was in the process of relegating the motorcycle to being a recreational item. Although Harley-Davidson was still outselling its major rival—still Indian, no other manufacturer had even come close to the big two—production at the Juneau Avenue factory was cut back: by 1924 it had slumped to 12,000. Sales, too, were down by more than 18,000 on 1920's record high. None of this was surprising: Ford's mass-produced Model T at this time was selling for almost the same price as a motorcycle and sidecar outfit—it was priced at

$300 for 1923. At around this time approximately 75 percent of Harley-Davidson's machines left the factory equipped with sidecars, so it is easy to understand why a big chunk of the market opted for the Model T in preference to a motorcycle.

The company made its first operating loss in 1921 because poor sales could not cover the expansion costs incurred to cater for the recent

ABOVE: The machine being ridden here is a Harley-Davidson Model FLXI racer with a sidecar attached.

ABOVE LEFT: The exposed nature of the rocker mechanism means the two inlet and exhaust valves on each cylinder head of the eight-valve racing engine can be easily seen.

LEFT: This 1920 board track racer was used by famous racer Dewey Sims.

boom. Immediate action had to be taken and so it was. The great Harley racing team—the "Wrecking Crew" was disbanded immediately to show that the core business, making and selling motorcycles, was the most important thing. In order to maintain profit margins and reduce price-cutting competition, the next step was a truce with Indian.

Price fixing discussions took place between Harley and Indian to ensure parity of pricing between similar models—a practice that would continue for many years. Harley then began to concentrate on three areas: aftermarket branded accessories—something that would grow and grow over the decades—the export market (see page 96), and fleet sales. It also went after the smaller opposition, trying to stop franchised dealerships selling smaller manufacturers, such as Henderson and Ace, who were already

struggling. Ace collapsed in 1924 and Harley employed its chief designer, Everett O. DeLong, to work on four-cylinder designs. The reason for this was that some police forces considered the Harley V-twins unsuitable for police work due to their excessive vibration. The police preferred four-cylinder bikes such as those produced by Henderson.

Police departments were a vitally important part of the shrinking motorcycle market and one targeted by Harley in the lean years (by 1924 Harleys were being used by 1,400 police departments in the United States). Unfortunately DeLong's ideas did not come to fruition following their rejection by William Davidson, who by this time had become a powerful voice within the company. Exactly why William rejected the work of DeLong, who was a designer with the highest credentials,

LEFT: Board track racers are rare machines— ones like this that remain in original condition are even more so.

BELOW LEFT: The lack of exhaust headers on board track racers meant they were very loud indeed—a whole pack of such machines racing together must have been an awesome and ear shattering spectacle!

BELOW: This meticulously restored 1920 board track racer now forms an important part of a museum display.

is still unknown, although production costs and an antipathy to model diversification are usually put forward as being the main reasons.

Towards the end of the twenties, as things seemed to be getting slightly better, the Wall Street Crash struck in October 1929. This was to have a devastating effect on America's

economy, leading to the Great Depression, that would last well into the thirties and mean that between 13 and 15 million Americans were out of work by 1932.

With hindsight we can see that the last years of the twenties also saw the quickening of a new phenomenon— the movement of townspeople into suburbs. The use of motor vehicles meant that people could work in a city and live at its edges—the start of suburban America. The result was growing road congestion, but increasing wealth meant that people could enjoy the personal freedom that motor vehicles allowed. Suburbia required the development of good vehicles and decent roads. This phenomenon was to offer something of a counterbalance to the effect that the Depression had on the motor vehicle industry. It would gradually bring about a major shift in many aspects of

continued on page 66

Racing

The twenties were a traumatic period for Harley racing. At the start of the period the Harley team—the so-called "Wrecking Crew"—was top dog and the 1921 season started with the "Crew" becoming the first factory team to win a contest at over 100mph on the boards at Fresno, California. Harley was also involved in the 300-mile National in Dodge City, Kansas on July 4.

Indian had seven riders mounted on Franklin's Powerplus models and Harley entered Ralph Hepburn on an eight-valve machine and five other riders on twin-cam pocket-valve Harleys. The win in what was the last ever Kansas 300-miler went to Hepburn and Harley-Davidson.

However, within a year the company had pulled out of racing, influenced possibly by the Norman G. Shidle report that was critical of the time and money that motorcycle manufacturers were spending on racing. In a difficult economic environment, Shidle argued, to spend too much time catering for the people to whom racing bikes—at that time heavyweight twins—appealed, missed out on a substantial part of the market. Concentrating on the thrills and spills of racing also gave motorcycling the wrong sort of image to compete with the Model T family car. The chief engineer identified the root cause—an engineering department that was spending a disporportionate amount of time on an area of the business that did not bring in the money that the company needed to stay afloat.

Specialized bikes for racing, such as the eight valve V-twin racers, were manufactured in limited numbers from 1920 but the 74cu in displacement FD and JD V-twins of 1922 onward were far more numerous. The eight-valve racer was powered by an overhead valve V-twin engine that displaced 61cu in (1,000cc). This 15bhp engine gave the race bike a top speed of 120mph. The bike comprised little more than an engine, steel loop frame, and a pair of wheels; it was equipped with a solo saddle, a set of leading link forks, and a pair of handlebars.

Despite this the board track phenomenon had not entirely passed and races were still promoted. By the mid-twenties, board track racing was an even more dangerous sport than it had been. Too often the tracks were badly maintained, the boards were soaked in oil from the total loss lubrication system of the engines, some of the riders had drunk away their nerves, and the racing was so close that death and injury was sudden, frequent, and violent. This and salacious press reports of the goings-on at the tracks led to a

decline in the sport. However, for the time being there were still enough reckless riders around who were prepared to risk all, out on the boards.

Crowds still came to watch their exploits and sample other attractions at the races—and it was the Press reporting of these that gave motorcycling a bad name for the first time. Newspapers reported on prostitutes openly soliciting the crowds, illegal betting, and bootleg liquor to be found on sale. Understandably the transitory nature of the racers lives and the excitement that the events would bring to town encouraged uproarious behavior. One group of racers on arriving in Chicago to race at the Riverview Park Motordrome are reported to have pooled all their money together and rented an entire brothel for the three days before the race!

Harley may have pulled its factory team out of competition, but it could not stop people racing Harleys—not only in the United States but also in Europe, where in Britain Harleys were particularly successful at Brooklands, Surrey. In 1923, for example, Freddie Dixon won the Three-Lap Solo race on an eight-valve Harley at a record speed. In the United States Harleys still took part—and won—many racing events without challenging Indian's

ABOVE LEFT: A static display of a board track racer in action shows that safety was not given much more than a passing thought, both for the riders and the spectators who came to enjoy the spectacle. Events could prove fatal for anyone attending the event as racers spun off the track and into the crowd.

ABOVE: The unusual handlebars of this 21cu in Peashooter show that this was also a racing machine. It now forms part of the Harley-Davidson factory's own collection.

works team or that of Excelsior that reentered competition in the 21cu in class. And it was in this engine size, on the flat, that Harley was to reign supreme in the later twenties as the Peashooter took over.

Harley officially reentered racing in 1925 and a brash young newcomer showed what had been missing as he won at Altoona on the boards. He was Joe Petrali and his exploits (see pages 114–115) would become legendary. It was not only in board track and flat dirt track racing that Harleys were popular: hillclimb competition increased steadily over the decade.

life and create more of a demand for automobiles and motorcycles.

The range of machines Harley produced in the twenties changed dramatically. Having dropped singles in 1918 (they would return in 1921 with the 37cu in CD—a "Seventy-Four" with one cylinder, which lasted only until 1923), it started the decade with a catalog of twins. Introduced in 1919, the Sports flat-twin had been designed to compete with Indian's Sports Scout, but proved more expensive to build although less powerful than its competitor: it had a production life of only five years. They would gain electric lighting in 1920.

The introduction in 1921 of the first 74cu in (1,200cc) displacement models had a profound effect. The large capacity of the engine made it more suitable for pulling a sidecar and matched that of models produced by Indian.

This first "Seventy- four" (a name that would be in use well into the eighties) was known as an F-head, indicating the position of the inlet and exhaust valves. The inlet valve was in the cylinder head while the exhaust valve was on the side of the

RIGHT: The early motorcycles still clearly show their bicycle antecedents and are not much more than a push bike with an engine bolted on to it.

BELOW RIGHT: Not all board track racers were V-twins—here a single cylinder OHV engine is installed in this Harley-Davidson Peashooter. High performance engines coupled with light weight and no brakes meant these machines were definitely not for the faint hearted!

cylinder head. Earlier models were known as IOE. The larger capacity engine was intended as Harley's competition to the Indian 74 and came in two versions: one featured a magneto and the other a generator, the FD and JD models respectively. The engine actually displaced 75cu in (1,220cc).

Other developments were also made throughout the twenties. These included dual spring forks, speedometers, ammeters, new types of piston, better exhausts, a redesigned frame, a new style of gas tank, and front wheel brakes.

In 1925, Harley-Davidson offered two twins of 61cu in (1,000cc) and 74cu in (1,200cc) displacement.

These were the F and J, and FD and JD models respectively. The basic configuration of the engine was the same; they were all of an F-head V-twin type. All were supplied finished in olive green (olive green gave way to Brewster green in 1922 but reverted to olive again in 1924) but there were further variations including sidecar models and those with electric lights. The overall styling was starting to look more streamlined, particularly the shape of the fuel tanks.

The single returned with the "Twenty-Ones" of 1926, small capacity single-cylinder motorcycles inspired by Indian's Prince model. The Model B—one of a range that included sidevalve models A and B, and their ohv partners AA and BA, —was powered by an engine that displaced 21cu in (340cc) and produced 10bhp. It featured a three-speed transmission and was capable of achieving 60mph.

The "Twenty-Ones" had problems in the United States, as they were more suited to the European markets. The Model A was prone to piston problems if ridden above 45mph but it was the pricing structure (between

Model	37
Code	CD
Years	1921–22
No. cylinders	1
Valves	ioe
Bore/stroke inch	3.424 × 4
Capacity cu in	37
Capacity cc	605
Ignition	magneto or coil
No of gears	3
Drive system	chain
Front suspension	leading link
Rear suspension	rigid
Wheel type	wire
Rear brake	drum

Model	Twin
Code	74F or 74J
Years	1921–29
No. cylinders	V-twin
Valves	ioe
Bore/stroke inch	3.424 × 4
Capacity cu in	74
Capacity cc	1,200
Ignition	F-magneto, J-coil
No of gears	3
Drive system	chain
Front suspension	leading link
Rear suspension	rigid
Wheel type	wire
Front brake	1928-drum
Rear brake	drum

Model	Twin
Code	61
Years	1921–29
No. cylinders	V-twin
Valves	ioe
Bore/stroke inch	3⁵⁄₁₆ × 3½
Capacity cu in	60
Capacity cc	980
Ignition	magneto
No of gears	3
Drive system	chain
Front suspension	leading link
Rear suspension	rigid
Wheel type	wire
Front brake	1928-drum
Rear brake	drum

$200 and $275) that was a problem when compared to secondhand cars retailing at less than $100.

It wasn't long, however, before the AA single gained a nickname best remembered on racetracks because of its distinctive noise. The Peashooter quickly became a favorite, especially in the new AMA-approved 21cu in racing class. The ohv singles were dropped after 1929 and the side-valve version was stretched to become the 1930 "Thirty-Five."

ABOVE: The layout of the left side of this 74cu in (1,200 cc) 1922 Model J engine differs little from that of big twins still produced today.

ABOVE LEFT: As engines became more powerful and brakes began to be fitted, so the tires had to be increased in size, as can be seen on this lovely 1928 F-Head.

LEFT: In the early 1920s 75 percent of all Harley-Davidsons left the factory equipped with a sidecar—such as the one shown here attached to this 1922 Model J.

By 1928, the JD and the smaller capacity model, the J, were made available in higher performance twin-cam versions; the JDH (61cu in) and JH (74cu in). Many riders recall these bikes as among the finest prewar Harleys, in spite of the age of the J's frame. By the time the Model J was retired it had sold over 70,000 units and had done much to establish Harley's reputation.

In 1928, a new model was announced that would open a fresh

ABOVE & LEFT: An original, unrestored Model J from 1922 with attached sidecar. While fully restored machines can be superb to look at, completely original bikes like this are a living piece of history.

OPPOSITE: The increasing use of electric lighting on motorcycles brought with it the associated reliability problems. The ammeter fitted here on top of the gas tank allowed the rider to monitor the charging system continuously.

chapter for Harley-Davidson. Aside from the front brakes attached to its products for the first time, the company also unveiled a new engine. It was a sidevalve design of V-twin that displaced 45cu in (740cc). This flathead V-twin would prove to be one of Harley's classic designs, still in service in the seventies.

The new model was designated the Model D. It didn't get off to the best of starts because of an unreliable gearbox and clutch, and it was only capable of 55mph. It was discontinued for 1929 while the problems were resolved and reintroduced as a 1930 model in three guises; the D, DL, and DLD. These three designations referred to the varying power outputs of the machines; 15hp, 18.5hp, and 20hp respectively. The D models featured a vertical generator at the front of the engine, which earned them the slightly disparaging name of the "three-cylinder Harley." The DLD was the "Sports Special Solo" and had a twin carburetor, large intake manifold, and an extra clutch plate.

Some of the second generation of Davidsons, Gordon, Walter, and Allan were photographed outside Dudley Perkins' dealership in San Francisco, California, with some of the so-called "three-cylinders;" the 1930 45cu in (740cc) sidevalve V-twins. The three riders were on an 8,000-mile coast to coast promotional trip in 1929. Gordon Davidson later became the production manager for Harley-Davidson while Walter oversaw the publicity and promotion. Allan did not enter the company's employ.

Events within the world economy took a turn for the worse when the Great Depression was heralded by the Wall Street New York Stock Exchange Crash of October 24, 1929. This dealt manufacturers of most commodities a severe blow and saw the thirties start less than optimistically for America as

Model	21		Model	21
Code	A & B		Code	AA & BA
Years	1926–29,		Years	1926–29
	1932–34		No. cylinders	1
No. cylinders	1		Valves	ohv
Valves	sv		Bore/stroke inch	2⅞ × 3¼
Bore/stroke inch	2⅞ × 3¼		Capacity cu in	21
Capacity cu in	21		Capacity cc	340
Capacity cc	340		Ignition	magneto or coil
Ignition	magneto or coil		No of gears	3
No of gears	3		Drive system	chain
Drive system	chain		Front suspension	leading link
Front suspension	leading link		Rear suspension	rigid
Rear suspension	rigid		Wheel type	wire
Wheel type	wire		Wheel size inch	20
Wheel size inch	20		Front brake	1928-drum
Front brake	1928-drum		Rear brake	drum
Rear brake	drum		Wheelbase inch	56.5
Wheelbase inch	56.5		Seat height inch	28.5
Seat height inch	28.5			

ABOVE: A Harley-Davidson equipped with a sidecar cost almost as much as a Model T Ford, but even so large numbers were sold. Pictured here is a 1922 61cu in (1000cc) Model FD.

LEFT: The 74cu in engines proved extremely successful for use with sidecars due to their enormous torque and smooth power delivery.

OPPOSITE TOP: Even though the Harley-Davidson factory had produced eight-valve racers and OHV engines for years, this 1925 Model JD still had inlet over exhaust valve-gear.

a whole. Harley-Davidson was no exception. Business was immediately affected and sales declined over the next years. By 1933, the country only produced 6,000 motorcycles—of these 3,703 were Harleys.

Despite all this it was the next decade, the thirties, that would guarantee Harley-Davidson a place in motorcycling folklore and give it the position as the strongest manufacturer in the United States.

Model	45
Code	D, R, W
Years	1929–51
No. cylinders	V-twin
Valves	sv
Bore/stroke inch	2¾ × 3¹³⁄₁₆
Capacity cu in	45
Capacity cc	740
Ignition	coil
No of gears	3
Drive system	chain
Front suspension	leading link
Rear suspension	rigid
Wheel type	wire
Wheel size inch	18
Brakes	drum
Wheelbase inch	57.5
Seat height inch	26.5

ABOVE & OPPOSITE: By the mid-1920s, the overall design of the Harley-Davidson big twin was set, and remained as such for many decades, as typified by this 1925 74cu in (1,200cc) Model JD. This JD still has IOE valve gear even though Harley-Davidson had for a long time been producing eight-valve racers and OHV engines.

OVERLEAF: The poor roads of the day meant that a journey was often long and slow—so bikes like this 1926 F-head came equipped with large seats, wide handlebars, and large section tires all to provide as much comfort as possible.

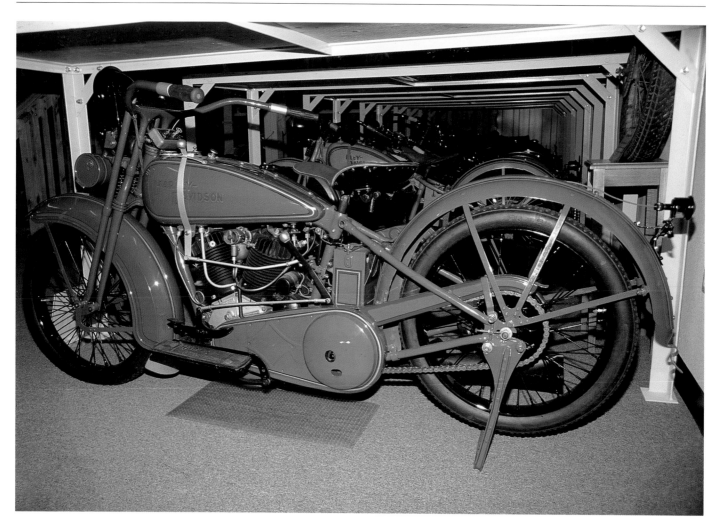

ABOVE: Like other Harleys of the time, the 1926 Model JD had no front brake. Since they started to appear more frequently on models supplied by other manufacturers, it wasn't long before the Harley-Davidson factory offered them as well.

LEFT: The overhead inlet valve made the engine very tall—in order to allow the gas tank to fit, it had to have special cutaways to provide clearance for the rocker gear.

OPPOSITE TOP: The 1925 Model J was produced with the 61cu in (1,000cc) F-Head engine. All the F, J, FD, and JD models were supplied painted olive green, although the purchaser could also specify electric lights and a sidecar.

OPPOSITE BOTTOM: This 1926 F-Head has electric lights fitted; these cut down the amount of owner maintenance required, since acetylene gas lamps needed a lot of care and attention.

RIGHT & OPPOSITE TOP: Harley-Davidson made utilitarian models as well as the more expensive bikes. This is a 1926 machine with a single-cylinder side-valve engine. The handlebar layout was clean and uncluttered, with controls kept to a minimum.

BELOW & OPPOSITE BOTTOM: These two 1927 J models would have been among the first production Harley-Davidsons to have been fitted with front brakes. The gas tank has been equipped with an ammeter and a speedometer.

TOP LEFT: Compare the handlebar layout of this J with that on page 80.

TOP RIGHT: The large electric horn fitted below the headlamp on this 1927 side-valve single was an optional extra.

ABOVE LEFT: The battery can be seen mounted behind the central frame-post.

ABOVE RIGHT: The gas tank on this Model J has been equipped with an ammeter and a speedometer.

LEFT: This beautifully restored 1927 21cu in side-valve single-cylinder machine would never have been this immaculate, even when new!

OPPOSITE TOP: A 1927 J Model.

OPPOSITE BOTTOM: As engines became more powerful and brakes began to be fitted, so the tires had to be increased in size, as can be seen on this lovely 1928 F-head.

ABOVE & OPPOSITE: This 1928 Model JDH is fitted with stands on both the front and rear wheels to allow flat tires to be attended to quickly and easily.

LEFT: The clutch was operated by the left foot, and the gears were changed using the lever on the side of the tank.

PAGE 86: It's always good to see bikes like this taken out and used.

PAGE 87: This 1928 side-valve single was produced with many of the features found on the more prestigious models—in particular electric lighting and a front brake.

PAGES 88–89: A 1928 single-cylinder Harley-Davidson.

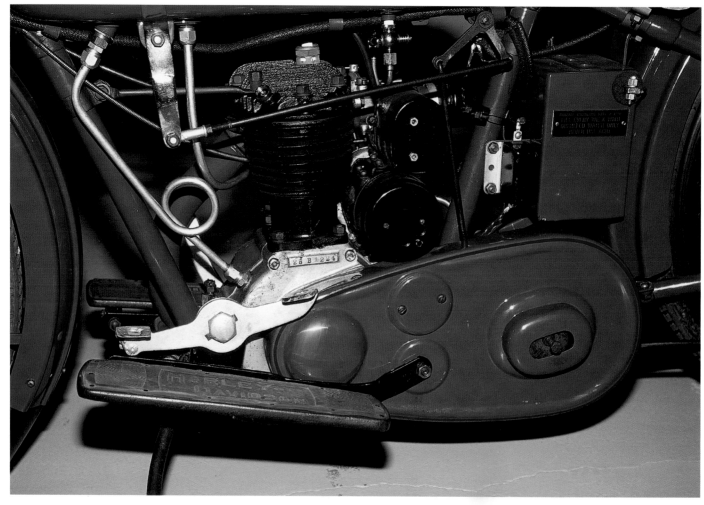

ABOVE: Cylindrical toolboxes were introduced in 1925, and were attached to the front of the bike below the horn. While these were a useful feature, many riders, complained that they rattled in use, and so removed them.

OPPOSITE, LEFT & BELOW: This utilitarian machine used a single cylinder engine and was intended for a wide variety of uses, including delivery riders and those who couldn't afford or manage a heavyweight model.

PAGES 90 & 91: This bike was produced using the 31cu in (500cc) engine in order to compete directly in the marketplace with the many European models of this size and configuration.

LEFT: This original condition machine is a 1929 single cylinder model.

BELOW LEFT, BELOW & RIGHT: Since the Europeans made a vast array of 45cu in (740cc) bikes, Harley-Davidson had to offer a competitive model to survive in the marketplace. This is the company's 1928 offering, which was nicknamed the "three cylinder" because the addition of a vertically mounted generator made it look as though another cylinder had been added. Note the twin headlights which could now be installed due to the improved power output of the uprated electrical system.

The Export Market

In the years immediately following the 1918 Armistice, sales to Europe were resumed. Exports were to provide Harley with a lifeline in the early twenties, as half the company's sales came from the overseas market. Harley machines gained their fame on the racing circuits of the world and this developed into sales. In 1921, for example, Douglas Davidson (no relation), aboard a Harley-Davidson, became the first person to exceed 100mph on a motorcycle in Britain. He recorded a speed of 100.76mph at Brooklands, the famous English racing circuit. As the domestic market retrenched in the early twenties the company embarked on a program to bolster sales around the

globe. An employee, Alfred Rich Child, went to Cape Town in South Africa and rode north the full length of the African continent on a Model J. En route he sold 400 motorcycles and established a number of new dealers. After this trip Child went to Japan and spent the next 13 years importing Harley-Davidson

ABOVE: The 45cu in (740cc) Model D was first introduced in 1928, but it suffered from many problems such as poor reliability and low performance. It was withdrawn for 1929, and reintroduced in 1930 when it went on to be a great success for the company.

ABOVE RIGHT: The clean lines of the rigid rear end on machines such as this late twenties model would later inspire bikes like the nineties Softail.

RIGHT: Sales of the 1929 74cu in (1,200cc) were affected badly (as were all models) by the start of the Great Depression.

motorcycles into the country. He also established a licensing agreement with Sankyo to enable Harleys to be made in Japan by the company.

The Japanese version of the Model VL was called Rikuo—King of the Road. But as economic conditions changed in the twenties, so the export market got tougher—in 1925, Winston Churchill, then British Chancellor of the Exchequer, levied a 33⅓ percent import tax against all foreign motorcycles. This pushed the retail price of American motorcycles so high that they were no longer competitively priced in the UK. This meant that the "Twenty-Ones" in general and the Peashooter in particular did not make the entry into the British market that Harley had hoped for. In 1929, sales were further hit by the introduction of an import tax in Australia and New Zealand, but in Europe, Japan, and other areas sales were consistently high.

ABOVE & RIGHT: Single cylinder machines were an important part of the model line up throughout the years between the two world wars. Two basic model sizes were offered: the 21cu in (340cc) and the 31cu in (500cc) —many of these bikes were destined for the export market.

LEFT: This 61cu in.(1,000cc) 1928 Model F was one of the last of these machines to be built— production ceased in 1929. The F range had been a mainstay of the company since 1909.

The Thirties

The United States in the thirties was a country beset by problems. The depths of the Depression were plumbed in 1933 as thousands of the dust bowl farmers of Oklahoma and the surrounding regions drove west in search of a better life. The Depression played havoc with the economy and manufacturing industry—not least motorcycle builders. Excelsior could not withstand the economic

ABOVE & BELOW: There were three versions of the 45cu in (740cc) engine—the sidecar version (Model D) which had a low compression, the standard version (Model DL), and the high compression version (Model DLD).

RIGHT: Note the contemporary Art Deco bird motif on the paintwork of this 1933 machine.

pressures of the times and closed in 1931 leaving Indian Motorcycles as Harley-Davidson's only domestic competitor. When industry is facing hard times the workforce has to protect itself. In 1935 the UAW (United Auto Workers) Union was formed and affiliated to the Congress of Industrial Organisations (CIO). The same year, 1936, Harley-Davidson Motor Company became unionized, further evidence of

ABOVE: This fine-looking machine is a 1930 45cu in (740cc) Model D.

ABOVE RIGHT: This is a 1930/1931 45cu in (740cc) Model D. Take note of the vertical generator and rear-facing air intake to the carburetor.

BELOW RIGHT: This pristine machine is a 1930 Model 30 VL. It even has an original tool-roll!

the uncertain times that were to characterize the decade. But as the thirties wore on there were signs that the worst was over as government schemes to get people back to work and kick start the economy began to take effect. One of the most enduring examples of this is the hydro-electric schemes that provided power and jobs too, such as the Hoover and Grand Coulee dams. The Hoover Dam in Colorado at the Nevada/Arizona border is the highest concrete dam in America—and was completed in 1936, the same year as Harley-Davidson unveiled the 61 EL Knucklehead, of which more later.

The decade started with the introduction in 1930 of new model big twins, designated V. These were the bikes that would put Harley-Davidson on the road to the success it has achieved today. The Model V 74cu in (1,200cc) was almost entirely new and shared few components with its

F-head predecessor. The V models featured a sidevalve engine where both inlet and exhaust valves were positioned alongside the cylinder bore. The cylinder heads, as a result, featured no moving parts and quickly earned the nickname of "flatheads," which became the term by which these models were differentiated from the other types of Harley-Davidson.

The cylinder heads were not completely flat: on the top they featured a number of cooling fins cast in during

ABOVE: This 1930 Model VL was supplied with stunning red and black paintwork with intricate pinstriping on both the bike and sidecar.

ABOVE LEFT & LEFT: The V series models were introduced in 1930, the year this fine machine was built. They had 74cu in (1,200cc) flathead engines, and were available in several different configurations.

production, while on their underside was a shaped combustion chamber. Each cylinder head was, of course, drilled and threaded for the spark plug.

Model	74
Code	V
Years	1930-36
No. cylinders	V-twin
Valves	sv
Bore/stroke inch	3.424 x 4
Capacity cu in	74
Capacity cc	1,200
Ignition	magneto or coil
No of gears	3, 1936-4 option
Drive system	chain
Front suspension	leading link
Rear suspension	rigid
Wheel type	wire
Wheel size inch	19
Brakes	drum
Wheelbase inch	60
Seat height inch	28

The V models featured a total loss lubrication system and were offered for sale in a number of guises, the V and the higher compression VL being two.

Model	80
Code	V
Years	1935-36
No. cylinders	V-twin
Valves	sv
Bore/stroke inch	3⁷⁄₁₆ × 4⁹⁄₃₂
Capacity cu in	80
Capacity cc	1,340
Ignition	coil
No of gears	3*
Drive system	chain
Front suspension	leading link
Rear suspension	rigid
Wheel type	wire
Wheel size inch	19
Brakes	drum
Wheelbase inch	60
Seat height inch	28
* From 1936 4 gears were optional	

These were followed by the magneto equipped VM and VLM as well as machines with varying compression ratios, the VS for sidecar work and the sporting VLD first mass-produced in 1934. A larger displacement model was also available—the VLH which displaced 80cu in (1,310cc). The sporting VLD featured a Y shaped inlet manifold rather than the T shaped one fitted to the earlier models.

Harley-Davidson used carburetors manufactured for them by Linkert and fitted a 1.25in M21 item to the VLD

ABOVE: This well-equipped 1931 Model VL even had a fire-extinguisher fitted!

ABOVE RIGHT & RIGHT: It's hard to imagine that this 1932 Model VLD resplendent in such glorious paintwork was produced at a time of great austerity, hunger, and genuine despair for many Americans.

which produced 36bhp. But while Harley-Davidson were still manufacturing total-loss lubrication engines their competitor Indian had advanced to dry sump lubrication.

The 1930 VL Model was an almost entirely new motorcycle when it was introduced, sharing few parts with its F-head predecessor. Around 13 variants of the sidevalve V Models were produced through the production run. These had differences in specifications such as those equipped with magnetos and higher compression engines. The VL had a capacity of 74cu in (1,200cc). Its engine was a four stroke V-twin flathead giving a top speed of 85mph. Transmission was three speed and a steel loop frame was used.

The 1931 Harley-Davidson range brochure includes the 45cu in (740cc) sidevalve V-twin, the Model D, and the 30cu in (490cc) single cylinder Model C. The Model D was available as the

ABOVE LEFT: The Harley-Davidson Servicar was popular as a delivery vehicle as it could carry many times the load of a solo machine.

BELOW LEFT: This is a completely original and unrestored 1932 74cu in (1,200cc) machine with a side-valve engine.

ABOVE & BELOW: The silver and blue paintwork of this 1933 Model VL blends in very well in these picturesque surroundings.

RIGHT: There's a superstition within the motorcycle fraternity that green is unlucky—the owner of this 1935 VDS would disagree!

D, DL, DLD, DC, and DS, of which the latter was the sidecar machine. The Model C was available as the C, CH, CMG, and CC. Also available at this time were the smaller 21cu in (340cc) single and the larger V and variants. The standard color across the range was olive green, though other colors were available for an extra cost.

The result of these new models—despite teething problems—was that 1932 was the best year for Harley for some time. Indeed, it was the best year for the motorcycling industry as a whole since 1919. Everything is relative, however; in 1932 only 31,000 machines were produced, half the 1919 figure, and half of the 1932 machines were exported.

The range of D models was redesignated R, RL, and RLD in 1932 when the generator was repositioned and the pistons were redesigned along with the oil pump, flywheels, and clutch. Harley-Davidson now was forced to

desperate measures to attract new customers, a choice of colors, extra chrome parts, optional accessories, and even an extra wheel were offered with the bikes. A new idea came in the form of the Servicar, a three-wheeled

Model	30-50
Code	C
Years	1930-34
No. cylinders	I
Valves	sv
Bore/stroke inch	3³⁄₂ × 4
Capacity cu in	30
Capacity cc	490
Ignition	magneto or coil
No of gears	3
Drive system	chain
Front suspension	leading link
Rear suspension	rigid
Wheel type	wire
Front brake	drum
Rear brake	drum
Wheelbase inch	57.5
Seat height inch	26.5

machine powered by the 45cu in (740cc) sidevalve engine. It was aimed at small businesses, garages, and police departments. Garages sent their mechanics out on them to break downs, small businesses used them as delivery vehicles, and policemen would hand parking tickets out from them. The first Servicars featured the D model engine, though this was later upgraded in line with the solo 45cu in (740cc) models.

The Enthusiast of August 1933 announced the 1934 range of Harley-Davidsons and trumpeted their new features, which included streamlined fenders, a new oiler, a redesigned exhaust (the Burgess muffler), new pistons, and a modern streamlined tank logo. The range included the 74cu in (1,200cc) big twin VLD which produced 36bhp at 4,600rpm and retailed at $310. The R model 45cu in (740cc) V-twin had a redesigned clutch and retailed at $280. In contrast, the

workaday three wheelers, the G and GD Servicars, retailed at $430. The designations indicated different sizes of rear bodies.

At the 24-hour race held in Atlanta, Georgia in 1933 William Bracy and O C Hammond won riding a stock 1933 Harley 45 by covering 1,366 miles in the allotted period. In second place were Bert Baisden and Todd Haygood, and in third were Jack Roberts and Hank Taylor, all of whom were also on Harley-Davidsons.

The company's 1934 brochure featured the same motorcycles as those announced in August 1933 but presented them in a form designed to help dealers move them off the showroom floors. Including sidecar and sports versions there were eight variants of the Model R offered and six variants of the VL, the big twin flathead. Competition with Indian was fiercer than ever and Harley soon upped the stakes with the introduction

of both dry sump lubrication and overhead valves in the EL model of 1936, the first Knucklehead.

Parallel to the development of its side valve or flathead engines the Milwaukee factory had been developing an overhead valve design of engine which went into production in 1936. This created a sensation when it was unveiled in 1936 as the 61cu in (1,000cc) EL model. It was a fast road-bike and although its production span was interrupted by the war it was to have a major effect on motorcycling and its introduction was one of the

ABOVE LEFT, ABOVE, & OVERLEAF: The style and sheer charisma of Harley-Davidsons such as this 1934 Model RLD are still influencing motorcycle design to this day. Their deep fenders, footboards, and sprung seats epitomise the era. A twin-cylinder side-valve 45, the RLD was the high-speed model of the R series produced 1932–36.

factors that gave Harley-Davidson a much needed advantage over Indian.

The engine soon became referred to as the "Knucklehead" because of the resemblance of the rocker covers to knuckles. Initially available as the 61E, from 1941 it would be available as the 61F at 74cu in (1,200cc), but production of both models was suspended in 1942 after the Japanese airstrike against Pearl Harbor.

The style established by the 1936 EL Knucklehead (soon incorporated into both displacements of flathead) has endured to this day and is still plainly evident in the design of current models. It is generally accepted that the 61E was the first of the modern Harleys, and was the model from which current Harley-Davidsons draw their styling. The bike was the first Harley to have dry sump lubrication, where oil recirculates between the oil tank and engine, instead of a total loss system. The oil tank, horseshoe

continued on page 117

Records & Racing

As mentioned earlier, the Model EL quickly made headlines when Joe Petrali broke the speed record with one at Daytona. The City of Daytona Beach had allowed record-breaking runs to be made on the hard tidal sands of the Atlantic shore for many years. Joe Petrali was one of the great names of motorcycle racing and became one of Harley-Davidson's star riders, winning the National Championship for the Milwaukee company in 1925.

Born in San Francisco in 1904, Petrali first came to prominence on an Indian before finding himself on the Harley-Davidson team. When Harley temporarily retired from racing, Petrali rode with Excelsior breaking three national speed records at Altoona,

Philadelphia. When Excelsior left motorcycle racing Petrali went back to Harley-Davidson with whom he stayed through the Depression. Between 1919 and 1950 he held a number of competition records on Harleys including:

- Board Track Solo Class A/61cu in 10-mile, 25-mile, and 100-mile
- 1-mile Dirt Track Solo Class A/21cu in 10-mile, 15-mile, and 25-mile
- ½-mile Dirt Track Solo Class A/21cu in 5-mile and 10-mile

His 1937 ride on Daytona Beach took a record previously held by an Indian machine. Petrali's Knucklehead-powered machine was clocked at 136.183mph, an American speed record and a world record for a non-supercharged-engined motorcycle. After retiring from racing Petrali worked for eccentric industrialist Howard Hughes and flew in the one and only test flight of the *Spruce Goose*,

Hughes' massive flying boat at Long Beach, California.

Speed records weren't the only area of excellence for Harley speedsters. As the United States emerged from the depths of the Depression, motorcycling again became a popular pastime. While the economy had suffered American motorcycle sport had been in the doldrums, and in an attempt to revitalize it the AMA's Class C had been born. To be raced in Class C a bike could displace no more than 45cu in (750cc) and would normally have two cylinders and side valves simply because that was what the big American factories—Harley and Indian—offered the man in the street through their dealers. The idea was to stop the few wealthy teams with exotic, specially constructed engines winning everything.

Class C was a great success and led to the enduring fame of events like the

Daytona 200. It also ensured that dirt-track bikes were based on the venerable "sidestick" 45cu in (740cc) Harleys and Indians and that every two-bit town had a dirt oval. The establishment of Class C gave motorcycle racing a wider appeal and was a success in that "ordinary" riders could compete without the expense of specialist race bikes.

This and the staging of a number of AMA-sanctioned 100- and 200-mile national races in places such as Savannah, Georgia, and Daytona, Florida, ensured that races began to attract huge crowds of spectators.

Many riders also emulated the style of the mildly modified race bikes for street use—Class C rules meant that race bikes were required to be street legal prior to the race—so that what can be termed "prewar customs" were usually bikes modified with a cut down or removed front fender and bobtailed (a term later shortened to bobbed) rear fender.

Sometimes a front fender was fitted to the back so that the flared end was much further around the wheel than normal and a pillion pad was fitted, the whole being supported by a modified or specifically fabricated fender strut. These modifications were made to both Harley-Davidson and Indian motorcycles, reflecting the fact that both were popular American bikes and that much of the racetrack rivalry was between the motor-cycles of the two companies.

In 1937 the City of Daytona Beach—famous for record breaking—invited the Southeastern Motorcycle Association to bring a 200-mile race to its area. The circuit would involve two straights, one along the beach and one along a surfaced road that ran parallel. The two straights were connected by sand turns making the total length 3.2 miles, 63 laps were required to cover

the total distance. As the race ran on both sand and pavement it would prove a testing combination for both the machines and their riders. The main event was the Class C race for almost showroom stock motorcycles—in this class wins meant sales. A win at Daytona in the spring meant that the manufacturers of the victorious marque were able to trumpet their victory through the entire selling season. The Daytona 200 was about to become an enduring institution.

Ed Kretz won the 1937 race—the first Daytona 200—on an Indian in front of a crowd of some 15,000 spectators. When the flag dropped Kretz took his Sport Scout toward the front of the pack. By the end of the first lap he was in third place and leading by the end of the second.

The top 20 finishers consisted of 11 Harley-Davidsons, seven Indians, and two Nortons. The new circuit only experienced one problem, which was the incoming tide. Due to the start time of the race, by the time the racers were in the later laps the incoming tide was forcing them to take a longer line through the softer sand further up the beach or risk running through the edge of the water.

The problem with the incoming tide was avoided for the 1938 running of the Daytona 200 simply by timing the start to coincide with the still ebbing tide rather than low water. Kretz was back, intent on defending his championship but crashed heavily

in practice injuring himself. Despite this he started the race along with 107 other riders and led for three laps before going out on lap 29 when his chain snapped.

After this the lead was a battle between Lester Hillbish, an Indian rider from Pennsylvania, and two Harley riders, Ben Campanale and Tommy Hayes. In the end Campanale took the win on a 45 just ahead of Hillbish who was trailed by Hayes.

A much smaller field of riders started the 1939 event, though there was considerable anticipation of a great dice for the win in view of the fact that both Kretz and Campanale were entered. It was also seen as a great Indian versus Harley-Davidson showdown. Kretz went into the lead from the start while "Campy" Campanale was well down the pack, but set about steadily working up toward the front. On lap seven he was in second place, a mere ten seconds behind Kretz and by lap nine Kretz's lead was less than six seonds. Disaster hit Kretz as the leaders went into lap ten, his Sport Scout caught fire and he lost four laps while successfully dealing with this.

Campanale of the Rhode Island Ramblers MC won his second successive Daytona 200 after a battle with Sam Arena, another famous Harley-Davidson rider from California. However, sn spite of the success of Daytona and Class C, racing in particular and motorcycling in general were soon to be curtailed by the outbreak of World War II.

shaped, was located under the seat, the engine was fitted into a double loop frame, and a new style of gas tank appeared. It was made in two halves, hid the frame tubes and had the speedo set into a dash plate that fitted between the two halves of the tank. The EL was soon in the news when Joe Petrali rode one to various speed records on the sands of Daytona Beach in Florida (see page 114). Despite its advanced engine much of the remainder of the machine was typical of Harley-Davidsons of the time. The frame was of the rigid type with no rear suspension, rider comfort was provided by means of a sprung saddle, and the forks were still of the springer design.

Despite the introduction of the EL the company did not abandon its production of sidevalve big twins. In 1937—the year that San Francisco's Golden Gate bridge was opened to traffic—the V range was redesignated

LEFT: A 1935 VLD, which was available with either a conventional four speed transmission for solo use, or a unit with three forward speeds and one reverse for sidecar use.

BELOW LEFT & BELOW: A 1935 Servicar—these were made until 1974.

PAGE 118 & PAGE 119 TOP: By 1934, the VLD, which had a side-valve engine of 74cu in (1,200cc), had developed a reputation for ruggedness and reliability—although it did tend to overheat if used at sustained high speeds making it unsuitable for police highway patrols. It was said to have a slight performance advantage over the Indian Chief, its main rival in the marketplace.

PAGE 119 BOTTOM: In 1936, the first Knucklehead (known as the Model EL) was produced—this was the start of a whole line of closely-related overhead valve big-twins that continue to this day.

U, UL, and ULH as it was upgraded to dry sump lubrication. The smaller capacity V-twins were also changed to

Model	74
Code	U
Years	1937-48
No. cylinders	V-twin
Valves	sv
Bore/stroke inch	$3\frac{5}{16} \times 4\frac{9}{32}$
Capacity cu in	74
Capacity cc	1,200
Ignition	coil
No of gears	4
Drive system	chain
Front suspension	leading link
Rear suspension	rigid
Wheel type	wire
Wheel size inch	18
Brakes	drum
Wheelbase inch	59.5
Seat height inch	26

Model	80
Code	U
Years	1937-41
No. cylinders	V-twin
Valves	sv
Bore/stroke inch	3⁷⁄₁₆ x 4⁵⁄₃₂
Capacity cu in	78
Capacity cc	1,310
Ignition	coil
No of gears	4
Drive system	chain
Front suspension	leading link
Rear suspension	rigid
Wheel type	wire
Wheel size inch	18
Brakes	drum
Wheelbase inch	59.5
Seat height inch	26

BELOW: The 74cu in (1,200cc) flathead was introduced shortly after its smaller brother, the 45, came into production. It was reasonably reliable, and sold in good numbers.

RIGHT: The introduction of the Model E OHV Knucklehead in 1936 also brought with it the recirculating oil system, which has remained almost unchanged right up to the present day (in the Evolution engine).

BELOW RIGHT: A 1936 Model VLH—see also overleaf.

dry sump lubrication and redesignated the W, WL, and WLD. The WLD was a sports version of the WL but the latter would later become famous in its military guise as the WLA and the WLC when it was adopted by the armed forces of several Allied nations.

The Enthusiast of October 1937 previewed the 1938 models which included 45cu in (740cc) flathead twins, 61cu in (1,000cc) OHV Knuckleheads, 74cu in (1,200cc) and 80cu in (1,310cc) flatheads, Servicars, and sidecars. Among the news it was noted that William Muehlenbeck Jr. of Saginaw, Michigan, had won the 13th Jackpine Endurance Run, a noted motorcycling competition of the time, on a 1937 Harley-Davidson 45.

In the September 1939 edition of *The Enthusiast* Harley-Davidson announced the new range of 1940 motorcycles. The bikes that "have what it takes" included the 45cu in (740cc), 74cu in (1,200cc), and 80cu in (1,310cc) sidevalve V-twins and the 61cu in (1,000cc) EL Knucklehead pictured in the magazine and on its cover with a rider in typical motorcycle club attire of the time. The OHV Knucklehead was a top of the range machine because of its advanced engine but the styling of the mudguards, tanks, and trim was similar across the range, and the bikes were all based around rigid frames and springer forks.

LEFT, BELOW & OPPOSITE: A wonderfully kept 1936 Model VLH. An 80cu in (1,310cc) version of the Model VL engine, its greater capacity brought with it increased torque which made it especially suited to sidecar use.

ABOVE & BELOW: A 1935 VLD, which had a generator version of the 74cu in (1,200cc) high compression side-valve engine.

OPPOSITE: The first Harley "Eighty," the 1936 VLH had a side-valve engine of 80cu in (1,340cc), and was the final model in a series which took the factory many years to perfect. This large capacity version of the 74cu in VL was only made for a short time, the UL and ULH twins taking over in 1937..

LEFT: Rear fender and streamlined Airflow taillight from a 1936 VLH.

ABOVE & BELOW: A 1937 80cu in (1,310cc) ULH—this was the first year of production for this model; it continued to be made until 1941.

ABOVE & BELOW: Speedo and gastank detail of the 1937 ULH seen on the previous page. Note instrument console on gastank and the gear lever mounted on the left of the tank.

ABOVE RIGHT: Pretty side view of a ULH.

BELOW RIGHT: Before the introduction of the Knucklehead EL, the oil tank was usually alongside the gas tank. Since the new model had a much improved oiling system, it required a smaller tank, which was relocated beneath the seat, freeing the main tank for extra fuel.

The Model E 61cu in Knucklehead

LEFT: Side view of a ULH.

BELOW LEFT: A 1937 UHS with sidecar, which operated as a service "truck" for Caterpillar.

BELOW: A Model E Knucklehead; note new Harley decal look (compare with those on earlier machines, for example those on pages 118–119) and the bolt-on saddlebags that were popular accessories on both civilian and police bikes.

Much has been written about Harley's successful Knuckleheads; as collector's items go, they are five-star rated and difficult to come by. They didn't last for very long— with the war effort intervening just after their introduction, there were only some dozen years of production until the engine was taken off the line in 1947. Although of only 61cu in (1,000cc) displacement, the Knucklehead, however, was more powerful than larger flatheads. The E models sported other novelties, too. As well as the idiosyncratic Knucklehead rocker cover, of course, that started with smooth domed bolts and later

received large hexagonal nuts as part of the oil leak fix, there was a teardrop gastank on which an instrument panel was mounted—civilian models were registered to 100mph, police vehicles to 120mph. This style of instrument panel would continue on Harleys to date. There was a new Harley decal as well, a gold and red winged creation that was used until 1939. Of the obvious outward styling features, only the

streamlined Airflow taillight remained from the past—it would be replaced by a chunkier "tombstone" light in 1947.

The "Knuck" had its teething problems: initially, the frame couldn't take the stress of a sidecar; there were oil leaks from the new recirculating lube system; the valve gear was inadequate and a fix had to be rushed out for the 1,900 models built in 1936. Indeed, on any quantitative success scale the Knucklehead wasn't the most successful bike of the period. However, when Joe Petrali set a record of 136.18mph on the Daytona mile, the Model E became a performance bike. Today, when the heritage style is perhaps more important than performance, the "Knuck" fulfills all the requirements needed for a Harley-Davidson classic.

PREVIOUS PAGE, ABOVE, & LEFT: A 1937 WL 45, with details of the tail light and the dash.

RIGHT: The 1934 Model VL was fitted with the high compression version of the 74cu. in. (1,200 cc) flathead engine.

PAGE 136 TOP: A gleaming 1937 side-valve UL.

PAGE 136 BOTTOM & PAGE 137: Three 1938 EL Knuckleheads. The "Knuck" motor enjoyed a long production run, from 1936 to 1952.

ABOVE & PAGES 142–143: A 1938 side-valve UH Police Special model with sidecar.

LEFT: A close-up of the dashboard on a 1938 Police Servicar.

ABOVE RIGHT: The 45cu in (750cc) side-valve WLD, as seen here, was the civilian version of the bike used by the military in World War II.

PAGE 138: Two 1938 EL Knuckleheads.

PAGE 139 TOP: A 1938 side-valve Model U with sidecar.

PAGE 139 BOTTOM: A 1938 80cu. in. (1,340 cc) side-valve UL.

Military Harleys

The thirties saw the clouds of war gathering over Europe, and the United States began to make preparations for a conflict as well. In the coming years the story of Harley-Davidson would become inextricably entwined with that of the military.

Mechanization of the US Army's cavalry units began in the late thirties although it was not until 1940 that sufficient funds would be available to procure the equipment to complete this process. During the second half of the decade the US Army had acquired numbers of Harley-Davidson 45cu in

(740cc) motorcycles starting with the R models in 1932. These were followed by RL models in 1934.

The US Army's reorganization involved a new divisional structure. Each division was to consist of three Independent infantry regiments and support units with enough transport to move regimental sized groups. There were also mobile reconnaissance troops, equipped with a variety of trucks and motorcycles—eight solos and three combinations per troop; unlike the German Army, the US motorcycle combos were not machine gun-armed.

During military expansion Harley-Davidson sought to supply motorcycles to the Army and shipped some WL models to Fort Knox—more famous as the nation's bullion depository—for

evaluation by the Mechanized Cavalry Board. The company received small contracts to supply motorcycles—as did Indian. Harley-Davidson would supply the WLA—an Army WL.

Because of its ties with Britain, Canada became involved in the war from 1939 and the Canadian military also ordered motorcycles—a machine tagged the WLC was specifically built for Canada, though it differed from the WLA only in details.

President Roosevelt declared a "limited emergency" within a week of the beginning of war in Europe and permitted further recruiting to both the US Army and the National Guard but it would only be in 1942 that US Army Harleys saw war service.

The Forties

As seen in the previous chapter, the United States started to make preparations for war in the thirties. As events unfolded in Europe, the United States were uneasy bystanders for the first two years, helping Britain in its solo fight against totalitarianism by providing much needed materiel.

War in Europe did not affect the production of civilian motorcycles for the US domestic market but the Japanese air strike against Pearl Harbor did. On December 7, 1941, the Japanese unexpectedly attacked America and propelled the US into World War II. The United States entered the war by Act of Congress within 24 hours of the bombing. Before many more days had passed the United States Marine Corps were fighting to hold Wake Island, a tiny Pacific atoll, which up to that point had been used almost exclusively by Pan American Airways to refuel their huge flying boats on around-the-globe services. The Marines determined stand for 16 days against overwhelming odds became the lead story in numerous editions of US newspapers, but was the first sign though that the road to victory would be long and costly.

Production of civilian motorcycles was suspended almost immediately as industrial companies, such as Harley-Davidson, turned their factories and production lines over to the war effort. Unlike the company's position in World War I, this time the involvement was total. The military specification WLs were produced in large numbers along with a tiny number of other models for police and "Essential Use" purposes.

The prewar 45cu in (740cc) side-valve engined Harley-Davidson WL motorcycle was militarized and supplied to Allied armies for the remainder of the duration of the war. There were two variants, the WLA and WLC. The two models differed only in details and were used all around the world throughout the war. In the years

ABOVE: This military bike is a 1942 WLC—the symbol on the gas tank indicates it belonged to the "Desert Rats," the nickname given to the British 7th Armoured Division, which fought against Rommel in North Africa.

RIGHT: During World War II the vast majority of US military motorcycles were WLA's—the machine shown here is from 1942, and was supplied complete with a rifle carrier.

PREVIOUS PAGE: A 1939 EL Knucklehead.

following the war, both also became popular as cheap civilian transport and helped popularize Harley-Davidsons in countries where American bikes were not normally widely available.

The WLA was an WL with an A suffix for Army that was supplied to both American and Chinese armies while the WLC was a WL with a C suffix. As seen in the previous chapter it was originally built for the Canadian forces but also supplied to Britain, Russia, Australia, and South Africa. Harley built in excess of 88,000 machines for the war effort—a large percentage of them for other Allied nations—and earned a special award from the US Army for doing so. Walter Davidson, who was one of the founders and had done so much to keep Harley at the forefront of the motorcycle industry, was sadly not to see the first of these as he passed away in February 1942. Another of the founders, William S. Harley, also died during the war, in September 1943.

The war proved momentous for Harley-Davidson, and it came out of the conflict strongly. Knucklehead production resumed in the immediate postwar years, but the technology had moved on: much had been learned during the war. The immediate effect

of this was another new overhead-valve Harley-Davidson big twin that soon made its appearance. It arrived to critical acclaim in 1948 and quickly became referred to as the Panhead.

As the Daytona 200 race was held in the spring it was becoming renowned as the first major motorcycle event of each year. This was the case in 1940 for the fourth running of the Daytona 200. This race looked set to be a close run affair; among others Campanale, Tancrede, and Arena were flying the flag for Harley-Davidson while Kretz and Jimmy Kelly were doing the same for Indian. There were 77 motorcycles at the start—only 15 finished. Kretz went out somewhere

around the midway point due to mechanical problems as did the Harley riders, Campanale and Arena. The lead developed into a dice between Babe Tancrede and Jimmy Kelly, the latter having caught the leader on lap 57. With only six laps to go Kelly was challenging for a win but his Indian developed mechanical problems forcing his retirement and leaving the race to Harley. Unfortunately for Jimmy Kelly history repeated itself in the last

ABOVE & RIGHT: Although Europe was embroiled in World War II when this UL was made in 1940, US domestic motorcycle production was unaffected.

Daytona 200 before World War II. Harley debuted its new 45cu in (740cc) Class C racer, the WRTT, but it retired due to mechanical problems. Jimmy Kelly again looked set for victory until mechanical problems.

Meanwhile Harley-Davidson found itself receiving more contracts from the Army than rival Indian and its WLA and WLCs soon became the workhorses of military policemen, other military motorcycle riders, and despatch riders. For the company this meant that there would be sufficient demand for Harley-Davidson military motorcycles to continue production for the duration of the war. The WLA and WLCs changed slightly from year

ABOVE LEFT & ABOVE: The production run of 1940/1941 was the last model year for the high compression flathead 80cu in (1,310cc) ULH Model.

BELOW LEFT: The factory continued to add new features each model year. The "Cats Eye" instrument warning lights on the dash panel on this 1940/1941 EL Knucklehead were introduced in 1939.

BELOW: Bikes such as this civilian model 1940 WL45 continue to be enjoyed on the road to this day.

WITH FACTORY DELUXE
SOLO PACKAGE

1941 ULH
80 CI FLATHEAD

208

to year as refinements were made; rubber parts, for example, were reduced due to the short supply of the commodity after numerous Japanese conquests. The factory received a number of accolades in the form of Army/Navy E for Excellence awards for these efforts. The first of these was awarded on May 12, 1943.

During the war years, Harley-Davidson produced a number of flat twin-engined motorcycles at the request of the US government and contributed to a number of other military projects. The XA was, for the company, an unusual experimental motorcycle. It was built at the request of the US government and closely styled on the flat-twin German BMW machines in use by the Wehrmacht at the time. Its technical specification was as follows; capacity was 45cu in (740cc) in a four stroke, flat-twin side-valve engine. The BMW-style twin

produced 23bhp at 4,600rpm. The XA had a four speed transmission and the engine and gearbox were fitted into a tubular steel plunger frame.

While Harley experimented with the XA, its competitors Indian developed a transverse-engined V-twin the Model 841 and Delco built a machine closely based on the BMW. Despite

ABOVE: The 45cu in (740cc) motor was introduced to the world in 1929, and continued with few changes until 1952, when it was revamped extensively. This is a 1941 WL45.

ABOVE LEFT: The designation "WL" indicates that this 1940/1941 model has the high compression 45cu in (740cc) engine.

LEFT: This 1941 ULH has an 80cu in (1,340cc) flathead engine and was supplied in the "Factory Deluxe" format.

acceptance of these bikes as practical motorcycles the US Army did not

Model	Boxer flat twin
Code	XA
Year	1941
Construction	Unit
No. cylinders	2
Valves	sv
Bore/stroke inch	3¹⁄₁₆ × 3¹⁄₁₆
Capacity cu in	45
Capacity cc	740
Ignition	
Primary drive	direct
No of gears	4
Final drive	shaft
Front suspension	leading link
Rear suspension	plunger
Wheel type	wire
Wheel size inch	18
Brakes	drum
Wheelbase inch	58.75
Seat height inch	30.5

ABOVE: The WL45 only had 25bhp, and with just three gears to move its 550lb, it was best suited to slow cruising.

BELOW: The 80cu in (1,310cc) U model was a low power machine intended for applications where a sidecar or cargo box would be fitted. This 1941 UHS was fitted with the slightly more powerful medium compression engine to help improve performance when hauling its sidecar.

ABOVE RIGHT: When the Knucklehead arrived, it had double the power output of the engine it replaced, firmly establishing it in the hearts of enthusiasts of the time. This is a 1941 74cu in (1,200cc) EL.

BELOW RIGHT: Although the design of the Knucklehead engine was heavily influenced by the factory's involvement with racing, most of the bikes it was fitted in were far from competition machines. This is a 1941 EL Knucklehead.

order vast numbers for its war effort as by the time it was ready for mass-production the army's requirement had changed. The success of the 4 x 4 Jeep and the number of WLA and WLC models already produced for America and her allies meant that there was little need for the new bike. As a result only 1,000 XA Harleys were built.

The noted World War II cartoonist, Bill Mauldin, recalled his wartime motorcycling experiences on a WLA while in Italy with the US 45th Infantry Division, in *The Brass Ring* (W. W. Norton Inc, 1971):

"I went to a big ordnance depot in Naples and asked if they had a couple of motorcycles which had run over mines or been mashed by shells. What I had in mind was putting together the halves of two machines which had been hit in different places. I hadn't grown up hanging

around those two mechanical geniuses, my father and brother, for nothing. 'Hell we hardly ever get anything that was busted in combat,' the man at the junk pile told me. 'Usually it's drunk driving.' I not only got the germ of a cartoon idea from this, but also ended up with a

ABOVE: The Model XA was an experimental design intended for use in the desert, where it was felt its flat-twin shaft-drive engine would perform better than more conventional arrangements. However, it never saw military action and only 1,000 were ever built.

ABOVE LEFT: Around 88,000 45cu in (740cc) Harleys were made for the war effort. This version is a WLC45.

LEFT: The "A" of WLA signified that it was a model produced for the US Army. The bike pictured here is a 1942 example.

slightly bent Harley-Davidson which I was told had run under the back of a truck, leaving its rider plastered on the tailgate. The ordnance boys lent me some tools and I got the thing running all right, though it crabbed slightly. During the next couple of weeks, I made two trips to the 45th on my bike. I would have kept on this way, except as I became a better rider I couldn't resist becoming a smart-ass. I would retard the spark going downhill to make backfires, squirrel my way through convoys, and plow through mudholes at high speeds. One of these finally trapped me. It was an old bomb crater full of water."

The Enthusiast of December 1944, published while the US Army was engaged in the Battle of the Bulge, featured Tom Henry of Stockton, California, on its cover, riding through the Yosemite National Park. News from 27 clubs around the US included numerous mentions of men in the forces. The mailbag was similarly biased toward the services, Lt. B L. Elliot (Canadian Army Overseas) wrote: "The army HDs are good, no doubt about it—they have proven their worth beside the other makes and made themselves popular with men who never rode bikes in civilian life. And that means a lot, for many of them will ride in peacetime now they have developed a liking for it in the army. But I long for civilian colors on the HDs again."

In the years immediately after World War II ex-army Harley-Davidsons were sold to transport hungry civilians around the world. In the USA new bikes, which had not been delivered to the army, went on sale, while in countries such as Holland, Harleys left behind by the

Allied armies were sold. Many owners preferred to repaint their old army machines and fit chromed parts and accessories. Some of these machines were so well refurbished that it is hard to tell them apart from genuine civilian

ABOVE RIGHT: The XA engine displaced 45cu in (740cc), and was very similar in format to the German flat-twins built by BMW and Zundapp.

BELOW RIGHT: The shaft drive on this XA would have been a great help in sandy environments where chains wear out remarkably quickly in the harsh conditions.

BELOW: The XA's plunger suspension was intended to make this bike more rideable in the rough conditions of desert warfare where rocky roads and rough conditions prevail.

models, such was the degree of care taken in their refurbishment.

Civilian production resumed after the cessation of hostilities but things only really got back to normal by 1947 when raw materials became more freely available again. Boom years followed, in 1948 the factory sold 31,163 bikes. It was not to last though, imports from Europe soon flooded the US market. In the postwar years the 45cu in (740cc) flathead models were reintroduced although their styling was upgraded to match the remainder of Harley-Davidson's range.

Production of the WL also resumed in almost the same form as the prewar models—once again the fenders were valanced, the diameter of the wheels was reduced to 16in, and the chromed parts at last returned. There were upgrades to the model however: the taillight and dash covers were

LEFT: The ELC Knucklehead was well suited to the roads of the day—it was tough, dependable, and when fitted with a windshield, as on this 1942 model, could cope with most weather conditions.

BELOW LEFT: By 1942 the Knucklehead engine had been improved to the point that most of the problems (such as lubrication failures) of the earlier models were no longer a concern.

RIGHT: Although the engine offered significantly improved performance over earlier models, this label on the gas tank warns the rider not to exceed 55 mph!

BELOW: The air filter fitted to this 1942 ELC is of the oil bath type, and was intended for use in particularly dusty environments.

redesigned and matched those on other models in the postwar range.

The WL was reintroduced, however, into a changed world where time was running out for the sidevalve design of engine as a viable motor in a modern motorcycle. It was only a matter of time before the small capacity side-valve was considered obsolete. The flathead solos were discontinued in 1952, although the Sportster would in time take its place. Production of the same 45cu in (740cc) flathead engine continued as the power plant for the three-wheeler Servicar which remained in production until 1973.

Harley had initially reintroduced the motorcycles from its old prewar range to satisfy pent up demand for new bikes from returning servicemen while it pre-pared new and updated models. The 1947 Knucklehead was another of the those machines and almost the last of the EL and FL Knuckleheads. It was to

be superseded the following year by the Panhead, albeit with a similar frame and cycle parts. As discussed in the previous chapter the Knucklehead was available as a 61cu in (1,000cc) machine from 1936 designated the 61E and as a 74 cu

ABOVE: The UL had a higher compression engine than the standard U model—ideal for hauling the sidecar attached to this bike.

ABOVE LEFT: The 1941 U Model was equipped with a generator and a standard compression ratio engine.

LEFT: This is the smaller 61 cu in (1,000cc) EL Knucklehead.

OVERLEAF: When the Knucklehead was first introduced to the American public in 1936, it had a 61 cu in (1,000cc) engine; by 1945 though, it was also offered as the FL, which had the larger capacity 74cu in (1,200cc) Knucklehead engine.

in (1,200cc), the 61F from 1941. Production of both models was suspended in the latter year, after Pearl Harbor.

Close scrutiny of the pre and post-war Knuckleheads reveal a number of styling changes that were made for the 1947 model year. Between 1936 and 1946 Harley-Davidson had fitted a rounded taillight to their machines, it was superseded for the 1947 bikes with a new design.

It's an unofficial tradition that Harley parts acquire nicknames to differentiate them from each other and the two taillights became referred to as the "beehive" and "tombstone" tail-lights respectively. The shapes of the two electrical components bear a distinct resemblance to the items they are named after. Other changes included a shift from the cat's-eye dash cover to a more modern looking one, known as the two-light dash. The "cat's-eye" and

1945
Model FL
Dennis Krueger
MILWAUKEE, WI

ABOVE: The fat tires, leading links forks, and sprung saddle on this 1945 FL Knucklehead were designed to make sure that it rode well over rough roads.

BELOW: The ES designation of this 1946 Knucklehead indicates it was supplied complete with a sidecar.

ABOVE RIGHT: Due to the combined effects of the Depression and the war, the Knucklehead was not the success (in sales terms) it should have been. When this 1946 F Model was made, the Knucklehead only had two years of production left.

BELOW RIGHT: The EL Knucklehead weighed 565lb, and needed the addition of a front brake—something that was new to many riders.

"two-light" descriptions refer to the type of ignition and oil warning lights used adjacent to the speedometer. Front fender lights were also changed and in place of the manually adjusted ride control a hydraulic damper was fitted instead.

The springer forks were replaced by hydraulic telescopic units in 1949 and the EL and FL big twins were renamed the Hydra-Glide. The new telescopic front end negated the need for the hydraulic damper, but the remainder of the styling changes introduced for 1947 remained current; tombstone taillights and similar are all to be found on early Panheads.

In many ways the Hydra-Glide was the crossover between the vintage-style Harleys and those perceived as being more modern. Whereas the springer forks looked vintage because of their exposed and spindly springs, the Hydra-Glide was much more up-to-date with

larger diameter telescopic fork legs and a cast headlamp nacelle. The sprung solo and buddy seats were still used according to customer preference in place of rear suspension but Harley's engineers were working on that as the next major update.

The Panhead superseded the Knucklehead models but retained the E and F designations for the 61cu in (1,000cc) and 74cu in (1,200cc)

ABOVE & ABOVE RIGHT: The oiling system of the Knucklehead engine probably received more factory development attention than any other aspect of its design. It was notorious for oil leaks in its early years, but by the time this 1946 EL was built, many of them had been sorted out.

RIGHT: Early models of the U engine had iron cylinder heads. This later model (1941) ULH 80cu in (1,310cc) was fitted with aluminum cylinder heads.

models. In fact, the bike was essentially a new top end on the existing Knucklehead bottom end and as the slang name implies its rocker covers look like upturned cooking pans. The cylinder heads were now cast from aluminum after problems with the all iron Knucklehead, while hydraulic lifters contributed to a quieter running engine, and a larger oil pump was used to improve lubrication. The improvements would not end there though; the cycle parts of the motorcycle would also be upgraded. For one year only Harley-Davidson marketed a Panhead engined motorcycle that featured a rigid frame and springer forks. Because of this short production run these "springer pans," as they are known, are very desirable motorcycles to collectors today.

The four stroke OHV V-twin Panhead-powered 1949 FL Hydra-Glide displaced 74cu in (1,200cc) and

had a top speed of 102mph and pro-duced 55bhp. It used a four speed transmission and a rigid frame made from tubular steel. The 1949 EL model

Panhead displaced 61cu in (1,000cc) but was externally similar to the FL.

Harley machines evolve over time, rather than each model being com-pletely different. The early machines that have just been discussed were the precursors to much later bikes. When Harley-Davidson introduced their Panhead engine in 1948, it was the successor to the overhead valve Knucklehead and it also had over-head valves. The new engine was originally fitted to Harley's springer fork equipped rigid frame rolling chassis, but this later benefited from

hydraulic telescopic forks and so became designated the Hydra-Glide. Later when a swingarm frame was used to give the Panhead front and

Model	61 OHV
Code	E & EL
Years	1936–48
No. cylinders	V-twin
Valves	ohv
Bore/stroke inch	3⁵⁄₁₆ x 3½
Capacity cu in	61
Capacity cc	1,000
Ignition	coil
No of gears	4
Drive system	chain
Front suspension	leading link
Rear suspension	rigid
Wheel type	wire
Wheel size inch	18
Brakes	drum
Wheelbase inch	59.5
Seat height inch	26

OPPOSITE & ABOVE: When the Knucklehead was first introduced in 1936, it was heralded as the fastest motorcycle in America. This claim was backed up when factory racer Joe Petrali managed to cover the flying mile at 136mph on Daytona beach. This is a much later 1946 model.

Model	74 OHV
Code	F & FL
Years	1941–48
No. cylinders	V-twin
Valves	ohv
Bore/stroke inch	3⁷⁄₁₆ x 3³¹⁄₃₂
Capacity cu in	74
Capacity cc	1,200
Ignition	coil
No of gears	4
Drive system	chain
Front suspension	leading link
Rear suspension	rigid
Wheel type	wire
Wheel size inch	18
Brakes	drum
Wheelbase inch	59.5
Seat height inch	26

ABOVE & BELOW: The speedometer on this 1946 Knucklehead goes up to 120mph, which was more of a marketing ploy than a reality!

RIGHT: This 1947 EL Knucklehead engine has been modified by the addition of a modern oil cooler—a very good idea due to the engine's habit of overheating when used on the highly congested roads of today.

rear suspension it was redesignated the Duo-Glide, to indicate two suspension systems and later again, in 1965, when an electric starter became available, the bike was redesignated the Electra-Glide.

The origins of the Harley chopper are inextricably linked with the period of American motorcycling that straddled World War II. As the country emerged from the depths of the Depression motorcycling again became a popular pastime and the establishment of Class C gave it a wider appeal in that "ordinary" riders could

Code	61 EL
Years	1949-52
No. cylinders	V-twin
Valves	ohv
Bore/stroke inch	3⅜ × 3½
Capacity cu in	61
Capacity cc	1,000
Ignition	coil
No of gears	4
Drive system	chain
Front suspension	teles
Rear suspension	rigid
Wheel type	wire
Wheel size inch	16
Brakes	drum
Wheelbase inch	60.5
Seat height inch	31

BELOW: The Servicar was initially aimed at the garage industry to act as a cheap form of service truck, it wasn't long, however, before it caught on with many other forms of industry and general commerce. This is a 1947 model.

ABOVE RIGHT: When the EL Knucklehead's capacity went from 61 to 74cu in (1,000cc to 1,200cc) the timing case was strengthened with stiffener ribs, as on this 1947 bike.

BELOW RIGHT: The EL Knucklehead was so much faster than its predecessors that those who rode this beast were often regarded as lawless hoodlums.

Code	74 FL
Years	1949-65
No. cylinders	V-twin
Valves	ohv
Bore/stroke inch	3⅞ × 3³¹⁄₃₂
Capacity cu in	74
Capacity cc	1,200
Ignition	coil
No of gears	4
Drive system	chain
Front suspension	teles
Rear suspension	rigid, 1958-s/a
Wheel type	wire
Wheel size inch	16
Brakes	drum
Wheelbase inch	60.5
Seat height inch	31

compete without the expense of special-ist race bikes. Class C and the staging of a number of AMA-sanctioned 100- and 200-mile national races in places such as Savannah, Georgia, and Daytona started to attract huge crowds of spectators.

Many of the people attending began to emulate the style of the mild-ly modified race bikes for their own use. Class C rules meant that race bikes were required to be street legal prior to the race so that what can be termed "prewar-customs" were usual-ly bikes modified with a cut down or removed front fender and bobtailed, (or bobbed), rear fender. Sometimes a front fender was fitted to the back so that the flared end was much further around the wheel than normal and a pillion pad put on that—the whole being supported by a modified or specifically fabricated fender strut.

ABOVE: The Servicar was popular for many reasons, not least that it was safe and easy to drive. Its large carrying capacity, advertised as 500lb, made it capable of performing many different roles. This is a 1947 machine.

OPPOSITE TOP LEFT & RIGHT: This 1947 EL Knucklehead has had many accessory items fitted, including lights, mirrors, saddlebags, engine bars, plus many other extras.

OPPOSITE CENTER LEFT: In 1945, 15,000 army surplus 45s were offered for sale to the American public and bought in numbers by ex-servicemen needing cheap transport. Many were converted to civilian specification, similar to this 1947 WL45.

OPPOSITE CENTER RIGHT & BOTTOM: 1947 WL45. When the 45cu in (740cc) engine was first released in 1929 it was a sales disaster as it was unreliable and under-powered. But, it went on to become one of the mainstays of the company for many years.

These modifications were made to both Harley-Davidson and Indian motorcycles reflecting the fact that both were popular American bikes and that much of the racetrack rivalry at the time was still between the motor-cycles of these two companies.

The war left a distinct influence on motorcycling in many ways; not only had technology been refined but it led to the superstition about green Harleys being unlucky. This probably came about because despatch riders were targeted by the enemy as they were likely to be carrying important infor-mation. The men assigned this duty also had to contend with dangerous journeys—land mines and wires strung across the road to decapitate them were menaces in forward areas.

For the survivors who came home and started riding motorcycles again for some it was back to normal and back to AMA-sanctioned events. For others it wasn't so straightforward; motorcycle club uniforms and rally games wouldn't have held the same appeal to restless combat veterans and those who'd buried their comrades in Europe and the Pacific Islands.

The author of *From Here to Eternity*, James Jones, summed it up: "About the last thing to go was the sense of *esprit*. That was the hardest thing to let go of, because there was nothing in civilian life that could replace it. The love and understanding of men for men in dangerous times and places and situations. Just as there was nothing in civilian life that could replace the heavy, turgid day-to-day excitement of danger. Families and other civilian types would never understand that sense of *esprit* any more than they would understand the excitement of the danger."

Some guys found what they were looking for in the saddle of a big motorcycle, with equally restless

BELOW: The 1947/1948 model year UL was much like the earlier models—it weighed 600lb and only had 30bhp to drive it along. Nevertheless, it was extremely popular as it was very reliable and provided masses of torque for a relaxed ride.

OPPOSITE TOP: The Panhead motor was introduced in 1948 and was an evolution of the Knucklehead engine, rather than a whole new design. It had aluminum cylinder heads, hydraulic lifters, and a generally more oil-tight engine.

OPPOSITE BOTTOM: The first Panheads were available in both 61cu in (1,000cc) and 74cu in (1,200cc) forms, although from 1953 only the larger engine size was offered.

buddies and the endless blacktop. For better or worse the world had changed.

The first postwar Daytona 200 was run in 1947, the same year as the AMA rally, races, and Gypsy Tour in

Hollister, California. The latter, a hitherto unremarkable event was about to become indelibly inked into the history books. Depending on which publications are consulted, the goings-on at Hollister over the 4th of July weekend in 1947 were anything from a full-scale riot to little more than an amount of general rowdiness and beer drinking. The *San Francisco Chronicle* of Monday July 7, 1947, described it as "The 40 hours that shook Hollister." The lines between fact and fiction have been blurred by time and the fact that *Life* magazine and subsequent movie maker, Stanley Kramer, picked up on the incident. Otherwise it probably would have faded into obscurity as the newsprint yellowed. The beer drinking, spinning donuts, racing in the street, and a few arrests for drunkenness would have simply been put down to "the boys having too much fun." Instead the

result was the 1953 Columbia Pictures film *The Wild One*. It starred Marlon Brando and Lee Marvin and, regardless of its interpretation of the facts, was pivotal in a number of respects. Firstly, it set the style for future motorcyclists in terms of clothing and bikes. Brando as the now legendary Johnny wore a peaked cap and highway patrol jacket while Marvin as his rival was every inch the up-and-coming outlaw biker in his sleeveless jacket, scruffy beard, cap comforter, and goggles. Brando's Johnny fronted the Black Rebels MC and rode a Triumph twin while Marvin did the same for the Beetles MC from the saddle of a chopped hog. As an aside, the latter club name is where the British pop group, The Beatles, took their name.

Apart from inspiring hundreds of youngsters to copy the riders' styles of both clothes and motorcycles, the film incurred the wrath of conservative America edging its way towards

McCarthyism. The country was becoming concerned about destabilization and to some the film appeared to be an abomination that apparently promoted subversion and antisocial

ABOVE: The name "Panhead" was derived from the shape of the rocker covers that resemble upside down saucepans.

ABOVE RIGHT: The hydraulic lifters on the 1948 Panhead not only reduced maintenance requirements, but also made the motor run a whole lot quieter.

RIGHT: Although the WL45 was a lot slower than Indian's 101 Scout, it was considerably more reliable, and its production out-lived its competitor by several decades.

OVERLEAF: The 45 earned a reputation the world over. Here members of the '45 Club of Great Britain show their respect for this much-loved machine.

behavior. It implied that all motorcyclists were no-good hoodlums intent only on disrupting the American way. This suggestion had already been made after the actual Hollister incident, and the American Motorcyclist Association keen to distance themselves from it declared that while 99 percent of all motorcyclists were up-standing citizens one percent were not. That one percent included clubs in Hollister, such as the Boozefighters MC.

This then, was the cultural background to biking at the time, but along with the style of clothing the style of the bikes was also changing. Close examination of the photographs from Hollister in the *San Francisco Chronicle* show prewar big twin Harleys with the front fenders removed, wide dresser bars on Flanders risers and at least one with a neatly bobbed rear fender cut back as far as the saddlebag hangers and fitted with a front fender trim. Class rides. The telescopic forked

Harley later seen in the film *The Wild One* is treated similarly although these machines were not in production in 1947.

One of the few companies in existence that did make what can be termed custom parts was the one started by Lucile and Earl Flanders. Earl was a regular motorcycle competition rider who after the war started making custom handlebars for other competitors. He bent the tube to suit his customer's requirements and manufactured them to specific widths. Another product which still bears his name are Flanders risers—sometimes known as dog bones because of their shape—which are a pair of extension bars to lift the handlebars above the stock handlebar clamp. Stroker motors became popular when mechanics started discovering that through mixing and matching of Harley engine components it was possible to increase the capacity of a twin. One way to

achieve this was to use the crank pin, flywheels, and con rods out of the VL flathead and incorporate them into the later engines. The VL had a longer stroke than the overhead valve engines and when used with the standard bore pistons increased the displacement without having to resort to expensive machining. The nickname of "stroker" is self-explanatory since capacity was increased by increasing the stroke.

ABOVE: Bobbed 45s not only went better due to their reduced weight, they also looked far nicer. In many ways this was the start of a split in the culture of motorcyclists—those who rode customized bikes, and those who didn't.

LEFT: After the war, many of the cheap ex-service 45s were stripped of unnecessary parts in an effort to improve performance by making them lighter. This process was known as "bobbing," and so a whole new style was born, as exemplified by this sweet little bobbed 45.

The scene was set for a splinter of the biking community to break away from the rest of the pack and in March, 1948, the inevitable happened, an event that would later propel the chopper and the Harley-Davidson far beyond California's freeways. The first chapter of the Hell's Angels was founded in Berdoo—San Bernardino, California. By 1954 the club was becoming established in San Francisco, California. It is recorded that in order to found another chapter, a rider known as Rocky traveled north on a classic chopper of the time. It featured tall apehanger bars and chromed XA springer forks. The latter components were the forks from an experimental World War II Harley-Davidson and four inches longer than stock springers. The cast VL springers from prewar big twin flatheads were equally desirable for early choppers for similar reasons. The mix and match concept of the chopper was firmly

ABOVE: At the end of the war, the Allies acquired the designs of many German motorcycle factories. This 1948 S-125 was based on the DKW engine and was intended for the economy market.

BELOW: The UL was very much the motorcycle equivalent of the Model T Ford. This 1948 machine has received a whole lot more loving care than most Model T's ever received!

ABOVE: Introduced in 1947, more than 10,000 S-125s were sold in the first seven months of production. This example dates from 1948.

BELOW: The wartime 45s were further developed to cope with every possible kind of environmental condition, from the snows of Russia to the deserts of North Africa. Reliability of the civilian bikes throughout the model range benefited extensively from this work, which increased their popularity enormously. This machine is a 1948 WL45.

ABOVE LEFT: An easy way to identify the 45 series of engines is by looking to see which side the drive train is on—big twins have the chain on the left: 45s such as this 1948 WL45 have it on the right.

BELOW LEFT: Servicars are still popular today—especially when solo riders are going on a run, as it gives them somewhere to stash their tents and sleeping bags. This machine dates from 1948, although you wouldn't guess from its condition!

ABOVE: The Model S 125cc was advertised as an excellent beginner's bike, which it undoubtedly was.

BELOW: Restoring bikes like this immaculate 1949 Panhead can take years, depending very much (among other things) on parts availability.

The Fifties

The 1950s was a time of plenty in an America that was enjoying a massive manufacturing boom. The only blot on the landscape was the Korean War. In response to the outbreak of this war in the Far East in 1950, the US Department of Defense reactivated the Ordnance Tank Automotive Center in Detroit, Michigan, with a view to mobilizing the automotive industry for war production. Most of the automakers had received military contracts of one sort or another but in excess of eight million cars, trucks, and buses were produced in the USA in 1950—estimated to be more than 75 percent of all the vehicles made in the world that year.

In 1951, the People's Republic of China sent troops and assistance to the communist North Koreans. This escalation in the war led to restrictions on certain metals including zinc, chromium, tin, and nickel that could be used by the American auto industry for work other than that concerning defense. The Korean War dragged on through 1952, the year that Republican Dwight D Eisenhower was elected president, and ended only after the agreement at Panmunjon in July 1953.

The federal program in the mid-fifties for interstate and freeway development within the US was to cause a shift in the buying patterns for motor vehicles of all types.

In 1957, Russia's Sputnik, the world's first satellite, went into orbit and started the space age. In recognition that such new technology would no doubt have a place in the automobile industry, various manufacturers produced futuristic vehicles. In the same year Harley-Davidson upgraded the K model motorcycle to overhead

continued on page 194

ABOVE: In 1949, the Harley factory finally replaced the leading-link front forks on certain bikes with the far more efficient hydraulic units used by just about every other manufacturer in the world. This 1950 Hydra-Glide has just such a front end.

LEFT: The Harley factory has always been keen on celebrating its birthdays, and in doing so has produced many such specials. It seems a bit strange, though, that this was celebrated in 1954, as by then it was 51 years since the beginning of the company.

RIGHT: A close-up of the front fender of a 1954 50th Anniversary. Panhead.

The S-125

The S-125 was advertised as a cheap and cheerful answer to local motoring needs in the postwar years. Based on a German design, the lightweight two-stroke single—a real departure for the Harley-Davidson list—was introduced in 1947. One thing was truly Harley, however: the tank shape is very similar to that used on the Sportster. Immediately successful, the S-125 would stay in the Harley list well into the fifties. It weighed 200lb, had a 50in wheelbase, the engine developed about 3bhp, and it was a perfect beginner's bike—so much so that in 1951 the Tele-Glide appeared (S-125 with telescopic forks) and in 1953 the engine was improved to 165cc (to produce the S-165). In total some 100,000 were built between 1947–59.

Model	Hummer
Code	S
Years	1947–59
No. cylinders	I
Valves	t/s
Bore/stroke mm	52 × 58
Capacity cu in	8
Capacity cc	130
Ignition	flywheel magneto
No of gears	3
Drive system	chain
Front suspension	girders, 1951-teles
Rear suspension	rigid
Wheel type	wire
Wheel size inch	19 and 19
Brakes	drum
Wheelbase inch	50

ABOVE LEFT: This S-125 dates from 1952.

BELOW LEFT: The S-125 was a departure for the factory in many ways, not the least of which was that it was a two-stroke.

ABOVE: The Model S-125 was introduced in 1947, and continued in production almost unchanged for 13 years. The model shown here is from 1950.

Model	Hummer
Code	ST
Years	1953–59
No. cylinders	I
Valves	t/s
Bore/stroke mm	60 × 58
Capacity cu in	10
Capacity cc	160
Ignition	flywheel magneto
No of gears	3
Drive system	chain
Front suspension	teles
Rear suspension	rigid
Wheel type	wire
Wheel size inch	19 and 19
Brakes	drum
Wheelbase inch	50

valves and redesignated it the XL. It also became known as the Sportster for the first time, a name that has endured until the present time. The development of this model paralleled that of the big twins.

Meanwhile, production of the Servicar continued largely unaltered. Its load carrying ability endeared it to numerous business users, including garage proprietors, who despatched their mechanics to breakdowns with tools and spares in the cargo body. Garages also used them to collect customers' cars for servicing, returning to the garage towing the Servicar with a special bumper attachment. The Servicar also found favor with numerous American police departments for a variety of duties including emptying parking meters and giving out parking tickets. The rider rode past parked cars and marked the windshields with chalk. After a suitable interval he

would return and any with the colored mark that had exceeded the allotted period for parking were ticketed.

The big twin-engined Harleys were sequentially upgraded throughout the fifties. The Panhead had superseded the Knucklehead in 1948 and would itself be superseded by the Shovelhead in 1966. There were numerous smaller upgrades to the Hydra-Glide between those dates. In 1952, a customer-specified option of a foot gear shift was made available. Panheads so equipped were designated as FLF, while the traditional hand shift remained as the FL.

ABOVE & ABOVE RIGHT: The K series model was first produced in 1952, in 45cu in (740cc) format. It had a flathead engine which was inherently not a very good performer. By 1954, the engine capacity had been increased to 55cu in (900cc) in an attempt to maintain sales until the new Sportster engine was available.

The basic E and F models were discontinued in 1952 and the smaller capacity EL, ELF, and ES in 1953. From then on Panheads were 74cu in (1,200cc) only. Details were redesigned, such as the change in 1955 to the three-light dash, which featured an extra warning light over two of the earlier models. The three lights were circular and located in different positions to the two rectangular lights used from 1947 to 1955.

The top of the range big twin for 1955 was the FLH with the stronger bottom end and higher compression. It was the FLH that coined the term "dresser" as owners of big twins used to accessorize their machines with saddlebags and windshields.

Initially these accessories were made from leather and canvas, but as times moved on they were manufactured from glass fiber and plastic and so the big bikes, which looked even

bigger with the accessories, became referred to as "dressed."

Harley-Davidson, who have always marketed a line of official accessories, began to offer such equipment off the showroom floor. The rigid frame was finally upgraded to swingarm rear suspension in the Duo-Glide in 1958.

The Duo-Glide was the logical extension of the Hydra-Glide. The Duo prefix referred to the two suspension systems, front and rear, basically an FL with a Glide at both ends. A chromed badge was also fitted either side of the front fender to emphasize this feature. The front end remained as before with hydraulic telescopic forks, while the rear was upgraded with the introduction of a swingarm and shock absorbers.

The Duo-Glide was renamed later when the electric start appeared in 1965. It became known as the Electra-Glide (the hyphen in the name was later dropped), in other words a Duo-Glide with electric start.

When the Duo-Glide was introduced in 1958 it was offered in both FL and FLH forms with a Panhead engine that supplied the get up and go. The original Panhead was upgraded in 1955 with a new bottom end that incorporated stronger bearings.

In order to satisfy the demands of all its customers including those whose tastes were largely traditional,

Harley-Davidson continued to keep both models in production. The earlier E and F models with lower compression were dropped and so the new bottom end was suitable for the more powerful FLH model. The FLF was a footshift hand clutch variant.

The styling of the Duo-Glide was typical of its time with chrome trims, whitewall tires, and two-tone paint. Such styling was apparent in both the products of two- and four-wheeled vehicle manufacturers, although by 1958 Harley-Davidson had been the sole domestic US motorcycle manufacturer for five years.

The FL Duo-Glide used a Panhead engine with a capacity of 74cu in (1,200cc) and its ignition system relied on contact breaker points. Its carburettor was made by Linkert and a Pancake air filter was fitted to it. The exhaust pipes were of a two-in-one design, known as fishtails because of their shape. Transmission was a four speed and the mechanical components were bolted into a tubular steel frame with the much-vaunted swingarm rear suspension. The swingarm was the biggest new feature of the Duo-Glide and was visible below the studded saddlebag, while the chromed shock absorber could be seen in front of it. At the front was a 16in spoked wheel and drum brake and at the rear, the same 16in spoked wheel and drum brake

with the addition of the drive sprocket. Suspension at the front was provided by telescopic forks. The styling of the bike was impressive, it incorporated wide handlebars, a headlight of 9in diameter and a tank mounted dash panel. The fuel tank itself was of the rounded "Fat Bob" style and the oil tank was of a chrome horseshoe design. A large solo saddle and footboards provided comfort for the rider.

Harley-Davidson were no doubt proud of the fact that they had produced a big twin with rear suspension to complement the similarly equipped, smaller capacity K models and announced it with the badge on the FL front fender. The provision of rear suspension by means of a swingarm and pair of rear shock absorbers meant the repositioning to vertical of the teardrop-shaped toolbox that had been a feature of Harley-Davidsons since before World War II. Wide handlebars were sited above the headlight mounted in the distinctive cast nacelle. The fuel tank held the dash-mounted speedo, while the oil tank was of a horseshoe design mounted between the frame rails under the seat, in this case a solo saddle.

Later Harley-Davidson upgraded the model into the Electra-Glide with the introduction of their first electric starter on a big twin (the Servicar had been upgraded to electric start a year

LEFT ABOVE & BELOW: The Hydra-Glide was the first Harley to receive a name rather than a model number. The "Glide" designation continues to this day and will undoubtedly continue for a good few years yet!

RIGHT & BELOW: Two views of a 1950 WL45. Even though the Harley factory was producing bikes like the Panhead by the early fifties, the humble 45 was still in great demand.

earlier). A year later the engine was replaced with the first of the Shovelheads, essentially a new top end on the Panhead bottom end.

Alongside these improvements and modifications to the frame and forks of the big twin powered motorcycles, there were numerous detail improvements made to the engine itself. In all there were six different Panhead engines. The first was made between 1948 and 1953 in both 61cu in (1,000cc) and 74cu in (1,200cc) capacities. The second type with a different pinion shaft was made only in 1954. The bearings on the engine sprocket shaft were altered in 1955. A spring loaded shock absorbing sprocket was incorporated and the lubrication system was changed very slightly. The next change happened in 1958 when the pinion shaft was altered in order to accept larger main bearings and this was how the motor stayed

RIGHT: The WR racer was built for Class-C dirt track racing, and was supplied ready to compete. This is the only 1952 model in existence, and is to be found in the Otis Chandler Collection, Oxnard, on the Pacific coast highway.

BELOW RIGHT: By the mid-fifties, the Servicar had been used by everyone from farmers to policemen. These days most surviving examples have been restored and are used purely for private leisure.

BELOW: 1958 saw the use of telescopic hydraulic dampers for the rear suspension of the big twins for the first time. The new model was called the "Duo-Glide."

until 1963. In that year the oil feed to the cylinder heads was taken through an external oil line. The final changes were made to the cases and covers of the Panhead to make it suitable for the fitment of the electric starter.

It was around this time that the "chopper" surfaced as an up and coming fashion. Some Harley riders were already heavily accessorizing their bikes to dress them up and others, who were probably reacting to that, decided to "undress" them by "chopping" everything off. These bikes bore a strong resemblance to the race-style bobbers of an earlier era, at least for a while, but later developed distinctive fashions including over-length forks, small tanks from scooters and mopeds, and jockey shift gearchanges among others. These unofficial styles became so important to Harley riders around the USA that later, in the Shovelhead era, Harley-Davidson started offering mildly customized models from dealers' showrooms, inventing the concept of the "factory custom."

Meanwhile, Indian could not compete with the rising tide of British imports and closed in 1953. They had

Corporation—would continue the manufacture of Indian Chiefs until 1953. In that year Titeflex closed down the motorcycle production operation as due to making insufficient profits. It was an ignominious end for a proud company that through its history had a reputation for innovation and engineering excellence.

In contrast, Indian's last domestic competitor, Harley-Davidson instead preferred to compete head-on with the newcomers and introduced motorcycles designed to do exactly that. The K model was one such machine and a curious mixture of old and new. The last 45cu in (740cc) W-series flathead

tried rebadging imported British bikes as Indians, but it was a shortlived and unsuccessful policy. The final blow to Indian's chance of survival came from something completely unrelated to motorcycles, when the British government devalued its currency, the pound, by almost 20 percent. This had the effect of drastically reducing the price of their exported motorcycles, mean-

ing that Indian were unable to compete on price. Considerable wrangling had gone on at management level, but the outcome was that the banks gained control of Indian and divided it into two companies. One was known as The Indian Sales Corporation and would distribute numerous British brands in the USA, while a subsidiary of The Atlas Corporation—The Titeflex

was made in 1951, but a new unit-construction flathead engine was fitted in the K model. The KH was a developed version of the K model, which itself was in some way an updated WL model. The K model was a unit construction side-valve V-twin built with a foot change hand clutch transmission. It was aimed at competing with the British bikes imported from Europe in the years after World War II and so had some similar features. The drum brake is very British in appearance and laced to a 19in rim, a popular European size.

The main drawback with the K model was that its performance did not match those of the imports so in 1954 the KH was introduced. It was a K model engine with a lengthened stroke, which meant its displacement went up to 55cu in (900cc). It also had new flywheels, cylinder barrels, an improved clutch, and was overall a

LEFT: This S-125 was originally a 1954 50th Anniversary Model.

BELOW LEFT: When the Hydra-Glide was first introduced, it had 50bhp, however, by the time this bike was built in 1955, the power output had risen to 55bhp.

BELOW: This very special machine is one of several Harley-Davidsons owned by Elvis Presley. It is a 1956 K Model, and is on display as part of a museum exhibition.

better motorcycle and one that could compete with the British imports on more even terms. It remained in production until 1956 when it was replaced by the models designated XL; the first of the motorcycles referred to as Sportsters.

The K-model resembled its foreign competitors in styling in that it had a swingarm rear suspension assembly, telescopic forks, foot shift gearchange, and neat compact lines. The smaller rounded gas tank precluded the mounting of the speedo in the tank dash so it was mounted in the top of

Model	45
Code	K
Years	1952-53
No. cylinders	V-twin
Valves	sv
Bore/stroke inch	2¾ × 3¹³⁄₁₆
Capacity cu in	45
Capacity cc	740
Ignition	coil
No of gears	4
Drive system	chain
Front suspension	teles
Rear suspension	s/a
Wheel type	wire
Wheel size inch	19
Brakes	drum

ABOVE: Simplicity and light weight was the order of the day when building a bobbed bike, such as this fine Knucklehead.

BELOW: This fifties style bobber was built by Warr's UK, one of the oldest Harley-Davidson dealers in Europe.

RIGHT: This close-up of a Panhead engine shows that much of the bottom end was more or less the same as that of the Knucklehead, the cylinder heads being the major difference.

LEFT, BELOW LEFT, & PREVIOUS PAGE:
The KHK was a sports version of the KH, with lower handlebars less chrome and a more powerful engine.

RIGHT: This 1956 Panhead has the handsome cast gastank badges which came in during the previous model year.

Model	55
Code	KH
Years	1954–56
No. cylinders	V-twin
Valves	sv
Bore/stroke inch	2¾ x 4⁹⁄₁₆
Capacity cu in	55
Capacity cc	900
Ignition	coil
No of gears	4
Drive system	chain
Front suspension	teles
Rear suspension	s/a
Wheel type	wire
Wheel size inch	19 and 18
	drum

the fork shrouds instead. Later Sportsters had the speedo mounted on a bracket from the handlebar clamp. The side-valve engine was of unit construction, but was vastly slower than the imports and the KK model was

ABOVE: The rigid frame on this 1957 Panhead Hydra-Glide was discontinued at the end of the year—this applied to all big twins in the model range.

ABOVE LEFT: The FL series was available both as a standard bike, or as the FLH version which had polished ports and higher compression pistons fitted. This added about five horsepower.

BELOW LEFT: Panhead Hydra-Glide—this model was fitted with the "Jubilee" horn as standard equipment.

introduced in response to criticisms of the speed of the K model. The KH model was introduced a couple of years later with an enlarged capacity, 55cu in (900cc) and capable of 95mph. Side-valve engines were decidedly old-fashioned by the late fifties and were being quickly superseded by overhead valve engines. The side-valve KH engine was the first of the unit

construction Harley-Davidson engines to displace 55cu in (900cc). This displacement is still found in Sportsters today, and some Evolution Sportsters use the figure as part of their designation. The KH evolved into the XL Sportster, which made its debut in 1957. The XL model was a 55cu in (900cc) overhead valve, V-twin engined motorcycle with an integral four speed transmission. It featured an oil bath primary chain drive and sealed dry clutch. The bike was based around a swinging arm frame and telescopic forks. It was soon followed by the XLCH model, which was a more basic motorcycle that debuted in 1958 and was followed by the XLH of 1960.

By 1958, the Sportster brochure mentioned that horsepower could be increased through bigger ports and valves. There were to be numerous versions of the Sportster over the next forty-plus years. The XLCH Sportster

continued on page 229

OPPOSITE, ABOVE & LEFT: 1957 saw the arrival of a very significant bike—the XL Sportster. For the first time in years, Harley-Davidson had a bike that could compete head to head with the European imports that were flooding in from factories such as Norton, BSA, and Triumph. The Sportster very quickly became the bad boy of the Harley range, especially since it appealed to younger customers who were looking for hot rod performance rather than low-speed workhorses. The Sportster engine was based on that from the KH, but instead had among the many design improvements, overhead valves and more efficient combustion chambers. The view from the seat shows that the Sportster's equipment was kept to the bare minimum, just as the customer required it.

ABOVE: The white-wall tires on this 1958 Duo-Glide matches its paintwork and gives the bike a more cohesive look.

BELOW: Many different factories acquired and used the DKW two-stroke design after the war. BSA produced the Bantam in 125 and 175cc forms, and while the Harley-Davidson version started out as a 125cc bike, it soon grew in capacity—this machine is a 1958 ST-165.

RIGHT: Although the XL Sportster was a massive improvement over its predecessors, its carburetor left a little to be desired. Many owners replaced this troublesome item with after-market versions, such as the later S&S unit on the bike (BOTTOM). The polished headlight (TOP LEFT) was faired in to suggest streamlining and so continue the performance theme and the swinging arm rear suspension (TOP RIGHT) was a big step forward in handling terms.

Code	XL
Years	1957–59
No. cylinders	V-twin
Valves	ohv
Bore/stroke inch	3 x 3¹³⁄₁₆
Capacity cu in	55
Capacity cc	900
Ignition	magneto or coil
No of gears	4
Drive system	chain
Front suspension	teles
Rear suspension	s/a
Wheel type	wire
Wheel size inch	19 and 18
Brakes	drum
Wheelbase inch	57
Seat height inch	30.5

PREVIOUS PAGE: This 1959 XL Sportster may look basic by today's standards, but it was a revolution to its customers. Separate exhausts were fitted to allow the high compression engine to breathe properly.

ABOVE: Another pretty 1958 Duo-Glide with white-wall tires.

LEFT: The bike is a Sportster and proud of it, so the name was emblazoned in many prominent places, such as here on the handlebar mount, as well as right across the primary chaincase in big cast letters.

Code	XLH & XLCH
Years	1958–71
No. cylinders	V-twin
Valves	ohv
Bore/stroke inch	3 x 3¹³⁄₁₆
Capacity cu in	55
Capacity cc	900
Ignition	magneto or coil
No of gears	4
Drive system	chain
Front suspension	teles
Rear suspension	s/a
Wheel type	wire
Wheel size inch	19 and 18
Brakes	drum
Wheelbase inch	57
Seat height inch	30.5

LEFT & ABOVE: The 1959 XLH sportster was relatively light, handled reasonably well, looked good and sounded better.

BELOW: A close-up of the dash on a 1959 XLH Sportster—although the speedometer went up to 120mph, this would have been very optimistic!

LEFT: The XL Sportster had 6-volt electrics and was started by kickstart only.

ABOVE: The KR factory racer came with a two-piece frame with a rigid rear end. This 1956 bike is in the Otis Chandler Collection.

BELOW: Even if the racing number plates were removed, it would be easy to see that this bike was built for speed. From the drilled engine plates to the lightweight wheel rims and sprockets, this bike is pure racer.

LEFT: The Sportster had a solo seat, although a dual was available as an optional extra.

BELOW LEFT: The 1959 XLH Sportster. The Sportster engine used a stroke of 3.8125in, the same as the K, although it had a larger bore which gave it a capacity of 55cu in (900cc).

RIGHT: The lovely WR dirt track racers were made between 1941 and 1951—this one has had many parts chromed and is undoubtedly in better condition than when it was first made.

BELOW: A 1958 Panhead engine in closeup. Two versions were available—the low compression engine ran cooler and was suited to heavy traffic, whereas the higher compression version was better on the open roads.

Racing in the Fifties

Following the demise of board tracks, dirt-track racing became the most widespread form of racing in the United States, the breeding ground for the great drivers. Postwar, in 1946, the AMA set up the national championship and for most of the years since then, dirt track, and in particular the Tourist Trophy—TT—races, have been important contributors to the winner's Number One plate.

Similar to the Class C events of the 1930s, dirt-track racing in the fifties and sixties was dominated to a remarkable degree by Harley—often by manipulation of the racing rules to ensure that opponents' machines could not run competitively and by blanket use of the check book to ensure the maximum

number of Harley-equipped entrants to each event. Starting with the 1941 WR flathead racer, Harley built specialist racers—the KR with a flathead V-twin in a rigid frame; the KRTT in a swinging arm frame for TT events; the KRM for desert racing. Great names included: Carroll Resweber from Port Arthur, Texas, national champion in 1958, 1959, 1960, and 1961. He retired after

ABOVE: Fine-looking 45cu in (740cc) WR dirt track racer.

ABOVE LEFT: The K Model was almost a completely new motorcycle—it had a double-loop frame, with a swinging arm and telescopic forks; this machine was converted for dirt-track racing.

LEFT: The KRTT dirt track racer was basically an improved and updated blend of the WR and the K models, with many relevant additions to help performance on the racetrack.

a bad crash at the Lincoln, Illinois, Half Mile Race while leading the 1962 championship. Al Gunter rode a KH model during 1955 and raced regularly at the famous Ascot track where he won the eight mile National Dirt Track Championship Race eight times. Johnny Gibson won at Daytona in 1956 in what was then nicknamed the "Handlebar Derby" because of its close racing. Joe Leonard was an accomplished rider who had a successful career racing Harleys. He won the Daytona 200 in 1957 and 1958 on a KR model as well as 25 other AMA National Championship races. He was the AMA Grand National Champion in 1954, 1956, and 1957. And then there was Bart Markel, aggression personnified, who won three championships and collided innumerable times with racers and crash barriers.

was new for 1958 and had been introduced in response to demands from
the West Coast for a stripped down
Sportster suitable for scrambling and
other types of competition. The competition version had the rear fender
bobbed just behind the strut and the
front fender removed. The Sportster in
this form was a brutal looking and
functional motorcycle.

*LEFT: The XLH Sportster of 1959 had bigger
valves and higher compression pistons to
improve performance.*

*BELOW LEFT: A fine-looking 45cu in (740cc) WR
dirt-track racer.*

*BELOW: The Duo-Glide was built to be ridden—
this 1959 example is being set free to cruise
the roads.*

The Sixties

The swinging sixties would be as much a roller-coaster ride for Harley-Davidson as it was for the inhabitants of the western world. The decade started with unbounded optimism, on the back of a peaceful decade that had seen the United States take its place as leader of the free world. When, on November 9, 1960, the youthful and vigorous Democrat John F Kennedy was elected President, it seemed that it was a time for new beginnings.

This is not the place to examine in detail the highs and lows of the sixties—Vietnam, the Cuba Crisis, JFK's assassination, in contrast to Martin Luther King's dream, the civil rights movement, and the moon landing. Suffice to say that the troubled decade mirrored Harley's ups and downs: on the one hand the US's favorite marque gained the man who would become its styling guru— "Willie G" Davidson, son of founder William A—in 1962 and the influential Electra-Glide.

On the other, the sixties would produce the least attractive Harley ever— the Topper scooter—encounter massive competition from Japanese imports, and end up in an unhappy relationship with the American Machine and Foundry (AMF) in 1968.

The Electra-Glide was introduced in 1965. It was essentially a Duo-Glide with the addition of an electric starter, as its name suggested. Power for the new model came from the proven Panhead engine although this was replaced by the new "Shovelhead" engine a year later and subsequently the Evolution and Twin Cam engines.

By the mid-sixties Harley-Davidson's share of the US domestic motorcycle market had contracted considerably and only three percent of its production was being exported. It became clear that Harley—the last American motorcycle manufacturer— would go the way of Indian unless it received a substantial cash injection.

By the end of the decade America was bitterly divided over the issues surrounding the Vietnam war as the viewpoints of the counter-culture became increasingly widespread. However, the belief that bikers and

ABOVE: A 1960s Knucklehead chop with ape hanger handlebars, slash-cut straight-through pipes, and 16in wheels.

RIGHT: The XLH Sportster was available with so many optional extras that it's unusual to find two that are the same!

Hell's Angels were the defenders of the generation of draft card burners and the flower people's guardians had been exposed as urban myth. A notable moment occurred when the Oakland Hell's Angels interrupted an antiwar protest march from radical Berkeley toward the Army depot in Oakland. The truth of the situation was that, in the main, bikers tended to be blue collar in upbringing and outlook while the radical liberals were, in general, from white collar families.

The Panhead-powered Duo-Glide for 1960 was an opulent touring motorcycle for which a dazzling array of accessories was available, including fiberglass rear panniers, tinted screens, chromed mudguard bars, whitewall tires, exhaust covers, dual seat, luggage carriers, and optional colors including Hi-Fi red and white. Chrome covers on the shock absorbers, trumpet horns, and suchlike were all typical of the era and led to the bikes being referred to as "dressers" or more disparagingly "garbage wagons."

The FLH designation had been new for 1955, the H indicating polished ports and Victory camshafts, ie. H for "hopped up" or "hot." The 74cu in (1,200cc) displacement Duo-Glide engine produced 55bhp at

7200rpm and was capable of 100mph. Furthermore, the machine had a four-speed transmission.

The 1961 Duo-Glide range brochure promoted the new year's models and highlighted the detail and option upgrades. The same can be said of the 1962 range brochure. It wasn't until the middle of the decade that real development could be seen, when in 1965 the electric starter was added.

Many US police departments of the sixties bought Harley-Davidsons for traffic duties. This was very important business to the company who went so far as to produce special police motor-cycle brochures. So popular have they proved that many departments still order bikes from Harley. Over the years police Harley-Davidsons have even achieved screen fame, appearing in movies such as *Electra Glide in Blue* and *JFK*. The bikes in use at the time the latter film was set would have been Duo-Glides.

By 1960, the three-wheeler Servicar was the only Harley-Davidson still using the 22bhp 45cu in (740cc) displacement side-valve engine as its powerplant. The basic concept of the Servicar as a utility machine remained unchanged although details had been upgraded—fiberglass load boxes, pressed steel rear wheels, and telescopic forks were all fitted. In the final years of the Servicar production even an electric start—from 1964—and a disc brake—from 1972—were

ABOVE RIGHT: The Topper scooter, was offered in 5bhp and 9bhp formats. It only lasted from 1960 until 1965.

BELOW RIGHT: The 1960 "Topper" scooter was powered by the engine from the ST-165, and although it had many novel design features, it failed to catch on.

BELOW: The factory's intention was to create a machine that would allow it to exploit the huge explosion in demand for scooters. Instead, they got the "Topper."

Model	Topper
Years	1960–65
No. cylinders	I
Valves	t/s
Bore/stroke mm	60 × 58
Capacity cu in	10.0
Capacity cc	164
Ignition	flywheel magneto
No of gears	automatic
Drive system	belt/chain
Front suspension	leading link
Rear suspension	s/a
Wheel type	disc
Wheel size inch	12 and12
Brakes	drum

fitted. The machine's ongoing 42 year production run didn't end until 1973.

Scooters were easy to ride and offered cheap transport to youngsters. Consequently the US scooter market flourished during the fifties and accordingly Harley-Davidson introduced their version in 1959 to compete with the European imports.

The Topper featured a centrifugal clutch, a two-stroke engine, a belt drive system that offered automatic gearing, and 12in diameter wheels. However, the 10cu in (160cc) Topper did not have the curvaceous lines of the Italian Lambretta and Vespa designs so was not a sales success. Good sales figures from the beginning of the decade slumped and the machines were dropped from Harley-Davidson's line in 1965. A Topper starred briefly in the TV series *77 Sunset Strip*.

Harley-Davidson also wanted to sell entry level bikes and had marketed

ABOVE: This 1960 XLH has the optional dual seat and grabrail fitted.

ABOVE RIGHT: The 1961 11cu in (175cc) Super 10 Hummer epitomized simple, cheap transport, where performance was not a priority.

Model	250 Sprint
Years	1961–67
No. cylinders	I
Valves	ohv
Bore/stroke mm	66 × 72
Capacity cu in	15
Capacity cc	245
Ignition	
No of gears	4
Drive system	gear/chain
Front suspension	teles
Rear suspension	s/a
Wheel type	wire
Wheel size inch	17 and 17
Brakes	drum
Wheelbase inch	51.2
Seat height inch	28.2

the 8cu in (125cc) two-stroke Hummer. The company then came to the conclusion that it could not build small bikes cheaply enough in the US so bought a controlling interest in the Italian firm of Aermacchi. One of the models that the company made was a four stroke 15cu in (245cc) single. Its cylinder projected forward horizontally and the machine had a four speed transmission, hand clutch, foot shift, and swinging arm rear suspension. The first Aermacchi for the US market was given the factory code of C, named the Sprint, and imported for the 1961 sales season. Between 1961 and 1967 there were CR, CRS, and CRTT versions of the roadgoing Sprint models. All were based around the 15cu in (245cc) displacement OHV single. The CR and CRS were the dirt track versions while the CRTT was the roadrace model.

The Sportster was initially an overhead valve version of the K-model and

displaced 53cu in (870cc) and in stock form produced 32bhp at 4,200rpm. The XL had a four speed transmission and was capable of 90mph. The bike, with drum brakes, telescopic forks, and a swinging arm rear suspension was comparable with the imported British bikes with which it had to compete for sales. In 1965 *Cycle World* magazine tested an XLH Sportster. It achieved 0-60mph in 7.4 seconds and in the standing quarter mile it achieved 84mph and an E.T. of 15.5 seconds.

The bike in question had 18in diameter wheels back and front, a wheelbase of 57in, a seat height of 30.5in, and a 3.75 gallon fuel tank. The 1966 XLH Sportster was one of the kick-start 54cu in (883cc) displacement Sportsters made between 1957 and 1967. Electric start was not available until 1967 and disc brakes were not fitted until 1973. Harley-Davidson considered the sixties XLH as a

sports-tourer, but it was outsold by the XLCH for the simple reason that the latter looked better—some said the CH indicated "Competition Hot." The

Model	Electra-Glide
Code	74FL
Years	1966–69
No. cylinders	V-twin
Valves	ohv
Bore/stroke inch	$3\frac{7}{16} \times 3\frac{31}{32}$
Capacity cu in	74
Capacity cc	1,200
Ignition	coil
No of gears	4
Drive system	chain
Front suspension	teles
Rear suspension	s/a
Wheel type	wire
Wheel size inch	16 and 16
Brakes	drum
Wheelbase inch	60
Seat height inch	31

XLCH had a classic Sportster tank and was a more basic, brutal bike.

The Electra-Glide was introduced in 1965. It was essentially a Duo-Glide with the addition of an electric starter as its name suggests. Power for the new model came from the proven Panhead engine although this was replaced by the new "Shovelhead" engine a year later. The Electra-Glide wasn't the first electric start Harley-Davidson, the Servicar was fitted with an electric start from 1964 and once proven on these utility machines it was fitted to the big twin. On the FLH a larger capacity battery and a volt electrical system were required to power the starter so these items were among the upgrades for the new model. In order to fit these electrical components especially the larger battery the oil tank had to be redesigned. The 74cu in (1,200cc) displacement Panhead fitted to the first Electra-Glides produced

60bhp at 5,400rpm and gave the motorcycle a top speed of 98mph.

The remainder of the Electra-Glide was traditional, period Harley-Davidson. It featured deep valanced fenders, the familiar fatbob fuel tank, sprung saddle, cast alloy headlamp nacelle, spoked 16in diameter wheels, and drum brakes. 1965 FLHs were the first big twins with electric starters and the only year of Electra-Glide production to use the Panhead engine. A year later the Shovelhead engine made its appearance and took the Panhead's place in the Electra-Glide. The early Shovelhead retained the Panhead's bottom end and generator but featured a new top end with a better lubrication system for the overhead valve assemblies. These so-called "generator Shovelheads" are easily identified by the ribbed timing cover on the engine.

Basically from 1948 to 1965, the Panhead was boss and its top end

RIGHT & BELOW RIGHT: The Panhead engine in the Duo-Glide worked well as long as it was well maintained. Should it suffer from owner abuse though, such as falling victim to unskilled hands working on the heads, or if the oil wasn't changed regularly, then all manner of problems would appear.

BELOW: This 1960 XLH Sportster has been modified since it was new; the forks have been lengthened, and the silencers have been replaced with short "chopper pots," along with many other detail changes.

clattered a familiar and beloved sound. Many bikers feel that the big V-twin motor looked at its best in a hardtail frame, ie Harley-Davidson frames that predate the introduction of the Duo-Glide. The looks of a rigid and a V-twin started it all, the only suspension was the 10lb rear tire pressure but the style was low, lean, and clean. A

righteous ride of the time consisted of the major components from the 74cu in (1,200cc) Harley-Davidson "hog" and as little else as possible.

Chopped hogs were little more than the heavy Harley frame, forks, and wheels, a 74cu in (1,200cc) V-twin engine, small gas tank, and tiny seat. Much more recently Harley-Davidson registered the word HOG as an acronym for the Harley Owners Group. They then set about litigating against all the chopper shops that had been using this particular slang in their shop names for decades.

The irony in this is that the company has regularly distanced itself from the One Percenters and their choppers but frequently takes aspects of their style for its own, even admitting to the notoriety of the past in advertising copy and equipping HOG members with back patches. It's hard to underestimate just how huge an influence

ABOVE LEFT: A close-up of the handlebar layout of a 1960 XLH Sportster.

BELOW LEFT: The Panhead engine continued to be used successfully in the sixties as can be seen with this 1961 Duo-Glide.

ABOVE: This 1961 Duo-Glide full dresser has been fitted with almost every accessory available at the time.

BELOW: Other models might be updated regularly, but the Servicar was still the same as models many years older—getting the job done for industry and commerce all over the world.

this chopper-styling had on the design and styling of the factory-stock bikes offered by the company from the late-eighties onwards particularly the nostalgic and custom models.

The Servicar was upgraded with the fitment of an electric start in 1964 when its model designation was changed from G to GE. This meant that the humble working Servicar was actually the first Harley-Davidson to come equipped with an electric starter, the mighty Electra-Glide did not appear until 1965. The difference between pre- and post-1964 Servicars are easy to spot as the later machines have a large alternator mounted on the frame downtube. The starter itself is mounted on top of the transmission and drives the outer clutch hub to start the engine. The large unit was deemed necessary to charge the battery enough to ensure sufficient power for starting. Some other changes to the

RIGHT: A close-up of the dash on a 1963 XLCH.

BELOW & BELOW RIGHT: The XLCH Sportster was produced to meet demand for a hot rod Harley-Davidson, and proved to be very popular.

Servicar were made in conjunction with those made to the solos and others independently. An example of the latter is the shift from spoked wheels to pressed steel ones at the rear and another was the shift from steel load boxes to molded glass fiber ones.

The OHV Panhead engine was superseded by the OHV Shovelhead engine in 1966 and once again it was a new top end on an existing bottom end. The new engine became known as the Shovelhead because the rocker covers bear a similarity to the backs of upturned shovels. Most of the models had designations that started FL,

there were bikes such as the FLB, FLHB and so on. The B suffix denoted electric start and was used until 1969; it was dropped for 1970 presumably because the backup kick starter had been discontinued. The Shovelhead engine as introduced in 1966 was a new type of top end on the latest style Panhead lower end. The new engine featured the same bore and stroke as all big twins back as far as 1941 but not all the parts of these engines were interchangeable. Some other components such as the dash panel and lights were redesigned in 1966 although the idea of a tank mounted speedo and ignition switch remained. The tombstone taillight disappeared in favor of a rectangular unit.

Possibly the biggest boost Harley-Davidsons in general and chopped ones in particular, have ever had came in the last year of the decade. Columbia Pictures released *Easy Rider*.

ABOVE: Although the engine and frame remained the same, the Sprint C had a larger fuel tank than its predecessors, along with covers for the rear shock absorbers and deeper fenders.

BELOW: An Aermacchi 350 Sprint road racer—it had more or less the same engine as the road bike, but had competition parts fitted. This bike has the long distance gas tank fitted.

ABOVE RIGHT: This 1961 Sprint has had a competition muffler fitted, along with racing style handlebars.

BELOW RIGHT: A 1963 Aermacchi Harley-Davidson 250 Sprint road racer—this would have had a race fairing fitted for the track.

Imports and Utilities

Any history of the company would be incomplete without a major mention of the many imported and utility motor-cycles marketed under the Harley-Davidson name. Many of them came from the factory's association with the Italian Aermacchi company in the sixties, but there were also models that came out of Germany's reparations to the Western Allies as a result of World War II.

These included a single-cylinder two-stroke engine, which was directly lifted from the DKW factory's prewar design. In 1947, the factory announced this motor would be the powerplant for a new 8cu in (130cc) utility bike. This was the start of an era of lightweight models that were perceived to be

necessary inclusions in the factory line-up due to the economic condi-tions of the day.

It is worth remembering that at this time most of Europe was more or less a bombed-out ruin. As a result of this exports to the European market were low, which had the knock-on effect of causing a slump in the US domestic marketplace. Motorcycle sales did not escape, and the factory had little choice but to offer machines that peo-ple could afford.

The Hummer sold well for the next decade, especially to younger riders, but the company still failed to offer any models for the incredibly important 350–500cc market. The management had been pressed for years by frustrated dealers for machines to compete with the vast numbers of mostly European imports. As a result of this, Harley per-formed a study and decided that the development costs of creating an up-to-

date range of machines did not make for a viable investment.

The simplest answer was to shortcut the whole process and form an alliance with a foreign competitor, thereby acquiring an entire range. The finan-cially troubled Aermacchi company was ideally placed for such maneuvers, and so in 1960 Harley started negotiations, eventually purchasing a 50 percent stake in the Italian factory. The Swiss-based Aermacchi-Harley-Davidson corporation was created out of this union for the purposes of handling the marketing and administration of the new alliance.

While the purchase was a lifeline to Aermacchi, it was also an enormous opportunity for Harley. Not only did it offer the chance to sell a wide range of models at minimal development cost, but since the Italian company had start-ed out as an aircraft factory, many of these bikes were superbly engineered.

One of these, a 15cu in (245cc) flat single four-stroke machine was marketed in 1961 as the Sprint, but it did at first it need a few minor modifications to make it appeal more to American riders. Poor spares back up and indifferent dealers did not help sales of this excellent bike.

During this period several variants of the American-made 8cu in (130cc) machine were also sold—they were marketed under the names Hummer, Ranger, Pacer, Scat, and Bobcat. Some of these were simple utility motorcycles, whereas others were produced as street scramblers to meet the huge popularity of such bikes.

The factory also produced a machine powered by the same 10 cu in (160cc) engine in an attempt to cash in on the enormous demand for scooters, called the Topper. An ill-conceived design from day one, it was underpowered and too heavy. This meant that it was not allowed

on freeways, considerably limiting its market appeal.

A 3cu in (50cc) machine called the Leggero was the next import offered for sale by the factory—this was first supplied to the market in 1965. Disappointing sales led to the motor's capacity being increased to 4cu in (65cc) a couple of years later, but it needed more than a couple of extra horsepower to improve sales.

While the Harley-Davidson factory was endeavoring to produce a range of lightweight motorcycles, fierce competition had arrived from Japan. Overnight, many of the factory's offerings became

ABOVE LEFT: An Aermacchi Harley-Davidson road racer proves rather too loud for some bystanders!

ABOVE: An Aermacchi Harley-Davidson road racer with the fairing removed to expose the engine for public scrutiny.

obsolete, including all the American made utility models. By the end of the sixties the company's financial situation was bleak, although the onslaught from the Land of the Rising Sun was just one of the many factors responsible.

The acquisition of the Harley-Davidson company by AMF in 1969 heralded a change of management, and was hailed as its salvation. Looking back—with the benefit of thirty years hindsight—it seems incredible how a company that made golf carts was thought to be capable of achieving this expected turnaround.

Nevertheless, it is unlikely that Harley-Davidson would have survived without the AMF takeover. While they did make some strange management and marketing decisions, they expanded the model range considerably, both of domestically produced machines and imports, but more on that subject in the following chapter.

Model	Leggero 50
Years	1965–66
No. cylinders	I
Valves	t/s
Bore/stroke mm	38.8 × 42
Capacity cu in	3
Capacity cc	50
No of gears	3
Drive system	gear/chain
Front suspension	teles
Rear suspension	s/a
Wheel type	wire
Brakes	drum

Model	Leggero 65
Years	1967–71
No. cylinders	I
Valves	t/s
Bore/stroke mm	44 × 42
Capacity cu in	4
Capacity cc	65
No of gears	3
Drive system	gear/chain
Front suspension	teles
Rear suspension	s/a
Wheel type	wire
Brakes	drum

LEFT: Several variants of the American-made 8cu in (130cc) machine were also sold—marketed under the names Hummer, Ranger, Pacer, Scat, and Bobcat. This is a 1964 Scat fitted with higher fenders and exhaust to allow it to be used off road. Compare this to the Pacer below.

BELOW LEFT: The 1964 Pacer had a 11cu in (175cc) two-stroke engine, and was intended for the road only, with low fenders and exhaust pipe.

Model	Super 10 & Ranger
Years	Super 10 1960–61, Ranger 1962
No. cylinders	I
Valves	t/s
Bore/stroke mm	60 × 58
Capacity cu in	10
Capacity cc	160
Ignition	flywheel magneto
No of gears	3
Drive system	chain
Front suspension	teles
Rear suspension	rigid
Wheel type	wire
Wheel size inch	19, Ranger-18
Brakes	drum
Wheelbase inch	50

Model	Scat, Pacer & Bobcat
Years	Scat & Pacer 1962-65, Bobcat-1966
No. cylinders	I
Valves	t/s
Bore/stroke mm	60 × 61
Capacity cu in	11
Capacity cc	175
Ignition	flywheel magneto
No of gears	3
Drive system	chain
Front suspension	teles
Rear suspension	rigid, 1963-s/a
Wheel type	wire
Wheel size inch	19, Pacer & Bobcat-18
Brakes	drum

budget movie, it had cost $375,000 to make and would go on to gross more than $20 million for its distributors. It didn't have a complex plot simply following Wyatt and Billy on their choppers and on the road, but it captured the mood, moment, and the movement perfectly. Hell's Angel Maz Harris writing in 1985 recalled when he first saw the film at its initial screening: "It was like drifting off into another world, a world which we desperately wished to experience for ourselves. In that single 94-minute, budget movie Dennis Hopper managed to encapsulate brilliantly the very spirit of freedom that we had all felt, at one time or another, out there on the road. He presented on screen a ceremonial vindication of what we'd known all along but were unable to articulate."

The film follows two enigmatic characters, Wyatt played by Peter Fonda and Billy played by Dennis Hopper, on their trip cross country aboard two Harley-Davidson choppers. The film gives no clue about their past, it's not where they've come from but where they are going to that is important. Their destination is ultimately Mardi Gras in New Orleans, but it could be anywhere. They are, as the Steppenwolf theme song says, "looking for adventure and whatever

comes our way." The film is set in the uncertain times of the Vietnam War era, the American Army was engaged in the struggle for Hill 937—Hamburger Hill—east of the Laotian border at the time of its release. The film underlines the conflicts within America's changing society and almost inevitably ends in tragedy. Their one and only companion on the road, George a whiskey drinking lawyer, played by Jack Nicholson, is

This film more than anything else propelled the image of the chopper and the Harley-riding biker beyond the boundaries of California and its outlaw clubs and San Francisco's Haight-Ashbury circles. It wasn't the first of the biker movies, Kramer's *The Wild One* had that distinction and there had been others through the sixties including *Wild Angels* and *Hell's Angels '69* and *Hell's Angels on Wheels*, which starred Jack Nicholson. *Easy Rider* was not a big

Three part-restored Duo-Glides—one from 1961 (ABOVE), another from 1962 (BELOW), another from 1963 (ABOVE LEFT), as compared with an original bike with only 10,000 miles on the clock (BELOW LEFT), which dates from 1961.

murdered as later are Wyatt and Billy. The tragic ending didn't alter the effect the film had on many of those who saw it. Another direct effect of the movie was that it spread the word about choppers internationally, notably to Australia and Europe. Great Britain had only one franchised Harley-Davidson dealer for many years, namely Fred Warrs in London. This number gradually increased but it was not until the advent of the Evolution range of Harleys in the eighties that dealers and customers became plentiful.

The bikes in *Easy Rider* are interesting and their styling has had noticeable influences on Harley-Davidson's factory customs of later decades. The film portrayed choppers completely typical of the time, both of the characters ride Panhead-powered, rigid-framed choppers, although they differ in style. The Captain America bike is Fonda's ride, it is a wishbone rigid framed bike with an overstock telescopic front end.

ABOVE & LEFT: Three 1965 Electra-Glides— it is easy to distinguish an Electra-Glide from a Duo-Glide simply by the presence of the massive battery required for the electric start. It can be seen where the oil tank used to sit.

Model	350 Sprint
Years	1969-74
No. cylinders	1
Valves	ohv
Bore/stroke mm	74 × 80
Capacity cu in	21
Capacity cc	340
Ignition	coil
No of gears	4
Drive system	gear/chain
Front suspension	teles
Rear suspension	s/a
Wheel type	wire
Wheel size inch	17/17
Brakes	drum
Wheelbase inch	51.2
Seat height inch	28.2

Apehanger bars are mounted on risers, there is no front brake or fender, a Mustang tank, dual seat and tall sissy bar are fitted and the chopper is finished with a stars and stripes flag paintjob. Hopper's ride is a flamed chop, it too features a wishbone frame and Mustang tank but the forks are not as long or as raked and have T-bars bolted to the top yoke. The bike has a small, English-style front fender and the stock drum brake. These two choppers are the machines that launched a style for choppers that irrevocably link choppers and long forks together. Fashion being what it is, while both bikes would still be welcomed at any custom bike event, Fonda's bike looks like a late-sixties or early-seventies chopper while Hopper's slightly more restrained bike hasn't really ever gone out of style with the possible exception of the type of handlebars fitted. As a result of the movie, rigid frames and high bars are as much a part of motorcycling for many as highways and Harley-Davidsons.

LEFT: Two more 1965 Electra-Glides; one with an S&S carburetor and air filter (BELOW) and the other in near stock form (ABOVE).

BELOW: The first "Sprint" arrived in the US in 1960, and had a horizontal 15cu in (240cc) single cylinder four-stroke engine.

ABOVE: A 1964 Panhead Duo-Glide.:

OVERLEAF: The Duo-Glide was in its final model year when this bike was built in 1964.

ABOVE LEFT: In 1965, the last Panhead-engined Electra-Glide was built. From this time on, Shovelhead engines would be fitted.

BELOW LEFT: 1965 Electra-Glides with white leather trim.

ABOVE: This Duo-Glide was the last "kicker" Panhead—from this point on they would have electric starts and be renamed Electra-Glides.

BELOW: 1964 Scat—when the Japanese started invading with their far superior machines, bikes like this were doomed.

OVERLEAF: A classic Knucklehead chop—high 'bars, upswept fishtail pipes, springer front end.

ABOVE: The 1964 Aermacchi Harley-Davidson Sprint-H was supplied in off-road specification.

LEFT: A detail of the rear suspension arrangement on the Scat and Pacer models, that was positioned in a manner similar to that of the much later Softail.

BELOW: When the M50 moped was brought out in 1965, it failed to sell. It was then enlarged to 4cu in (65cc), but this didn't help either, so the final batch of machines were heavily discounted.

ABOVE RIGHT: This immaculate Sprint was built in the mid-sixties. It was fitted with a four speed transmission and had about 18bhp.

RIGHT: 1964 Scat designed to be used both on and off the road.

LEFT: For some years, the factory discontinued the practice of marking their speedometers with actual mph figures—instead they used the numbers 1 to 12, as can be seen on this 1964 Panhead Duo-Glide.

BELOW: Through the sixties, Servicars continued to ply their trade – this one dates from 1966.

RIGHT: The Electra-Glide is probably the most famous motorcycle of all time. Every small boy and many housewives know the name; this example is a 1966 Shovelhead-engined machine.

BELOW RIGHT: The 1966 Bobcat was a close relation to the Scat and the Pacer; it too was outclassed by the Japanese imports, and was withdrawn from the market in 1966.

LEFT: The Duo-Glide was in its final model year when this bike was built in 1964.

BELOW LEFT: A 1965 Aermacchi Harley-Davidson Sprint street model—it has low fenders and exhaust and street handlebars, all of which separate it from the off road versions with their higher level components.

RIGHT: A close-up of the engine of a 1965 Aermacchi Harley-Davidson Sprint. The contact breakers live behind the small round cover on the side. Below this is the gear lever.

BELOW: The 1966 BTH Bobcat was a departure from conventional styling—it had a fiberglass seat, tank cover, and fender but the rest of the machine was essentially the same as the Scat.

OVERLEAF: The 1964 Panhead Duo-Glide had plenty of storage—from the massive panniers on either side of the rear wheel, to the much smaller toolbox mounted in front of the left shock absorber.

OPPOSITE & LEFT: These three bikes were built in 1966, the first year of the Shovelhead-engined Electra-Glide.

BELOW: This 1967 FLH Electra-Glide has had an S&S carburetor fitted—a very sensible modification.

Racing in the sixties

Racing in the sixties continued as it had in the fifties with dirt-track racing unchanged and road racing only beginning to gain importance—it wouldn't be until the mid-1980s that a separate road racing championship was set up. The bikes were also similar—the venerable KR needed a more modern replacement: it wouldn't arrive until 1970 (see next chapter about the XR750)—and it wouldn't be until 1970 that dirt-track bikes gained brakes! The KR was still the racing version of the K-model introduced in 1952. It had a long production run and was increasingly tuned during it. The first models produced approximately 38bhp and the last in 1969 around 60bhp. The fact that side-valve engined motorcycles were still being

raced competitively during the mid-sixties was largely down to a quirk of the motorcycle racing rules set by the AMA.

1961's Daytona 200 race was to be the first year that riders would use the new purpose-built speedway track. The AMA had reservations about motorcycles racing on the 33-degree banked turns so a two-mile course in the infield was used. The event was won by 22-year-old, Roger Reiman on a Harley-Davidson KR750, the side-valve-engined racer. He covered the 200-mile distance in two hours, 53 minutes, 17.15 seconds, averaging 69.25mph having held the lead from the second lap onward.

Also in 1961 Texas rider, Carroll Resweber, won the national title for the fourth consecutive year after his win at the Springfield, Illinois, event. He rode a rigid framed KR flathead (it is noteworthy that the tuned flathead racers

outlasted the roadgoing versions), but his luck ran out in 1962 when a practice session crash ended his fantastic career while he was leading the championship. Instead Bart Markel, never the most successful of Harley racers on surfaced race tracks, won the title. One of the all-time greats of dirt track racing, he won 28 National Championship races and was AMA Grand National Champion in 1962, 1965, and 1966.

Part of the overall championship, the TT races were a real crowd pleaser. In American racing, TT indicates Tourist Trophy though a TT event is considerably different from European events such as the famed Isle of Man TT races. The US type of TT is held on a dirt track but incorporates jumps and turns in both directions. As a result brakes and suspension were needed so Harley-Davidson built a TT version of the KR model, known as the KRTT with both brakes and suspension. Road racing

Harley-Davidsons used the KRTT frame and brakes that were additionally equipped with fairings and larger capacity fuel tanks. The former items were only sanctioned by the AMA for road- and circuit-racing from 1963 and their first competitive use was at Daytona in spring 1964. Roger Reiman had one fitted to his winning machine, the year he won the AMA championship.

Among the famous names in this discipline was a young Evel Knievel who rode for Harley. In 1963 *Cycle World* magazine track-tested Dick Hammer's KRTT (with rear suspension and brakes) and revealed that the flathead produced 48bhp at 6,800rpm and could attain 145mph.

In 1968, another famous racing name won at Daytona, repeating the success the next year: Cal Rayborn from Spring Valley, California, would go on to become a Grand Prix driver of note; his

teammate Mert Lawwill won the AMA title.

The sixties Aermacchi linkup led to the arrival of the Sprint to take part in the new lightweight 15cu in (245cc) classification. In 1969 Harley Davidson Aermacchi increased the displacement of the Sprint to 21cu in (340cc) by increasing the stroke. The models offered were the SS-350 (SS designating street scrambler) and the CRS for off-road riding—a scrambler that took part in TT races. The first

ABOVE LEFT: An Aermacchi 350 Sprint dirt track racer shows just how versatile the little engine could be—it would perform on the street, the road race track, and dirt tracks as well.

ABOVE: The beautiful lines of this KR road racer are partly due to the aerodynamic seat, which legend has it was first used on a motorcycle by the Harley factory.

national race won by the CR short-track racer was by Carroll Resweber at Sante Fe in 1961. But a few successful years were all that the CR and CRTT notched up: in 1965 Yamaha won its first national; by 1965 Daytona's lightweight race was a Yamaha whitewash and from then on Harley—like everyone else—was snapping at the Japanese heels.

Finally, Harley's streamliners. Built by James Mangham they were powered by short-stroke 15cu in (245cc) Harley-Davidson Sprint engines. The streamliners were clocked at 149.78mph (1964, Roger Reiman) and 176.817 mph (1965, George Roeder) on the salt flats at Bonneville, Utah.

OPPOSITE TOP LEFT: It's unusual to see a Sportster with hard luggage fitted, since most owners wanted performance rather than utility.

OPPOSITE TOP RIGHT: This Servicar has been modified by adding a handlebar fairing. Note the car alternator mounted in front of the engine to allow the fitment of modern lights and ancillary electrical equipment.

OPPOSITE CENTER LEFT: In an attempt to make the M-50 moped more marketable, a conventional gas tank was fitted to make it look like a proper motorcycle.

OPPOSITE CENTER RIGHT: The Rapido Sportster was first imported in 1968; it had a different engine to its predecessor, although it was the same capacity at 8cu in (130cc). This machine dates from 1969.

OPPOSITE BELOW: A late sixties Shovelhead FLH; it is said the kerb weight of such a machine was around 780 lb., approximately twice that of its European rivals.

ABOVE LEFT: Late in 1967 the XLH was fitted with an electric start, which was said to have added around 40lb to the bike's weight.

BELOW LEFT: The 1968 FLH Electra-Glide had a power output of about 60hp, which gave it a top speed of around 95mph.

RIGHT: Early Shovelheads had the Panhead bottom end—this meant that they still had generators. This example is an Electra Glide of 1966/1967.

BELOW & LEFT: Two 1968 XLCH Sportsters. Both are essentially the same model, but one has a solo seat, the other has a dual seat. They both have aftermarket exhausts fitted.

OPPOSITE BOTTOM RIGHT: The speedometers of 1965 Electra Glides were marked 1 to 20, possibly in an attempt by the factory to mask their poor top speeds.

OPPOSITE BOTTOM LEFT: A close-up of the dash of a 1967 XLH shows that it had a revcounter as well as a speedometer.

The Seventies

After some negotiation, Harley-Davidson was bought by American Machine and Foundry (AMF) in 1969, a huge conglomerate that owned a variety of leisure and industrial companies. AMF took over on January 7, 1969. The takeover was not an entirely happy one and led to quality control problems, a strike over job losses, and all the other symptoms of an unsettled industry. Despite the problems, the early seventies were boom years for

ABOVE: The 74cu in (1,200cc) FLH Electra-Glide typifies Harley's tourers of the seventies.

RIGHT: In the late sixties and early seventies, long front ends were de rigeur, as shown on this Shovelhead chop.

BELOW: This early seventies' FLH has stopped for fuel; when it was first supplied, the world more or less stopped for fuel as well, as the Middle-East oil crisis deepened.

motorcycle sales and the AMF-controlled company upped production enormously. In the long term this was to compound quality control problems, but this did not become immediately apparent. AMF is often criticized for its ownership of Harley-Davidson and the way it ran things, but with hindsight it is now generally accepted that if AMF had not bought Harley-Davidson in 1969 the company would not have survived. The new

Model	Super Glide
Code	FX, FXE
Years	1971-78,
	1974-81
No. cylinders	V-twin
Valves	ohv
Bore/stroke inch	3⁷⁄₁₆ x 3³¹⁄₃₂
Capacity cu in	74
Capacity cc	1,200
Ignition	coil,
	1979-electronic
No of gears	4
Drive system	chain
Front suspension	teles
Rear suspension	s/a
Wheel type	wire
Wheel size inch	19 and 16
Brakes	drum,
	1973-discs
Wheelbase inch	62.7
Seat height inch	29

ABOVE: In 1970 the 74cu in (1,200cc) FLH Electra Glide was produced with an alternator, which replaced the previous model's generator.

LEFT: These two 1970 XLH Sportsters had engine capacities of 55cu in (900cc), but in 1972 this was increased to 61cu in (1,000cc).

generation of Japanese superbikes during the seventies were to make AMF begin to consider withdrawing from the Harley-Davidson operation.

The Super Glide was an early factory custom from Harley-Davidson combining the lighter Sportster front end with the muscle of the big twin Shovelhead engine. Its design in a sense acknowledged the existence of choppers and customized motorcycles, and was produced by Willie G

Davidson, the grandson of one of the founders. At the time, in 1970, it was seen as a watershed in US motorcycling. *Cycle* put it on the cover of the November 1970 issue and an article inside the magazine said: "The members of the Harley-Davidson styling team, in response to the genius of Dick Hirschberg, the impact of the chopper phenomenon, and the success of *Easy Rider*, have savaged the venerable Electra Glide like tigers at a goat and herewith present to you the . . . Super Glide, Sonnet on Extravagance."

What had brought this machine from a Milwaukee drawing board and onto the street? William G Davidson, according to *Cycle*, put it down to: "the influence of the California bob-jobs; not full choppers as such, but lightened, leaned-down bikes that were recognizable as 74s."

The Super Glide was launched with a red, white, and blue paint job but, despite the very evident parallel with Fonda's ride in *Easy Rider*, the manufacturer was keen to distance itself from the whole chopper scene. Davidson had this to say: "As a company we're leery of the chopper image and any kind of extremism."

It was an uncertain period for the red, white, and blue because times were changing quickly. President Nixon, inaugurated in 1969, took a completely different approach to the Vietnam War and his scaling down of US military involvement was one aspect of this. Despite the ongoing controversy about the Vietnam War, some dealers clearly knew who bought the Harley-Davidsons they sold. Adverts in 1970 for Dudley Perkins Co, a San Francisco dealer since 1914, included the line, "Returning servicemen welcome."

ABOVE: In 1970 the street version of the 8cu in (130cc) Rapido was dropped from production, but this off-road version survived until 1972.

ABOVE RIGHT: This is an original, unrestored 1972 74cu in (1200cc) AMF Electra Glide.

BELOW RIGHT: This is the last Servicar ever made; it was built in 1973, ending a continuous production run since 1932.

Harley-Davidson had introduced a refined overhead valve 74cu in (1,200cc) engine in 1966 and it had quickly become known as the Shovelhead because of the resemblance of the rocker covers to the backs of upturned shovels. It may seem contrived, but as a nickname it is now universal. This engine was used in the Super Glide which was, without doubt, the factory's interpretation of a custom bike. Harley had taken an FL Electra

Glide, removed the cumbersome front end and replaced it with the lighter one from an XL Sportster, hence the FX designation. They had fitted a 3.5-gallon "fatbob" tank and a custom-styled dual seat unit with an integral frenched taillight.

Amid talk of the lack of frame flex, of rake and trail, and cornering, *Cycle* said, "Everybody likes it; everybody has to like it for one reason or another." They went on to predict that the Super Glide would succeed like no other motorcycle the company had ever built. The magazine was completely right, the Super Glide has been in Harley-Davidson's range ever since and the concept of the factory custom motorcycle was proven beyond all doubt. Subsequently, most of the world's major motorcycle manufacturers, especially the Japanese ones, have at one time or another included factory customs in their ranges.

The biggest refinement to the Shovelhead engine came in 1970 when Harley-Davidson changed from using a DC generator to an AC alternator. This upgrade required major alterations to the crankcases and a number of subtle changes to other parts. As a result of this redesign early Shovelheads are often referred to as Generator Shovels, while later ones are known as Alternator Shovels.

The timing case side of the engine gives an at-a-glance identification of the two types. The way models were numbered changed at this time too, letters and numbers were substituted for models and years. The Shovelhead engine was refined almost continuously: for example, between 1966 and 1980 there were five different oil pumps used within the engines and they are not all interchangeable.

Of all the models ever produced by Harley-Davidson, the mighty Electra

PREVIOUS PAGES: The production of the 1971 FX 74cu in (1,200cc) Super Glide boat-tail was the first time a motorcycle maker had offered anything resembling a custom bike for sale. It had an FLH frame and a Sportster front end.

RIGHT & BELOW RIGHT: These two gleaming 74cu in (1,200cc) Super Glides were built during the AMF era.

BELOW: The boat-tailed Sportster was only produced as an option for a short time before the factory withdrew it and reverted to offering the original design only.

Glide is the most recognizable and the one most likely to be regarded as an American icon. The Electra Glide was used by many Police Departments around the United States and beyond and was immortalized in the film *Electra Glide in Blue*. The model designated Electra Glide has had a

long production run, from its introduction in 1965 to the present time. During this period there have been no fewer than four different Harley-Davidson engines used to power this, the biggest of the Harley-Davidsons. Somehow though it is the seventies' Shovelhead-powered Electra Glides that typify the model most of all. The Shovelhead was to take Harley through the seventies and the years of AMF ownership.

The seventies' Harleys were built under the auspices of AMF. The conglomerate owned a glassfiber plant so fairings, saddlebags, and top boxes were made from glassfiber and the large saddle is designed for two people. As this progression continued, Harley-Davidson's big twins gained weight and size, especially when the FLH models were fitted with hard glassfiber bags. This style of dresser was not to every rider's taste and, in a changing world, a rethink was called for.

LEFT: A proud owner displays his 1976 74cu in (1,200cc) Shovelhead-engined Super Glide.

RIGHT: Motorcycle paintwork comes in many forms—the gas tank on this 1976 74cu in (1,200cc) Super Glide celebrates the Bicentennial—two hundred years of American Independence.

BELOW: There's over the top, and there's way over the top! These two full dressers have just about every conceivable accessory in the catalog fitted.

The 1972 Harley-Davidson FLH Electra Glide was powered by the company's mighty Shovelhead engine with a capacity of 74cu in (1,200cc). The bike's transmission was a four-speed type and both engine and gearbox were installed in a swingarm frame. The model designation of FLH had been used before but the Shovelhead-powered Electra Glide was considered a development of the FLH rather than a completely new motorcycle. The suspension systems were similar to the Duo-Glide; at the front were telescopic forks and at the rear, a swingarm and shock absorbers. The wheels and brakes were upgraded slightly; at the front was a spoked 16in wheel with a single disc brake while at the rear was a spoked 16-inch wheel with a hub-mounted brake drum.

Accessories typical of the seventies were items such as a chromed brake disc cover. The 12-volt battery was

LEFT: These two Shovelhead engines have been fitted with aftermarket air filters. They probably also have non-standard carburetors behind.

BELOW: Comparing this Electra Glide with those on pages 293–295 shows the level of individuality that can be gained on what are, essentially, identical bikes.

carried beneath the upper frame tube and concealed behind a square chrome cover. The oil tank is positioned in the corresponding position on the other side of the machine. During AMF's ownership of Harley-Davidson a popular trademark was the #1 stars and stripes logo used on the points cover of the alternator Shovelhead engine.

Willie G Davidson, grandson of one of the founders was employed within Harley-Davidson's design department and considered the possibilities of a new big twin that would sit in the company's range between the Electra Glides and the smaller Sportsters.

Model	Electra Glide
Code	74FLH
Years	1970-80
No. cylinders	V-twin
Valves	ohv
Bore/stroke inch	3⁷⁄₁₆ × 3³¹⁄₃₂
Capacity cu in	74
Capacity cc	1,200
Ignition	coil, 1978-electronic
No of gears	4
Drive system	chain
Front suspension	teles
Rear suspension	s/a
Wheel type	wire
Wheel size inch	16 and 16
Brakes	drum, 1972-discs
Wheelbase inch	61.5
Seat height inch	33

The new Harley-Davidson emerged in 1970, as a 1971 model designated the FX Super Glide. This was an alternator Shovelhead with the slimmer Sportster front end and none of the big dresser's glassfiber bags or fairings. The first models featured an unusually shaped dual seat and tail-piece manufactured in glassfiber but it was discontinued for the second year of production in 1972 when the Super Glide appeared with a scalloped dual seat, and XL style rear fender.

In many ways the FX Super Glide was the first factory custom and also an attempt to compete with the unauthorized and non-official chopper builders who were thriving on chopping the dresser-style machines. Later there was a succession of FX models each designating a particular detail such as electric start or disc brakes; FXE, FXWG, FXDG, FXR, FXEF, and FXB. The Super Glide (FXE) was

BELOW, RIGHT & OVERLEAF: More fantastic Electra Glides! Although basically the same bike, these examples show just how the selection of a few optional extras or aftermarket components can change the look of a motorcycle to tailor it to the wants and needs of its owner. Some riders clearly want to be heard as well as seen, as they've fitted drag pipes, whereas the others have stayed with stock systems. Some bikers—albeit few!—want the breeze in their face, most others go for windshields. While the list of differences could go on, it all helps to illustrate why Harleys have found their way into the hearts and minds of their owners, and why a complete counter-culture has evolved around them. While dressers may not be to everyone's liking, it would be hard to find a motorcycle that is better suited to riding the long distances of the seemingly endless roads in the US.

Model	Electra Glide
Code	FLH80
Years	1978–84
No. cylinders	V-twin
Valves	ohv
Bore/stroke inch	3½ × 4¼
Capacity cu in	80
Capacity cc	1,310
Ignition	electronic
No of gears	4
Drive system	chain, 1983-belt
Front suspension	teles
Rear suspension	s/a
Wheel type	cast alloy
Wheel size inch	16 and 16
Brakes	discs
Wheelbase inch	61.5
Seat height inch	33

followed by the Low Rider (FXS), which was another factory custom. With its distinctly chopper styling,

forward-control foot-pegs, a low seat height, and a raked out telescopic front end it was poles apart from the full

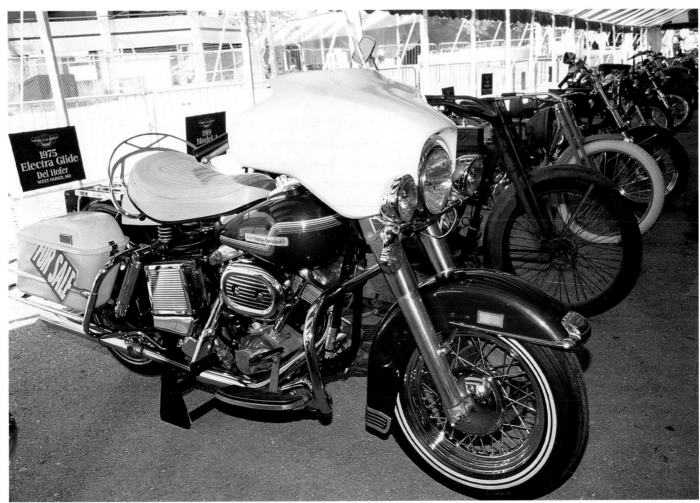

Model	Low Rider
Code	FXS-80
Years	1979-82
No. cylinders	V-twin
Valves	ohv
Bore/stroke inch	3½ × 4¼
Capacity cu in	80
Capacity cc	1,310
Ignition	electronic
No of gears	4
Drive system	chain
Front suspension	teles
Rear suspension	s/a
Wheel type	cast alloy
Wheel size inch	19 and 16
Brakes	discs
Wheelbase inch	63.5
Seat height inch	27

LEFT: Two more Electra Glides.

BELOW: The FXS Low Rrider was released to an unsuspecting public in 1977. While it seemed to buck the trend for sports and touring bikes, it was an immediate success, proving that at least someone at the factory was in tune with the wishes of many Harley customers.

Model	Low Rider
Code	FXS
Years	1977-79
No. cylinders	
Valves	ohv
Bore/stroke inch	3⁷⁄₁₆ × 3³¹⁄₃₂
Capacity cu in	74
Capacity cc	1,200
Ignition	coil, 1979-electronic
No of gears	4
Drive system	chain
Front suspension	teles
Rear suspension	s/a
Wheel type	cast alloy
Wheel size inch	19 and 16
Brakes	discs
Wheelbase inch	63.5
Seat height inch	27

Glide (FXWG) and Fatbob (FXEF) which took the factory custom Harley a way further along the road towards factory choppers—it featured a longer raked front end in which the fork legs were more widely spaced, a stepped seat, and back rest. But—most telling of all—there was a flame paint job on the tank.

Such machines were seen as acceptance by the factory of just who bought the Harley-Davidson motorcycles they made. Prior to this they had tried to

dress Electra Glide (FLH). It was instantly popular and Harley-Davidson followed it with the Wide

disassociate themselves from the chopper riding bikers. This had done them few favors as there was some resentment from

ABOVE, RIGHT, & FAR RIGHT: Throughout the seventies, Sportsters continued to sell well—for many they were the first step toward the world of the Harley big twin fellowship; as such, many regarded them as junior beginner Harleys, not to be taken too seriously. This is a shame as they were (and still are) an important part of the factory's model line-up, and were generally damn good motorcycles.

such riders who rightly felt they alone had stuck with Harley-Davidsons when its market share had contracted drastically.

The 1976 FLH dates from the year of America's bicentennial and is typical of the style of motorcycle constructed by Harley-Davidson. The method of construction and the fact that many parts are interchangeable has helped to promote a growth in aftermarket parts manufacture and therefore encourages riders to slightly customize their motorcycles to suit their own tastes and riding styles.

Model	Fat Bob
Code	FXEF
Years	1979
No. cylinders	V-twin
Valves	ohv
Bore/stroke inch	$3\frac{7}{16} \times 3\frac{31}{32}$
Capacity cu in	74
Capacity cc	1,200
Ignition	electronic
No of gears	4
Drive system	chain
Front suspension	teles
Rear suspension	s/a
Wheel type	cast alloy or wire
Wheel size inch	19 and 16
Brakes	discs
Wheelbase inch	63.5
Seat height inch	27

The lines of the fatbob tank and the dash mounted in it are timeless Harley-Davidson, although the precise details have changed significantly over the years. The FLH at this time was powered by a Shovelhead engine with a capacity of 74cu in (1,200cc). Ignition was by means of points and coil while transmission was four-speed and both units were installed in a tubu-lar steel frame with swingarm rear suspension. Suspension at the front is provided by telescopic forks. The wheels and brakes are traditional spoked 16-inch diameter wheels with

LEFT: The Sportster was another Harley that rarely stayed stock.

BELOW LEFT: The 74cu in (1,200cc) FX1200 Super Glide was advertised as "The Road King." The 1973 model shown here was an improvement over the previous year's model which had suffered from poor brakes and front suspension that was too soft.

RIGHT & BELOW RIGHT: The model range of Super Glides and Low Riders soon acquired a loyal following—these were people who didn't want a tourer or a sports bike, but instead wanted a motorcycle with boulevard cruising style.

disc brakes bolted to the hubs. The caliper used to brake seventies' AMF era Harley-Davidsons such as this was also used on Cessna aircraft. Modern calipers are more compact although the design of disc rotor has not been significantly changed. The rear suspension and disc brake is partially concealed behind the saddlebags. The hub is designed to accept the brake disc on one side and the drive sprocket on the other and is known as a dual flange hub.

The name Electra Glide lost its hyphen down the years (we haven't used it at all in this chapter) and gained weight as it became equipped with larger saddlebags and fairings usually made from glassfiber—to some extent

Model	Fat Bob
Code	FXEF
Years	1979-82
No. cylinders	V-twin
Valves	ohv
Bore/stroke inch	3½ × 4¼
Capacity cu in	80
Capacity cc	1,310
Ignition	electronic
No of gears	4
Drive system	chain
Front suspension	teles
Rear suspension	s/a
Wheel type	cast alloy
Wheel size inch	19 and 16
Brakes	discs
Wheelbase inch	63.5
Seat height inch	27

because of AMF's part ownership of a glassfiber manufacturing plant. The motorcycle in this form became famous to many as "the" Harley-Davidson and was immortalized on film in *Electra Glide in Blue*. By 1979 it had been powered by the "Shovelhead" engine since 1966 and after 1984 would be powered by the Evolution engine. The 1979 FLH 1,200 Electra Glide was powered by a 74cu in (1,200cc) four-stroke OHV V-twin Shovelhead that gave a top speed of 105mph (170kph) and produced 66bhp at 5,200rpm. The transmission was four-speed and the whole motorcycle was constructed around a tubular-steel frame.

Choppers began to seriously diversify in the mid-seventies; as well as the

varying low rider and long forked styles there was a less obvious but possibly more important divergence. Show bikes were becoming increasingly less like rideable street bikes and ever more extravagant, so a style of chopper emerged designed for riding. This successful formula incorporated a mixture of factory-manufactured Harley parts —such as engine, transmission, and maybe the forks and frame—with a combination of custom parts from companies such as Jammer and Paughco; perhaps the tank, frame, forks, and saddle. The custom bikes that resulted were usually Panhead or Shovelhead-powered choppers using rigid or swingarm frames and telescopic or springer forks. When finished with a combination of smaller parts from either custom suppliers or OEM accessories this ensured considerable diversity in the appearance and detail of finished choppers, albeit after a certain general style.

In 1979, as the decade drew to a close, Drag Specialties were supplying many of the custom components to build a chopped Harley. The adverts claimed that the company was the No 1 motorcycle accessory leader in the world with over 9,000 dealers worldwide. In the same year Jammer offered items such as belt primary drive conversions and stamped steel custom wheels that bolted to a hub assembly, in

ABOVE: A late seventies Shovelhead-engined 74cu in (1,200cc) FXs.

LEFT: This heavily customized early seventies style Sportster chop has apehangers, rigid (hardtail) rear suspension and a springer front end.

PREVIOUS PAGE, LEFT: Two Super Glides—note the logos on the tank, AMF Harley-Davidson.

PREVIOUS PAGE, RIGHT: The FX Super Glide may not have been the most popular of Harley's machines, but it debuted a name style that would prove extremely popular.

later years this type of wheel would be machined from billet alloy.

The overall style of the rideable chopper was reflected in the factory's successful Super Glide models. These in their component form can be considered as a Shovelhead engine in a swingarm frame with a telescopic front end, minimal fenders, and other cycle parts. This combination of parts was available through use of an AMF Harley and a number of custom components added on.

Various FX models were manufactured and sold throughout the seventies including the decidedly custom-looking FXS Low Rider of 1977. This machine incorporated shorter forks with greater rake, cast wheels, and a fatbob gas tank. A crinkle finish black Shovelhead engine and silver painted tank and fenders completed the custom look. With ersatz choppers rolling off the factory's assembly lines and selling off the dealers' showroom floors the chopper entered the eighties with something of an identity crisis.

ABOVE & OPPOSITE: In 1977 the 61cu in (1,000cc) XLCR 1,000 Cafe Racer was introduced—it caused a real stir at the time, but even though it was a very pretty motorcycle, it failed to sell in any numbers. The excellent styling was done by Willie G Davidson, who used design cues from flat track racers and sports bikes alike.

BELOW: Shovelhead engined 74cu in (1,200 cc) FX.

In the mid-seventies Harley-Davidson released a range of small-capacity two-stroke, single-cylinder bikes that were similar in appearance to many similar capacity Japanese motorcycles of the time. They had a look of the street scrambler about them and were intended to appeal to the growing market for this type of motorcycle and to attract younger riders to Harley-Davidsons.

The machines were not a great success. The two models introduced in 1974 were the SS and the SX and each was available as a 8cu in (130cc) and a 11cu in (175cc) machine. A 15cu in (245cc) version capable of 85mph followed in 1975. Production ended by 1978 when Harley-Davidson sold off its interest in Aermacchi.

The SX-250, a two-stroke single-cylinder motorcycle, was built in Italy by Aermacchi and marketed by Harley-Davidson in the US to compete with Yamaha's DT-1 street/trail machine that appealed widely to youngsters. The SX-250 displaced 15cu in (245cc) and had a four speed transmission which meant it was capable of 75mph. It was not made after 1978. The SX-250 was one of a succession of small off-road styled bikes from Harley-Davidson.

There was the TX-125 of 1973, the SX-175 of 1974, the SX-250 of 1975 and the street only SS version all of which had little in common with the MX-250 motocrosser also made for Harley-Davidson.

RIGHT: The cone shape of the timing case on the alternator version of the Shovelhead-engined Electra Glide was to become a hallmark feature of big twin engines from 1970 to the present day.

OVERLEAF: A late seventies' Shovelhead-engined 74cu in (1,200 cc) FX.

BELOW: A close-up of the 74cu in (1,200cc) Shovelhead-engined Electra Glide.

Sportsters

The first XL Sportster engine displaced 54cu in (885cc) although by the early seventies there was a 61cu in (1,000cc) version available in a range of models—such as the XL, XLCH, XLT, and XLX amongst others—that stayed in production until the introduction of the Evolution-engined Sportsters in 1986.

Unlike the big twin Harley-Davidsons Sportsters feature "unit" construction, meaning that the engine and gearbox are both part of one casting rather than two separate items. The earlier Sportsters were noted for being fast yet fragile although these characteristics were modified as the years passed. The Sportster received a redesign in 1978 when it was given a new frame.

One Sportster noted as being different from the others in the range was the XLCR of 1977. This was an attempt to put contemporary race styling onto the street, it was not a particularly popular motorcycle at the time, which means that such machines are now desired by enthusiasts.

In late 1977, Harley-Davidson introduced a radically restyled Sportster. It featured European cafe racer styling, which basically gave it racetrack looks for the street. The CR suffix to the XL Sportster designation, standing for "Cafe Racer," was prominently displayed on the primary cover.

The new Sportster was gloss black all over with the exception of the Siamesed exhaust pipes which were matt black. The remainder of the bike was finished in chrome and polished alloy. Items such as the gas tank had been redesigned and the seat was clearly racetrack inspired. The

ABOVE: This early seventies'-style Sportster chop has straight-through pipes, an unusual type of long forks, a molded frame, along with a sissy bar, and psychedelic paint.

RIGHT: This Sportster chop was built in the style of the mid-seventies with a plunger frame, girder forks, prismatic gas tank, and a wild paint job.

LEFT: Although this Panhead chop has a sixties' engine, it was built much later—but since it's pretty well unique, it is hard to say when. The owner seems at home with it—but those tiller bars must have taken some getting used to!

Model	Café Racer
Code	XLCR
Years	1977-78
No. cylinders	V-twin
Valves	ohv
Bore/stroke inch	3³⁄₁₆ × 3¹³⁄₁₆
Capacity cu in	61
Capacity cc	1,000
Ignition	coil, 1978-electronic
No of gears	4
Drive system	chain
Front suspension	teles
Rear suspension	s/a
Wheel type	cast-alloy
Wheel size inch	19 and 18
Front brake	disc
Rear brake	disc
Wheelbase inch	58.5
Seat height inch	31

Model	Roadster
Code	XLS
Years	1979-85
No. cylinders	V-twin
Valves	ohv
Bore/stroke inch	3³⁄₁₆ × 3¹³⁄₁₆
Capacity cu in	61
Capacity cc	1,000
Ignition	electronic
No of gears	4
Drive system	chain
Front suspension	teles
Rear suspension	s/a
Wheel type	cast-alloy or wire
Wheel size inch	19 and 16
Front brake	disc
Rear brake	disc
Wheelbase inch	58.5, 1982-60
Seat height inch	30

Code	XLH & XLCH
Years	1972-85, 1972-79
No. cylinders	V-twin
Valves	ohv
Bore/stroke inch	3³⁄₁₆ × 3³⁄₁₆
Capacity cu in	61
Capacity cc	1,000
Ignition	coil, 1978-electronic
No of gears	4
Drive system	chain
Front suspension	teles
Rear suspension	s/a
Wheel type	wire
Wheel size inch	19 and 18, 1980-19/16
Front brake	drum, 1973-disc
Rear brake	drum, 1979-disc
Wheelbase inch	58.5, 1982-60
Seat height inch	29.5

rear portion of the frame was based on the styling of the XR-750, but the whole unit was stretched to allow the oil tank and battery to be fitted, and as a result, the shock absorbers were mounted further back than on other models. Rear set brake and gear-change mechanisms allowed the rider to assume a sportsbike riding position and cast alloy Morris wheels and Kelsey Hayes disc brakes completed the sporting look.

Model	Tourer
Code	XLT
Years	1977-78
No. cylinders	V-twin
Valves	ohv
Bore/stroke inch	3³⁄₁₆ × 3¹³⁄₁₆
Capacity cu in	61
Capacity cc	1,000
Ignition	coil, 1978-electronic
No of gears	4
Drive system	chain
Front suspension	teles
Rear suspension	s/a
Wheel type	wire
Wheel size inch	19 and 18
Front brake	disc
Rear brake	drum
Wheelbase inch	58.5
Seat height inch	29

RIGHT: An immaculate 74cu in (1,200cc) Electra Glide dresser.

BELOW: A 1970 55cu in (900cc) XLH Sportster with twin exhausts and engine crash bars.

Sportsters could be chopped too! These three represent the middle and opposite ends of the decade. This (BELOW) is a relic of the sixties with wild paint, high pipes, hardtail rear suspension, and a long, long springer front end. Note the prismatic gas tank (RIGHT) on a bike that represents the style of the mid-seventies, with stark graphics, and lots of chrome. The other (RIGHT) is a much more subtle late seventies' machine with understated paint, a stretched "gooseneck" frame, mustang tank, forward controls, and drag pipes.

RIGHT: A close-up of the 61cu in (1,000cc) motor installed in the XLCR.

FAR RIGHT: The XR750 road racer was an awesome beast to see in action—the glorious sound it produced was matched by impressive graphics and classic styling.

BELOW: The last Shovelhead engines were made for the 1984/1985 model year. The last few Electra Glides were dependable machines as more or less all their problems had been ironed out in by the early eighties.

Racing Bikes

The XL Sportster was the basis of Harley-Davidson's competition bikes because it suited the most popular forms of competitive motorcycling in the United States—dirt track and flat track racing. In 1969, the rules governing dirt track racing had been altered: 45cu in (740cc) Class C dirt track racing for the first time allowed OHV-engined motor- cycles to race; prior to this racing had been for sidevalves only, hence the longevity of the competition KR models.

As a result of this rule change, Harley-Davidson's racing department had to find a replacement racer for the KR sidevalve machines in order to keep the marque competitive on the dirt ovals around the States. The motorcycle that Harley came up with was the XR-750. It was based loosely on many of the components of the XL series of Sportsters—hence its XR

designation; X from the Sportster, R for racing. It used a unit construction 45-degree V-twin engine and gearbox and initially was styled along similar lines to the KR models. Introduced in 1970, the XR-750 at first used an iron engine, but after numerous problems with heat dissipation among others it was manufactured with an alloy engine. It became a racing legend.

The internals of the engine were considerably different to the XL models for street use. The flywheels were different, as was much of the rest of the engine. For the first time, a production Harley-Davidson had a forward-facing exhaust on its rear cylinder and a rear-facing inlet port. The revised format was far more successful for racing and the bike went on to become a legend of the dirt tracks especially when ridden by men such as Jay Springsteen, Ricky Graham, Scott Parker, and Chris Carr. Evel Knieve, who had started as a racer

before moving on to more extreme sports, used an XR-750 on which to perform many of his stunts.

Cal Rayborn raced at Daytona in 1970 on the so called "waffle iron," an iron XR-750. Rayborn had won the Daytona 200 in 1969 but in 1970 there was considerable competition from the British and Japanese factories. The AMA now allowed 45cu in (740cc) displacement bikes, regardless of valve configuration, to race. Gene Romero qualified fastest aboard a Triumph Trident at 157.34mph.

On the new XR-750 Harleys Bart Markel qualified at 147mph and Cal Rayborn at 145mph, but in the actual race both Markel and Rayborn retired with holed pistons as did, similarly mounted, Mert Lawwill and Mark Brelsford. Dick Mann won the race on a Honda 750.

1969 Chamiponship winner Mert Lawwill raced at the Peoria TT in 1970 aboard an XR-750 on a version with twin disc brakes at the front and a disc rear. The event was won by Jim Rice on a BSA. In attempting to defend his title Lawwill was hampered by the unreliable iron XR-750 engine so on a number of occasions rode the more reliable flathead models. It was to little avail, he finished sixth in the point standings as a result of strong challenges by riders on British bikes.

Overall 1970 wasn't a good year for the XR-750. Mert Lawwill, won a half-mile dirt-track race on an XR-750 at Ascot, California when the bike made its first appearance on a dirt track. This was one of few wins for Harley-Davidson in 1970 because the iron XR-750s were plagued with mechanical problems that were not eliminated until the engines were modified later.

Mark Brelsford won at the 1971 Ascot TT, on *Goliath*, the potent 54cu in (885cc) TT bike built by Mert

RIGHT: One of the most beautiful motorcycles ever made! The XR750 dirt-track racer.

BELOW RIGHT: A sight made in heaven! Two gleaming XR750 road racers with spoked wheels, Supertrapp exhausts, and full race fairings.

BELOW: This is a very rare 1975 AMF Harley-Davidson RR250 two-stroke water-cooled racing bike. Original and unrestored, it is number six of only 25 ever built.

Lawwill and Jim Belland. It was lighter, had more power, and triple disc brakes. Following an AMA rule change in 1973 it displaced more than the rules allowed for TT competition so was outlawed by the AMA. Following its enforced retirement from racing *Goliath* was converted into a powerful street bike. Dirt track bikes have a functional style all their

own and have distinct appeal as cool street bikes. Harley-Davidson later exploited this with the introduction of the XR-1000, which was a powerful Sportster variant.

In the seventies, The Grand National Championship still consisted of a specific series of competitive events—TT, short track, half mile, mile, and road race events. Bart Markel's last National win, his 28th, came at Columbus, Ohio in the half-mile event of June 1971. Despite this win Markel did not finish in the top ten that year but his 28th win beat Joe Leonard's record of 27 National wins.

During 1971, the iron XRs were notoriously unreliable and frequently retired from events. At the Loudon, New Hampshire road race in 1971 Mark Brelsford managed to win by less than a wheel's length even as his engine failed. This victory was the only National road race victory

achieved on a "waffle iron." Cal Rayborn was in the same race; in 1971 his engine blew and he was thrown off and injured but in 1972 he fared better. On an alloy XR, he qualified on pole position and finished eighth, while Brelsford finished second. Harley-Davidson debuted its new alloy construction XR-750s for the 1972 season although they weren't ready for Daytona. Cal Rayborn, Mark Brelsford, Mert Lawwill, Dave Sehl, and Renzo Pasolini were all members of Harley-Davidson's factory team in 1972.

Mark Brelsford debuted the new XR-750 at the Colorado Springs Mile on April 30, 1972. The specification of the new all-alloy construction engine included twin 36mm Mikuni carburetors bolted to rear-facing ports and, on the other side of the engine, twin forward-facing exhaust ports from which exhausts curved back into

reversed-cone megaphone exhaust pipes. Brelsford qualified fastest and won his heat race but in the 25-lap final was beaten into second place by Jim Rice on a BSA. Third was Kenny Roberts on a Yamaha. Having first ridden the alloy XR-750 at Colorado Springs, Colorado in April, Mark Brelsford went on to win the Ascot, California TT in May 1972 and later in the season won the half-mile events at Louisville, Kentucky, and Salem, Oregon. These wins helped this cheerful and popular rider clinch the Grand National Championship for 1972. Cal

ABOVE: Team Obsolete now run this ex-Cal Rayborn factory racer, here being prepared at the Daytona racetrack.

LEFT: The late, great racer of the early seventies, Cal Rayborn sits astride a Harley-Davidson factory racing bike.

Rayborn was killed racing in New Zealand when the engine of his Suzuki seized and threw him off the bike in 1973 and Roger Reiman died after a crash in a Battle of the Legends race at Daytona in 1997.

The highest placed Harley-Davidson at Daytona in 1972 was ridden by Larry Darr who finished 17th. Harleys had all but disappeared from the top 20. The later seventies would see all that change—thanks to a shy youngster from Michigan named Springsteen. He had put in a good showing in an invitation-only event at Ascot, California in late 1974 and would soon change the face of dirt-track racing.

In the interim the HD team for 1975 included Scott, Lawwill, Beauchamp, Keener, and Sassaman. Kenny Roberts was on a Yamaha as was Gene Romero. Through the season all these guys raced neck and

neck out on the dirt mile and half-mile ovals around the States; Houston, San Jose, Louisville, Harrington, Columbus and so on. The term "freight train" abounded as the Harleys cleaned up, crossing the line in quick succession with only occasional upsets from Roberts hanging onto the notoriously wild Yamaha TZ750. The XRs were making almost 90hp and pulling more than 120mph on the straights.

By 1978, the engine capacity of the XR-750 was 45cu in (740cc). It was a four stroke V-twin fitted with alloy cylinder heads and twin carburetors and was of an OHV configuration. The machine had a top speed of

LEFT: This is George Roeder's XR-750 road racer. Note the large air-scoop on the front brake, the treaded race tires, megaphone exhausts, and long distance gas tank.

BELOW: The 61cu in (1,000cc) XL Sportster was criticized in the mainstream press for having poor oil consumption and being too heavy. It still looked good though!

130mph dependent on gearing, and some riders changed the sprockets to suit specific tracks. The power produced by the engine also varied ranging from 70-90bhp depending on the tune. The transmission was four-speed and the whole machine was

constructed around a tubular steel frame. The single backbone tube frame was made from 4130 steel tubing. The fuel tank held two gallons and it, and the seat and rear fender, were made in glassfiber by the Wixon brothers. The bike rolled on 19in diameter wheels, had a 54in wheelbase and weighed 317lb dry. The standard Harley-Davidson frame was often replaced by a specially constructed one that offered better handling characteristics for specific dirt-tracks.

Although the XR-750 was similar in appearance to the street Sportster, close examination reveals few similarities at all. The fuel tank was

smaller than the Sportster one and held enough fuel for each race. A racing style seat and lightweight fiberglass tailpiece were fitted to allow the rider to move about in the bends and the twin-carburetor engine was especially engineered for these bikes. An alloy oil tank could be found under the seat, mudguards were omitted as was a front brake, the exhaust pipes swept up the left side of the bike, and lights were unnecessary.

Dirt-track racing is an American institution that has evolved rather than changed massively over the years. XR-750s are still raced and nowhere is the experience of the dirt track greater than at the Del Mar Mile near San Diego in California. The final round of the Grand National Dirt Track series happened in the late nineties. There on the mile-round dirt oval was played out the last act in a

RIGHT & BELOW RIGHT: This 1980 XR-750 was once ridden by Jay Springsteen, one of the most famous dirt-track racers of all time.

BELOW: Imagine having your name on not one, but two of the most beautiful racing bikes ever made!

drama that sees dreams come true, hopes dashed, and a champion crowned. Even the venue is theatrical: the dirt oval is really a horse racing track within the Del Mar Fairgrounds. Most of the racers are mounted on XR-750 Harley-Davidsons and if that sounds slow, then think again; they go anticlockwise around the oval, touch speeds well over 100mph on the straights and opposite lock around the turns. It's been a long road—around 60,000 road miles— from the start of the season at Daytona in March to its

October finale at Del Mar; 23 events on mile and half mile tracks in more than 15 states although some were rained off. Amid the Winnebagos in the pits some of the guys in baseball hats have long ago emerged as strong contenders, the names on everyone's lips were Scott Parker, Kevin Atherton, and Jay Springsteen. As it happens they are all from Michigan so maybe there's something in the water there that makes grown men want to hurl themselves sideways into bends on bikes without front brakes.

By Del Mar, the six times champion, Parker who won the 1995 Championship and hence the Number 1 plate, was leading the championship to the extent that he had to only place 15th or better to pick up the trophy. The 35-year-old who had been racing Grand Nationals since 1979 finished 23 races in 1995 of which ten were wins and 16 were in

the top five placings. At the beginning of the season he was quoted as saying, "Racing is more exciting than ever. I've set new goals for myself, and can't wait to see what I can accomplish in the coming year."

By the Del Mar race he had six wins to his credit and it was clear that his goal was the unprecedented Seventh National Championship win. Parker had heavyweight sponsorship behind him including Harley-Davidson themselves, this year he was their only factory rider as his team-mate Chris Carr had turned all his attention to the VR1000 racer.

Another legendary name was on the entry list; Jay Springsteen, remembered among other things for his dices with Kenny Roberts including the times Roberts rode the Yamaha TZ750 two-stroke. Springsteen, then 39, had three consecutive championships go his way starting in 1976. He too was riding a trick-framed XR-750 but sponsored by Bartels' Harley-Davidson dealership, Bell, and others.

The third Michigan resident on an XR-750 was Kevin Atherton (23) racing for Total Control Racing along with Will Davis (21), a team owned by Benson Ford, Henry Ford's great grandson. The team was a strong one and chasing Parker, Tom Cummings the general manager said prior to the final, "Our team has finished third or better in 16 of the 20 races. All in all it's been a terrific season."

The qualifying heats started and for ten laps half a dozen or so riders gave their all to get into the next round. They all went into turn one together and within a lap the group got strung out, drafting down the "straightaways" and sliding around the outside of each other in the turns.

It's all about hooking up in the dirt, staying off of the cushion and staying on the groove, which meant getting traction, staying out of the loose dirt on the outside of the turns, and keeping the bike on the fastest line. Parker, Atherton, and Springsteen were in separate qualifying heats and unsurprisingly all qualified, although Springsteen's heat developed into a six-lap dice with

Steve Morehead that saw the lead change numerous times.

The race bikes were predominantly Harley-Davidson XR-750s, but there were a few Honda RS750s and a Ducati in contention. The top three from each heat qualified for the final while the rest went into three semis from which the top two qualify. This gave a field of 18 for the Grand National final but there was a hitch as the track was too wet.

As the track dried out, the semis were run; Californian Andy Tresser on the Ducati missed qualifying for the final by one place and six more Harley-Davidsons won places on the grid. There were other formulas for the dirt track event, namely a 600

BELOW LEFT: The 1971 55cu in (900cc) XLH was the last version of the Sportster to be made with an external ignition timer. From this model year on they had contact breakers mounted behind a cover plate.

BELOW: The AMF Harley-Davidson SX250 was imported from the Aermacchi factory in Italy and was designed to challenge the similar Yamaha.

class and an 883 class, guess whose bikes filled the latter class.

The almost stock 883 class looked almost pedestrian when compared to the heavily tuned 750s even though there are rules about what can be done to the bikes. The 750 class bikes usually ran twin Mikunis although

they had to use 33mm inlet restrictors to conform to the AMA's rules.

The AMA Grand National Final was something akin to the chariot race in *Ben Hur* and at a strangely appropriate place, the thirties Hollywood stars' own horseracing track. There are 18 unsilenced V-twins in three rows on the grid, 400 yards away is turn one; Springsteen's intention was to be in fourth gear by that turn: "The light goes green, 18 rooster tails of dirt arc into the air and the next second there's 18 bikes sideways, handlebars touching going into turn one. Unbelievably no one goes down and there's 25 laps to go. 130 mph on the straights, right hand on the throttle, left hand on the fork leg,

chest on the tank down the straight-aways. Sit up, flick the back end out, steel shod left foot down, keep the throttle open through the turns. If it twitches open it's up some more and wrestle those wide bars out of the turn."

When the pack stretches in single file drafting each other from the outside wall back to the exit from the turn, it's called a freight train. But no freight train ever looked or sounded this good: noise, dust, action on each lap, then suddenly all over. It's hard to believe the riders have done 25 miles, but suddenly the marshal is waving the flag. Atherton, Parker, Kopp. Butler, Coolbeth, Davis, Camlin, and Springsteen were all on XRs. Kevin Atherton (23) won the race but Scott Parker (1) won the championship.

Code	Z90
Years	1973-74
No. cylinders	I
Valves	t/s
Bore/stroke mm	48 × 49
Capacity cu in	5
Capacity cc	80
Ignition	coil
No of gears	4
Drive system	gear/chain
Front suspension	teles
Rear suspension	s/a
Wheel type	wire
Wheel size inch	17 and 16
Brakes	drum
Wheelbase inch	46.5
Seat height inch	29.7

Model	Rapido
Years	1968-72
No. cylinders	I
Valves	t/s
Bore/stroke mm	56 × 50
Capacity cu in	7
Capacity cc	II5
No of gears	4
Drive system	gear/chain
Front suspension	teles
Rear suspension	s/a
Wheel type	wire
Brakes	drum

Code	X90
Years	1973-74
No. cylinders	I
Valves	t/s
Bore/stroke mm	48 × 49
Capacity cu in	5
Capacity cc	80
Ignition	magneto
No of gears	4
Drive system	gear/chain
Front suspension	teles
Rear suspension	s/a
Wheel type	disc
Wheel size inch	10 and 10
Brakes	drum
Wheelbase inch	40.7
Seat height inch	26.8

LEFT: One of the unsuccessful Z90 imports.

BELOW & BELOW LEFT: These two SX 125s were imports from Italy, and were intended to meet the Yamaha trail bikes head to head.

Although the SXs were sturdy and competitive bikes, they could not match the price of their Japanese counterparts..

The Eighties

The Shovelhead V-twin engine appeared in 1980 powering one of the first factory custom bikes from Harley-Davidson, the Sturgis (FXB), named after one of America's huge annual biker gatherings. The Sturgis was a belt-drive Shovelhead painted almost entirely black but highlighted with orange detailing.

In 1980, AMF Harley-Davidson took this concept of the factory custom a long way further down the chopper road when they announced the FXWG

ABOVE: A Shovelhead-engined Super Glide and a Sportster cruise through town.

RIGHT: A pair of 80cu in (1,310cc) Evolution-engined machines.

BELOW: An 80cu in (1,310cc) FLH Electra Glide.

for 1981. This was an FX Super Glide with a Wide Glide front end—hence its WG suffix. It was, Harley claimed, "the only factory built custom in sight" and

featured a 21in front wheel, 16in rear, extended front forks with Electra Glide sliders, staggered short dual pipes, and a bobbed rear fender. To round off the custom appearance the FXWG was available with a flame paintjob over black or in four different metallic colors. For years Harley dealers had been helping themselves out by marketing unofficial aftermarket parts, but now the factory were at last offering their own choppers as well as lines of aftermarket custom parts.

ABOVE LEFT: The 1982 FXB Sturgis was so named because it was first introduced at the famous Sturgis rally. It had belt drives, both for the primary transmission and to the back wheel.

ABOVE RIGHT: The Evolution engine was just that—the next generation of big twin; it soon acquired the nickname "Blockhead." This example is installed in a flamed-tank Wide Glide.

BELOW: The Sportster was produced in two forms in 1980—the XLH and the XLS, as shown here. This had dual shorty exhausts, a 3.3-gallon gas tank, and buckhorn handlebars.

RIGHT: Two views of the Electra Glide. The 80cu in (1,310cc) half-dresser was built to be ridden all day, mile after mile.

A new model Harley-Davidson for 1980 was the FLT Tour Glide powered by an 80cu in (1,310cc) displacement Shovelhead engine and featuring five-speed transmission, an oil-bath enclosed rear chain, and a vibration isolated engine mount system. This FLT also featured a fairing and glass-fiber panniers. The following year another special Shovelhead was unveiled—the FXWG Wide Glide. Based around a duplex tubular steel frame, the FXWG was available with a custom "flamed" paint scheme similar to the contemporary work of custom

Model	Sturgis
Code	FXB
Years	1980-82
No. cylinders	V-twin
Valves	ohv
Bore/stroke inch	3½ x 4¼
Capacity cu in	80
Capacity cc	1,310
Ignition	electronic
No of gears	4
Drive system	belts
Front suspension	teles
Rear suspension	s/a
Wheel type	cast alloy
Wheel size inch	19 and 16
Brakes	discs
Wheelbase inch	63.5
Seat height inch	27

ABOVE: The Evolution engine fitted in this full dresser had many design improvements, including far superior combustion characteristics, easily removed rocker covers, better lifters, improved piston design, and so on.

ABOVE RIGHT: When the factory management bought the company back from AMF, most of the model line-up received serious attention, and as a result they were improved considerably. The late model Sportster here was just one such example of this process.

RIGHT: The 80cu in (1,310cc) Evolution engine was the product of years of development, much of it in conjunction with external companies who specialized in performance or emissions work. The result was a strong, reliable motor which was well-suited to machines like this 1988 Electra Glide Classic.

Model	Wide Glide
Code	FXWG
Years	1980-86
No. cylinders	V-twin
Valves	ohv
Bore/stroke inch	3½ x 4¼
Capacity cu in	80
Capacity cc	1,310
Ignition	electronic
No of gears	4
Drive system	chain, 1984-chain/belt
Front suspension	teles
Rear suspension	s/a
Wheel type	cast alloy/wire, 1985-wire
Wheel size inch	21 and 16
Brakes	discs
Wheelbase inch	65
Seat height inch	28

Model	Café Racer
Code	XR1000
Years	1983-84
No. cylinders	V-twin
Valves	ohv
Bore/stroke inch	3³⁄₁₆ × 3¹³⁄₁₆
Capacity cu in	61
Capacity cc	1,000
Ignition	electronic
No of gears	4
Drive system	chain
Front suspension	teles
Rear suspension	s/a
Wheel type	cast-alloy
Wheel size inch	19 and 16
Front brake	disc
Rear brake	disc
Wheelbase inch	60
Seat height inch	28.7

RIGHT: The 74cu in (1,200cc) Shovelhead engine fitted to this FXE Super Glide was phased out of production in 1981, and replaced by the 80cu in (1,310cc) version.

BELOW: The last Shovelhead engines were made for the 1984/1985 model year. The last few Electra Glides were dependable machines as more or less all their problems had been ironed out by 1982.

builders and painters. Its Shovelhead engine had a capacity of 80cu in (1,310cc), a top speed of 102mph, and produced 49bhp at 5,800rpm. This was connected to a four-speed transmission. Harley-Davidson traditionally produced air-cooled engines rather than being a motorcycle manufacturer per se. So the Evolution engine introduced in the eighties could conceivably have been the final chapter for the company. New anti-pollution laws concerning emissions were producing increasingly stringent regulations that meant that liquid-cooled engines would have to power the Harley-Davidson bikes of the future.

This change was duly noted and in recent years Harley-Davidson have been trialing a liquid-cooled race bike—the VR1000. This has not been without problems but few development machines are, and it is common practice to iron out technical problems on the racetrack prior to turning to mass production for ordinary road consumers.

Also in 1983 Harley-Davidson introduced two new models—the FXR Super Glide II and a redesigned Sportster. One of the Sportsters was a special 25th anniversary machine to mark the fact that the company had been making Sportster motorcycles for a quarter of a century.

Another landmark was created in 1983 with the founding of HOG—an acronym for Harley Owners' Group. At the time of its foundation this was the

Model	Tour Glide
Code	FLT80
Years	1980-83
No. cylinders	V-twin
Valves	ohv
Bore/stroke inch	3½ x 4¼
Capacity cu in	80
Capacity cc	1,310
Ignition	electronic
No of gears	5
Drive system	chain
Front suspension	teles
Rear suspension	s/a
Wheel type	cast alloy
Wheel size inch	16 and 16
Brakes	discs
Wheelbase inch	60.6
Seat height inch	32

RIGHT: The belt drives fitted to this FXB Sturgis proved to be popular both with the motorcycling press and Harley's customers. Requiring far less maintenance than chains, they were also lighter, quieter, and smoother.

BELOW: The Evolution-engined FLTC was supplied with a five-speed transmission, belt drive, and a full set of touring equipment.

OVERLEAF, LEFT & TOP RIGHT: The Shovelhead-engined FXR was made until 1983; from then on, they all had Evolution engines.

OVERLEAF BOTTOM RIGHT: This well cared for FXWG is a Shovelhead engined Wide Glide that has had a lot of detail work performed on it; the visible work includes having the primary chaincase engraved, high performance ignition, and an oil cooler fitted, and so on.

helped reverse the company's declining fortunes because of its focus on after sales care for customers—something that had taken a lot of criticism while under AMF ownership.

The hip and aggressive marketing of the Evolution Harley-Davidsons, the founding of HOG, as well as the increasing numbers of a new generation of "celebrities" seen posing on Harley-Davidsons suddenly made Harley ownership more than simply desirable. Suddenly out of the blue it became the hottest fashion accessory anyone could have.

Meanwhile the true bikers who had stuck with Harley through the bad times were somewhat bemused by the whole turnaround in fashion. They'd been ostracized and shunned for so long by mainstream society, discriminated against, and snubbed, that seeing their reason for living turned into a fashion statement wasn't what a lot of

only factory-sponsored motorcycle club in the world—and was seen by some as an attempt by Harley-

Davidson to reclaim the family motor-cycling tradition. Many people now firmly believe that this organization

the guys wanted. They didn't dig the pre-ripped jeans and designer T-shirts and were surprised by the posh nightspots suddenly welcoming "bikers." They had been raised on choppers, flatheads, Knuckles, and Pans—we're talking way before even the Shovelheads for many. *Mask*, the 1984 biker movie starring Cher and Sam Elliot, typified this era of acceptable custom bikes and biking.

Back in the real world, as a result of the popularity of dirt-track racing, competition inspired models such as the XR-1000 featured in Harley-Davidson's range in 1983. This was a competition-inspired bike manufactured and marketed for the street.

In many ways it was a styling exercise as the bike was a clever mixture of Sportster XL-1000 street parts and XR-750 race parts. The engine used an XL-1000 bottom end with cylinder heads, exhausts, and carburetors from

TOP LEFT: This is a 1982/1983 FLH Electra Glide full-dresser with the trademark fishtail exhausts.

TOP RIGHT: This bike is an early 1980s' FLH Classic.

CENTER LEFT: Although sidecars were less popular in the eighties than in previous decades, they continued to sell to a diehard core of enthusiasts. The example shown here is a 1981 Heritage Edition FLH

BELOW & BELOW LEFT: Many of the FXWG Wide Glides produced were supplied with flamed paint jobs. This 1980 example has an S&S carburetor and air filter fitted.

the XR-750 racing engine. The cylinder barrels were new components. The dual race-type carburetors with K&N air filters were positioned on the right of the engine, and the exhaust pipes, unusually for a Harley-Davidson, were

on the left; this was necessitated by the fitment of the twin carburetors on the other side. The engine used coil and points ignition. The remainder of the machine was almost all the then stock XLX Sportster including the steel swingarm frame, which was the basic entry-level model.

The front wheel was a 19in cast alloy nine-spoke item fitted with twin disc brakes; at the rear was a 16in cast nine-spoke wheel with a single disc brake. The fenders were stock XL front and rear. The handlebars were flat and featured handlebar clamp-mounted speedometer and tachometer. The fuel tank was a stock Sportster item as was the oil tank, positioned under the solo seat. Because the XR-1000 was a limited edition model and made from an unusual combination of parts, it retailed for a higher price than the other Sportsters in the early eighties' range. Despite this it was a fast

motorcycle and the first Harley that, off the showroom floor, achieved drag strip quarter mile-elapsed times (ET) of less than 13 seconds.

The 1984 61cu in (1,000cc) XR-1000 was also an exercise in both engineering and marketing in that it was the closest street bike that a customer could buy to a race bike. As before the engine was derived from the XR-750 racer with a Sportster XL-1000 bottom end and a set of iron cylinders and alloy heads. Dual carburetors were fitted on the right of the engine and twin exhausts on the left. This OHV ironhead V-twin engine was capable of 120mph (193kph) and produced 70bhp at 6,000rpm. The remainder of the bike was the basic XLX Sportster.

The FXRT was a new (for 1983) touring model, while the FXR was something of an FLT Tourglide stripped of its touring paraphernalia

and an upgraded FXE at the same time. The most immediately obvious difference was the appearance of

ABOVE: The 1982 FXB Sturgis Model seen here being ridden in the country was ideal for just cruising around on. This wise owner has fitted high performance ignition and an oil cooler to help make the bike just that little bit sweeter!

ABOVE RIGHT: The FXR was born out of the remnants of the Tour Glide chassis; it was, however, much more than just that—a whole new generation of bikes had been born. This example is a 1982 model.

OVERLEAF: The lovely 61cu in (1,000cc) twin-carb XR-1000 was fast as well as good looking. It was the first stock Harley ever to break into the 12-second class at the drag strip.

triangulated frame tubes behind the gearbox. The engine used was the rubber mount Shovelhead from the

Model	Disc Glide
Code	FXRDG
Years	1984
No. cylinders	V-twin
Valves	ohv
Bore/stroke inch	3½ × 4¼
Capacity cu in	80
Capacity cc	1,310
Ignition	electronic
No of gears	5
Drive system	chain
Front suspension	teles
Rear suspension	s/a
Wheel type	wire/disc
Wheel size inch	19 and 16
Brakes	discs
Wheelbase inch	63.1
Seat height inch	26.8

FLT along with a five-speed transmission, the FX/XL style front end and dual shock absorber swinging arm rear

Model	Low Glide Custom
Code	FXRC
Years	1985
No. cylinders	V-twin
Valves	ohv
Bore/stroke inch	3½ x 4¼
Capacity cu in	80
Capacity cc	1,310
Ignition	electronic
No of gears	5
Drive system	chain/belt
Front suspension	teles
Rear suspension	s/a
Wheel type	wire
Wheel size inch	19 and 16
Brakes	discs
Wheelbase inch	63.1
Seat height inch	26.8

suspension. It took a new frame to make these components work and look good together.

Initially the bike was known as Super Glide II but the name disappeared in only 12 months and the FXR designations appeared. The motorcycle was an FX with a rubber mount engine—hence the R suffix. The FXR was fitted with wire wheels and finished with a single color paint scheme. The FXRS was similar except for having a pair of cast alloy spoked wheels, highway pegs, sissy bar, and a two-tone paint job.

The Evolution engine was in many ways a much improved 80cu in (1,310cc) Shovelhead engine, a new top end on the old alternator Shovel. It initially gained the nickname of Blockhead continuing the tradition of referring to the types of rocker covers but soon became generally referred to as the "Evo." It uses alloy cylinder barrels with iron liners and heads that

permit greater and more even heat dissipation than the iron and alloy combination of the Shovelhead. The valves were redesigned to allow better flow on both the induction and exhaust strokes of the four-stroke cycle and the combustion chambers were redesigned to meet emissions regulations and take unleaded gas.

The redesign allowed higher compression with lower octane fuel. Also improved were levels of quality control, oil consumption, and frequency of maintenance. The engine has become noted for reliability, gas-mileage, and lightness—in short for being a good steady piece of engineering. The entire range of big twins benefited from the new engine and the range was later extended with the introduction of a new model—the Softail in 1984.

Harley-Davidson won a California Highway Patrol (CHP) contract in 1984—the first time it had done so

ABOVE LEFT & RIGHT: The heart of the 61cu in (1,000cc) XR-1000 was the top end—the two large carburetors with their racing style air filters allowed the motor to breathe really well, and in doing so produced lots of power!.

LEFT: A 61cu in (1,000cc) XR-1000 with XR-750-style tank and seat.

ABOVE RIGHT: A street-legal XR-750—properly ridden on canyon-type roads, there would be few bikes that could match its performance.

BELOW LEFT: An immaculate 61cu in (1,000cc) XR-1000 with Corbin seat.

Model	Sportster
Code	XLX-61
Years	1983-85
No. cylinders	V-twin
Valves	ohv
Bore/stroke inch	3³⁄₁₆ × 3¹³⁄₁₆
Capacity cu in	61
Capacity cc	1,000
Ignition	electronic
No of gears	4
Drive system	chain
Front suspension	teles
Rear suspension	s/a
Wheel type	cast-alloy
Wheel size inch	19 and 16
Front brake	disc
Rear brake	disc
Wheelbase inch	60
Seat height inch	28.5

in ten years—and this was taken as tangible proof of Harley-Davidson's improved product line and standards. Further CHP contracts followed.

The FLHTC of 1984 incorporated the new rubber engine mount frame, five-speed transmission, and Tour Glide front end—partially concealed behind a fairing. Final drive was by means of a chain. Engine aside, the FLHTC was the same as the Shovelhead-powered Tour Glide.

The new machine was tested by American motorcycle magazines to critical acclaim. The engine was referred to as the V2 by Harley-Davidson and by 1985 the company had incorporated a five-speed belt final drive in the FL models. For the remainder of the eighties the range was

altered subtly as improvements were incorporated. One of the few that is obvious was the move to the use of a circular air cleaner.

The V2 engine powered the swingarm-framed Super Glides, including Fat Bob, Low Rider, and the Wide Glide, but the Softail frame was about to change all that. The new Softail models such as the FXST Softail were essentially Superglides based around a specific new type of frame, these had the appearance of a vintage rigid frame but featured suspension. The shock absorbers were positioned horizontally below the gearbox between the bottom frame rails. The pivot for the suspension was mounted in the rear section of the frame behind the gearbox.

The nostalgic look received another boost with the introduction of the Softail Springer in 1988 and the Softail Custom. That same year Harley-Davidson astounded the motorcycling world by reintroducing springer forks—most people had assumed they were a thing of the past having been superseded by telescopic forks. Harley-Davidson had by then started advertising a significant percentage of their motorcycles as ideal for the nostalgia market. As a result the reintroduction of components that had last been seen on their motorcycles in 1948 was a shrewd move.

Nostalgia and heritage were the main selling points for the new Harley-Davidsons that looked like old ones. The Springer forked motorcycles had by then been in production for well over a decade and the old style forks were used on more than one model. The Bad Boy, the nearest

BELOW: This bike is an early eighties' FXE with an S&S air filter and straight pipes.

BELOW RIGHT: In 1980, the factory released the FLT 80cu in (1,310cc) full-dresser. The design of this bike was a radical change from the way previous big twins had been engineered—the entire powertrain and swing arm were bolted together and then suspended from anti-vibration mountings, leading to the nicknames "Rubber-Mount" and "Rubber-Glide." A very similar system had been used on the Norton Commando, where it also worked well at isolating the rider from the vibes generated by a twin-cylinder engine.

Model	Sport Glide
Code	FXRT
Years	1984-92
No. cylinders	V-twin
Valves	ohv
Bore/stroke inch	3½ × 4¼
Capacity cu in	80
Capacity cc	1,310
Ignition	electronic
No of gears	5
Drive system	chain,
	1985-chain/belt
Front suspension	teles
Rear suspension	s/a
Wheel type	cast alloy
Wheel size inch	19 and 16
Brakes	discs
Wheelbase inch	64.7
Seat height inch	27.7

motorcycle to a factory-built chopper, was one of the models to use Springers. The springer forks used on Evos are a

modernized design of the originals designed by William Harley decades previously, although they have been

Model	Super Glide		Model	Super Glide II		Model	Low Glide
Code	FXE		Code	FXR, FXRS		Code	FXRS
Years	1981-84		Years	1982-83		Years	1984-85
No. cylinders	V-twin		No. cylinders	V-twin		No. cylinders	V-twin
Valves	ohv		Valves	ohv		Valves	ohv
Bore/stroke inch	3½ x 4¼		Bore/stroke inch	3½ x 4¼		Bore/stroke inch	3½ x 4¼
Capacity cu in	80		Capacity cu in	80		Capacity cu in	81.78
Capacity cc	1,310		Capacity cc	1,310		Capacity cc	1340
Ignition	electronic		Ignition	electronic		Ignition	electronic
No of gears	4		No of gears	5		No of gears	5
Drive system	chain, 1984-chain/belt		Drive system	chain		Drive system	chain, 1985-chain/belt
Front suspension	teles		Front suspension	teles		Front suspension	teles
Rear suspension	s/a		Rear suspension	s/a		Rear suspension	s/a
Wheel type	wire		Wheel type	FXR-wire, FXRS-cast alloy		Wheel type	cast alloy
Wheel size inch	19 and 16		Wheel size inch	19 and 16		Wheel size inch	19 and 16
Brakes	discs		Brakes	discs		Brakes	discs
Wheelbase inch	62.8		Wheelbase inch	64.7		Wheelbase inch	63.1
Seat height inch	26.6		Seat height inch	28.9		Seat height inch	26.8

updated from those used on Knuckleheads and Panheads and are now made with the assistance of computer aided design and modern materials, as well as being fitted with a single disc brake.

The 1985 Harley-Davidsons received a special AIW/IAM union sticker. The initials belong to the two

LEFT, BELOW & RIGHT: Produced in 1984 this FLHX Special Edition was the last Shovelhead ever made!

biggest labor unions, Allied Industrial Workers of America and International Association of Machinists and Aerospace Workers, and this was seen as an endorsement of the products for the consumer by those who made it. Bigger news for 1985 was the introduction of the re-engineered Sportster, the Evolution 883. It featured a four-speed transmission and a chain final drive and was Harley-Davidson's first bike in a decade to be launched into the less than 61cu in (1,000cc) class.

The 1986 FXST Softail was a restyled 80cu in (1,310cc) displacement big twin from the Harley-Davidson factory. Its engine was the four-stroke OHV Evolution engine that had been introduced in 1983–84. The engine had first appeared in the FX models and then spread across the range over the next three years. In traditional swingarm models, the engine was rubber-mounted into the steel Softail frame to minimize vibration. Transmission was

ABOVE: This Softail belongs to Peter DeSavary, a millionaire businessman, who is also a Harley fan.

ABOVE LEFT: A 1980 80cu in (1,310cc) FLT Tour Glide.

BELOW LEFT: A 1986 80cu in (1,310cc) FLHT Electra Glide.

Model	Low Rider
Code	FXSB
Years	1983-85
No. cylinders	V-twin
Valves	ohv
Bore/stroke inch	3½ × 4¼
Capacity cu in	80
Capacity cc	1,310
Ignition	electronic
No of gears	4
Drive system	belts, 1985-chain/belt
Front suspension	teles
Rear suspension	s/a
Wheel type	cast alloy
Wheel size inch	19 and 16
Brakes	discs
Wheelbase inch	63.5
Seat height inch	27

Model	Fat Bob
Code	FXEF
Years	1985
No. cylinders	V-twin
Valves	ohv
Bore/stroke inch	3½ × 4¼
Capacity cu in	80
Capacity cc	1,310
Ignition	electronic
No of gears	4
Drive system	chain/belt
Front suspension	teles
Rear suspension	s/a
Wheel type	cast alloy
Wheel size inch	19 and 16
Brakes	discs
Wheelbase inch	63.5
Seat height inch	27

ABOVE: An Evolution-engined 80cu in (1,310cc) FLHT Electra Glide.!

LEFT: An Evolution-engined FXR.

RIGHT: Detail of the light and agile FLT 80cu in (1,310cc) Tour-Glide. Despite weighing in at 780lb it was an agile machine.

Model	Springer Softail
Code	FXSTS
Years	1988-99
No. cylinders	V-twin
Valves	ohv
Bore/stroke inch	3½ × 4¼
Capacity cu in	80
Capacity cc	1,310
Ignition	electronic
No of gears	5
Drive system	chain/belt
Front suspension	leading link
Rear suspension	s/a
Wheel type	wire
Wheel size inch	21 and 16
Brakes	discs
Wheelbase inch	64.5
Seat height inch	26.1

four-speed. The bike's top speed is 112mph and the power produced by the engine is 67bhp. The Softail models take their styling from an earlier age as they have the all appearance of the early rigid frame models due to the hidden suspension. The Softails feature a chrome horseshoe oil tank and traditional fenders. One model—the FXSTS—took nostalgia a step further by using springer forks. The Evolution and the Softail styling made Harley-Davidson motorcycles huge sellers during the late eighties and nineties.

New for 1987 were four motorcycles, the FLHS Electra Glide Sport, the FXLR Low Rider Custom, the FLSTC Heritage Softail Classic, and the 30th Anniversary XL Sportster. Of these the FLHS was intended to be a more nimble sports-tourer and the FXLR marked the tenth anniversary of the Low Rider.

The FLST Heritage Softail Classic of 1988 was very much a fifties-inspired Harley-Davidson big twin motorcycle, redesigned for modern roads and traffic conditions, and to sell to the rapidly growing nostalgia market. It featured the Softail frame—a Harley-Davidson-designed frame that looked like a traditional rigid frame—but featured rear suspension to increase the rider and passenger's comfort. The way this was done was to have a pivoted triangulated rear section to the frame in place of the more usual swinging arm. The shock absorber for the new frame design was hidden underneath. This kept the triangular lines of the frame clearly visible and not unlike pre-'58 Harley frames. The remainder of the bike was styled in an old-fashioned way too, big valanced FL fenders, studded saddlebags and saddle, and a nostalgic two-tone paint scheme.

Alongside the Softail models sat the FXR range—the R suffix designates a rubber mounted engine and a redesigned frame—a continuation of the rubber-mount series started in 1982 by the Shovelhead powered FXR and FXRS. By 1987 the FXRs were acknowledged to be better machines than the rigid mount FXs so Harley-Davidson combined the FXR with the chopper-look of the FX. The result was a V2-powered, five-speed, belt-drive motorcycle with a solid rear wheel, a 21-inch front wheel, an XR-1000 front fender, and a small XL-type headlight. The bike was called the FXLR—FX Low Rider Custom.

For 1989 there was a logical extension to the FXR range—the FXR Low Rider Convertible. This machine converted between being a Low Rider custom and a touring bike through the use of removable saddlebags

and windshield.

Despite all the alterations to the FX, FXR, and FLST models the more standard-looking big twins such as the Electra Glides were not ignored. Having been upgraded through the use of the V2 Evolution engine it was simply fine tuned for each model year; the 1984 and 1985 FLHT Electra Glide had a lower seat for the rider, stepped for the pillion, and a variation on the normal glassfiber fairing fitted. The 1985 models were five-speed and had final belt drive and a new clutch. For 1987 there was a new model, the FLHS Electra Glide Sport which was the bottom of the Electra Glide range in terms of price and featured a windshield rather than a fairing. Two years later

LEFT: The Softail was designed to combine the looks of a rigid rear end with the practicality of modern suspension. The rear shocks were hidden under the transmission

BELOW: The 61cu in (1,000cc) Sportster continued to receive development time from the factory. In 1982 it was given a new, lighter and stiffer frame which helped improve the handling.

another two new models were added to the line up, the FLTC Tour Glide Ultra Classic and the FLHTC Electra Glide Ultra Classic, both these models remained in the range and stayed in production into the next decade.

A new Sportster debuted in the

1988 range of motorcycles. It had a 74cu in (1,200cc) displacement engine and featured a 40mm constant-velocity carburetor. A redesigned version of the FXRS Low Rider appeared alongside using the proven rubber-mount frame. A limited number of 85th anniversary bikes were offered including the FXSTS Softail Springer.

The 1989 range of motorcycles was as follows. In the FXR models there were: FXR Super Glide, FXRS Low Rider, FXRS-SP Low Rider Sport, FXLR Low Rider Custom, and FXRT Sport Glide. The Softail models on offer in 1989 were: the FXST Softail, the FXSTC Softail Custom, the FXSTS Springer Softail, the FLST Heritage Softail, and the very nostalgic

FLSTC Heritage Softail Classic. The Electra Glide range comprised: the FLHS Electra Glide Sport, the FLHTC Electra Glide Classic, the FLTC Tour Glide Classic, FLHTC Ultra Classic Electra Glide, and the FLTC Ultra Classic Tour Glide. There were four motorcycles in the Sportster

ABOVE LEFT: A stretched frame and long narrow gas tank make this an eighties Bay Area Lowrider.

ABOVE RIGHT: An 80cu in (1,310cc) Shovelhead engined FLH Electra Glide half-dresser.

BELOW: Hiding the rear suspension under the transmission creates the clean lines of this Softail..

range: the XLH 883, the XLH 883 Deluxe, the XLH 883 Hugger and the XLH 1200.

The Buyout

The merger with AMF had not turned out to be a happy one and in 1981 Vaughan Beals—who had joined Harley-Davidson in 1975 as a vice-president—and a group of 13 Harley-Davidson executives raised $100 million and bought the company from AMF. Beals said of the former owners, "AMF helped the motor company through a critical stage of growth . . . the most tangible evidence of their success is the company's ability to now stand on its own again and look to the future with pride and expectation."

To get the news through to the public at large the Harley-Davidson factory's advertising shouted evocative lines such as "The eagle soars alone." *Easyriders* magazine reported in April 1982 that "Harley currently sells only 31 percent of bikes in the over 61cu in (1,000cc) market. Honda has a 26-percent share, Kawasaki has 16 percent, and the other Japanese manufacturers are coming on like Yamamoto at Pearl Harbor."

Vaughan Beals was interviewed on the reasons for AMF wanting to part with Harley-Davidson and was quoted as saying: "Aggression is the key word in this industry, without it you lose your market and AMF had lost the will to fight for Harley-Davidson's share of the market." According to Beals, AMF had spent vast sums on plant building

and modernization soon after buying Harley-Davidson but had then decided it was not going to pump any more money into the firm. "It had to justify Harley-Davidson's expenses against those of its 30 or 40 other businesses." Beals recalled, "But those of us who were running AMF's motorcycle products group had to justify what was right for Harley against what was right for AMF. It was a stand off." He also added that, "AMF considered our offer as a sort of last resort."

Soar alone, though, the eagle did, flying strongly through stormy skies. Between 1980 and 1982 Harley-Davidson had been reluctantly forced to lay off a portion of its workforce and the management appealed to the government to increase tariffs on imported Japanese motorcycles of over 43cu in (700cc) displacement. Harley-Davidson felt that heavyweight garbage wagons from Japan such as the Honda Goldwing were their main threat. The US government under the presidency of Ronald Reagan imposed tariffs of up

ABOVE LEFT: The Evolution engine was easily powerful enough for this full dresser to tow a small trailer.

ABOVE RIGHT: Retro styling continues to be popular to this day, just as it was when this Evolution engined Classic full dresser was built in the late 1980s.

to 50 percent on such imports and Reagan showed his support by visiting one of Harley-Davidson's plants.

Better days were around the corner for the company and in 1983 another new engine was announced, officially designated the Evolution. This engine was to be Harley-Davidson's salvation. By 1984 motorcycle magazines were able to report that Harley-Davidson's laid-off workers were reemployed, its market share had increased, and that the company had made a profit for the first time in three years.

Vaughan Beals of Harley-Davidson was quoted as saying that, "We're not out of the woods yet but we're working hard to get there. We have an obligation to the American people and the government to take advantage of the breathing room the tariffs provide. We intend to fulfill that obligation by finishing up the job at hand."

One of the ways they went about this was by aggressively marketing the new engine; the Evolution—a name that is entirely appropriate as the bottom end of the 80cu in (1,310cc) engine can trace its origins back through the Shovelhead and Panhead to the original 61E Knucklehead of 1936. This engine was the one major factor above all else that saved Harley-Davidson from going out of business and turned the company again into a major force in the ranks of the world's motorcycle producers. Suddenly

everyone, it seemed, wanted a Harley. From then on things only got better for the company. On July 1, 1987, Harley-Davidson Inc was listed on the New York Stock Exchange. Diversification was also on the agenda and the company acquired a British motorcycle manufacturing company—Armstrong Equipment—in October 1987. Armstrong made military motorcycles with a single-cylinder 31cu in (500cc) engine and Harley-Davidson, with a tradition of making motorcycles for the US Army, were looking towards resuming such production. Since World War II, military motorcycles had moved away from heavyweight road bikes toward motocross-inspired cross-country machines, such as the Armstrong MT500. The company went forward into the nineties on a high, and Richard Teerlink was elected president of Harley-Davidson Inc.

Model	Hugger
Code	XLH
Years	1980-85
No. cylinders	V-twin
Valves	ohv
Bore/stroke inch	3³⁄₁₆ x 3¹³⁄₁₆
Capacity cu in	61
Capacity cc	1,000
Ignition	electronic
No of gears	4
Drive system	chain
Front suspension	teles
Rear suspension	s/a
Wheel type	cast-alloy
Wheel size inch	16 and 16
Front brake	disc
Rear brake	disc
Wheelbase inch	58.5, 1982-60

ABOVE: Some Harleys were just made for weekend runs! This Softail Custom sits covered with the morning dew awaiting its owner's appearance.

ABOVE RIGHT: Another view of the Softail belonging to the millionaire businessman Peter DeSavary.

Model	Sport Glide
Code	FXRT
Years	1984-92
No. cylinders	V-twin
Valves	ohv
Bore/stroke inch	3½ x 4¼
Capacity cu in	80
Capacity cc	1,310
Ignition	electronic
No of gears	5
Drive system	chain,
	1985-chain/belt
Front suspension	teles
Rear suspension	s/a
Wheel type	cast alloy
Wheel size inch	19 and 16
Brakes	discs
Wheelbase inch	64.7
Seat height inch	27.7

Model	Low Rider
Code	FXRS
Years	1986-92
No. cylinders	V-twin
Valves	ohv
Bore/stroke inch	3½ × 4¼
Capacity cu in	80
Capacity cc	1,310
Ignition	electronic
No of gears	5
Drive system	chain/belt
Front suspension	teles
Rear suspension	s/a
Wheel type	cast alloy
Wheel size inch	19 and 16
Brakes	discs
Wheelbase inch	63.1
Seat height inch	26.5

Model	Low Rider Sport
Code	FXRS-SP
Years	1986-93
No. cylinders	V-twin
Valves	ohv
Bore/stroke inch	3½ × 4¼
Capacity cu in	80
Capacity cc	1,310
Ignition	electronic
No of gears	5
Drive system	chain/belt
Front suspension	teles
Rear suspension	s/a
Wheel type	cast alloy
Wheel size inch	19 and 16
Brakes	discs
Wheelbase inch	64.7
Seat height inch	27.5

Model	Super Glide
Code	FXR
Years	1986-94
No. cylinders	V-twin
Valves	ohv
Bore/stroke inch	3½ × 4¼
Capacity cu in	80
Capacity cc	1,310
Ignition	electronic
No of gears	5
Drive system	chain/belt
Front suspension	teles
Rear suspension	s/a
Wheel type	cast alloy, 1993-wire
Wheel size inch	19 and 16
Brakes	discs
Wheelbase inch	63.1
Seat height inch	26.5

Model	Low Rider Custom
Code	FXLR
Years	1987-94
No. cylinders	V-twin
Valves	ohv
Bore/stroke inch	3½ × 4¼
Capacity cu in	80
Capacity cc	1,310
Ignition	electronic
No of gears	5
Drive system	chain/belt
Front suspension	teles
Rear suspension	s/a
Wheel type	wire/disc
Wheel size inch	19 and 16
Brakes	discs
Wheelbase inch	63.2
Seat height inch	26.5

Model	Softail
Code	FXST
Years	1984-90
No. cylinders	V-twin
Valves	ohv
Bore/stroke inch	3½ × 4¼
Capacity cu in	80
Capacity cc	1,310
Ignition	electronic
No of gears	4, 1985-5
Drive system	chain, 1985-chain/belt
Front suspension	teles
Rear suspension	s/a
Wheel type	wire
Wheel size inch	21 and 16
Brakes	discs
Wheelbase inch	66.3
Seat height inch	25.2

Model	Softail Custom
Code	FXSTC
Years	1986-98
No. cylinders	V-twin
Valves	ohv
Bore/stroke inch	3½ × 4¼
Capacity cu in	80
Capacity cc	1,310
Ignition	electronic
No of gears	5
Drive system	chain/belt
Front suspension	teles
Rear suspension	s/a
Wheel type	wire/disc
Wheel size inch	21 and 16
Brakes	discs
Wheelbase inch	66.3
Seat height inch	25.2

LEFT: A close-up of the springer forks on a 1988 Springer Softail; the damping unit is between the spring assemblies.

Model	Heritage Softail
Code	FLST
Years	1987-90
No. cylinders	V-twin
Valves	ohv
Bore/stroke inch	3½ × 4¼
Capacity cu in	80
Capacity cc	1,310
Ignition	electronic
No of gears	5
Drive system	chain/belt
Front suspension	teles
Rear suspension	s/a
Wheel type	wire
Wheel size inch	16 and 16
Brakes	discs
Wheelbase inch	64.2
Seat height inch	26.5

Model	De Luxe
Code	XLH883
Years	1986-95
No. cylinders	V-twin
Valves	ohv
Bore/stroke inch	3 × 3¹³⁄₁₆
Capacity cu in	54
Capacity cc	883
Ignition	electronic
No of gears	4, 1991-5
Drive system	chain, 1991-chain/belt
Front suspension	teles
Rear suspension	s/a
Wheel type	wire
Wheel size inch	19 and 16
Brakes	discs
Wheelbase inch	60.2
Seat height inch	28.5

Model	Hugger
Code	XLH883
Years	1988-2002
No. cylinders	V-twin
Valves	ohv
Bore/stroke inch	3 × 3¹³⁄₁₆
Capacity cu in	54
Capacity cc	883
Ignition	electronic
No of gears	4, 1991-5
Drive system	chain, 1991-chain/belt
Front suspension	teles
Rear suspension	s/a
Wheel type	cast alloy, 1993-wire, 1995-cast alloy, 1998-wire
Wheel size inch	19 and 16
Brakes	discs
Wheelbase inch	59
Seat height inch	26

The Nineties

The success of the FLHS Electra Glide Sport released in 1987 led to a widening of Harley-Davidson's motorcycle range in the nineties. Another two new models were added to the line up, the FLTC Tour Glide Ultra Classic and the FLHTC Electra Glide Ultra Classic, both these models proved popular and by the mid-nineties the latter were available with sequential-port fuel-injection systems. The FLHTC Ultra Classic models were presented in both carburetor and fuel injection models—the injection models designated FLHTCUI.

Out of Milwaukee something altogether different first appeared in 1990—the FLSTF Fat Boy. This machine took the factory custom concept out in a new direction and caused a stir on its introduction for several reasons, not least of which was its unusual name. The Fat Boy also caused a commotion because of its unusual appearance—it was a factory custom from a completely different mold. The appearance was of a heavyweight solid motorcycle with squat stance and solid cast alloy wheels.

Mechanically it was a Softail, but with cast alloy 16in disc wheels, fully valanced front fender, shotgun exhaust pipes, and wide FLH bars. In the first year the Fat Boy was only available in silver metallic paint with yellow detailing. Subsequently, on becoming a regular in the Harley-Davidson range, it is now sold in a number of different colors.

The FLSTF Fat Boy somehow projects an old style look while being completely modern, its overall shape may be almost vintage but its solid

ABOVE: A bit of light-hearted drag-racing between two Evo-engined big twins.

LEFT: Relaxed ride in the country—this is what the Evolution engine was made for!

RIGHT: Having your picture taken outside the Harley-Davidson factory makes for a good memento.

wheels, Evolution engine, and custom-style parts—including the front fender and shotgun dual exhaust pipes—are right up to date. The Fat Boy had been heralded as a spectacular motorcycle when it was unveiled. By 1991, the FLSTF Fat Boy featured solid 16in diameter wheels back and front, and with the Evolution engine power in a Softail frame it all added together to present a very solid motorbike. Its unusual name caught on quickly, and since then Harley-Davidson named another of its range the Bad Boy. Powered by a 80cu in (1,310cc) capacity four-stroke OHV V-twin Evolution engine, it boasted a top

speed of 115mph that produced 58bhp at 5,000rpm; five-speed transmission, and a steel Softail frame.

While much of Harley-Davidson's nineties' range was based around the 80cu in (1,310cc) so-called big twin, Evolution engine, the company had another range of engines in production. The Sportster range is based around a unit construction engine of which two displacements are available: the 53cu in (870cc) and 74cu in (1,200cc) versions. The 883 is seen by many riders as an entry level Harley-Davidson, but its success on racetracks and the specific race series for this model indicate otherwise (see also pages 410–419).

A new model that shared little with the existing Sportsters (beyond its displacement) debuted at the Daytona, Florida Speedway. It was the VR1000, a liquid-cooled racing bike. The machine has been raced at numerous events and although success has eluded it there was much speculation that the VR1000 may be a rolling testbed for a new generation of Harley-Davidsons as it is not unlikely that increasingly stringent noise and emissions regulations will make the production of air-cooled motorcycles impossible within the foreseeable future. For more on the VR1000 see pages 420–421.

Harley-Davidson's 1991 range was announced in the fall of 1990. The biggest news was the introduction of the Dynaglide series that had been developed from the ground up using computer-aided design (CAD) techniques. The first of the Dynaglides was a reintroduced Sturgis model—celebrating the 50th anniversary of the famed Black Hills Motorcycle Classic rally and races held in Sturgis, South Dakota.

Harley-Davidson claimed that the new model had been five years in the making and although reminiscent of the earlier Shovelhead-powered Sturgis, it was in fact a new bike deep down. The new square top-tube,

TOP LEFT: Harley gatherings are very popular—whether they are hundreds or even thousands of miles away, or just around the corner.

CENTER LEFT: A Harley, a proud owner, and a bar.

CENTER RIGHT: The Evolution-engined version of the FXR was built from 1986 to 1994.

ABOVE & RIGHT: The FXSTB Bad Boy was just one of the many different m odels based on the Softail chassis. This clean looking design first originated in 1984, and was produced right through the nineties.

Model	Heritage Softail
	Classic
Code	FLSTC
Years	1988-99
No. cylinders	V-twin
Valves	ohv
Bore/stroke inch	3½ x 4¼
Capacity cu in	80
Capacity cc	1,310
Ignition	electronic
No of gears	5
Drive system	chain/belt
Front suspension	teles
Rear suspension	s/a
Wheel type	wire
Wheel size inch	1⁹⁄₁₆
Brakes	discs
Wheelbase inch	62.5
Seat height inch	26.5

frame, and engine isolation system were the key to the whole machine but for extra special individuality numerous custom touches were engineered into the bike.

The oil tank was mounted under the transmission for a cleaner overall appearance, while the filler cap featured a built-in dipstick to make checking the oil level easy.

ABOVE: The polished fins on the Evolution engine in this Convertible contrast well with the matt black cases.

RIGHT & OVERLEAF: The Fat Boy—an evocative name for the popular FLSTF was introduced in 1990.

Furthermore, the oil filter was repositioned so that it was easier to change at the recommended service intervals. Better ignition and steering locks were built into the new bike and the big twin Evolution engine was coated in crinkle-finish black paint for the first time. The staggered dual exhaust pipes were designed in such a way that their appearance didn't clutter the lines of the bike or detract from the appearance of the engine. The machine rolled on 19 and 16in diameter wheels, front and rear respectively, and the cycle parts were finished in gloss black, set off by a red Sturgis Harley-Davidson logo on the fuel tank.

The proven FXR series continued for 1991 with a line up that included

the FXR Super Glide, FXLR Low Rider Custom, FXRS Low Rider, FXRS-SP Low Rider Sport Edition, FXRS-Conv Low Rider Convertible, and FXRT Sport Glide. These bikes were all based around the welded, tubular steel frame with a rubber mounted 80cu in (1,310cc) big twin engine, five-speed transmission, and belt final drive. Up front were 39mm diameter telescopic forks and most of the FXR series had nine-spoked alloy wheels front and rear. Exceptions were the traditional spoked front wheel and solid alloy rear wheel of the FXLR Low Rider Custom.

The FX Softail line up for 1991 was impressive, including the FXSTS, Softail, the FXSTC Softail Custom, the FLSTF Fat Boy, and the FLSTC Heritage Softail Classic. This range of bikes played heavily on Harley-Davidson's heritage of bike building with springer forks and two-tone paint jobs. Some of the range, especially the FXSTS Springer Softail, hinted at

Model	Dyna Glide Sturgis & Daytona
Code	FXDB
Years	1991 Sturgis, 1992 Daytona
No. cylinders	V-twin
Valves	ohv
Bore/stroke inch	3½ x 4¼
Capacity cu in	80
Capacity cc	1,310
Ignition	electronic
No of gears	5
Drive system	
Front suspension	teles
Rear suspension	s/a
Wheel type	cast alloy
Wheel size inch	1⅞
Brakes	discs
Wheelbase inch	65.5
Seat height inch	26.6

LEFT: Another three Fat Boys!

BELOW: An FXDB Sturgis Special Edition built for the 1991 model year.

Harley's unofficial styling department of yore—the chopper builders. The FXSTS featured springer forks with a minimal front fender/mudguard and a "bobbed" rear fender. In later years Harley-Davidson would go further down this factory chopper road.

The touring models, the FL range for 1991 included: the FLHS Electra Glide Sport, the FLHTC Ultra Classic Electra Glide, the FLHTC Electra Glide Classic, the FLTC Tour Glide Classic, and the FLTC Ultra Classic Tour Glide. All these bikes were based around 80cu in (1,310cc) big twin engines and a variety of touring paraphernalia including fairings, hard panniers, windshields, and sidecars.

The Dynaglide was introduced in 1991 with the FXDB Sturgis, named after one of America's biggest biker gatherings which was celebrating its fiftieth anniversary in 1991. Ten years earlier there had been a Shovelhead-powered belt drive Sturgis. This Harley-Davidson was also based

around a new frame and some saw it as the "most significant new Harley-Davidson to come out in almost a decade." It ran the quarter mile in 13.58 seconds. The FXDB designation indicated Super Glide (FX), Dynaglide chassis (D), and Belt drive (B).

The 50th Anniversary Sturgis model was followed by a 50th Anniversary Daytona model. A limited edition of only 1,700 of this model were produced. Also an FXDB, it featured a number of custom touches including 50th anniversary graphics on the tank, air cleaner insert, sissy bar, and a serialized nameplate. The wheels and rear sprocket were trimmed in gold. The use of the Dynaglide chassis in the pearl-painted limited edition FXDB Daytona was entirely appropriate in

view of the fact that custom Harley-Davidsons gathered in huge numbers at the annual spring event in Daytona, Florida—and the FXDB Daytona was named in commemoration of the event's 50th anniversary. The bike went on sale in August 1991 as Harley's first 1992 model, although it had been shown during the 50th Anniversary of the races at Daytona in Florida during Bikeweek in March. It was discontinued by 1992.

Harley's new range for 1992 came in August 1991 with the announcement of two new models. As well as the FXDB Daytona the company

ABOVE & RIGHT: Only 1,700 examples of this 1991 Daytona 50th Anniversary Dynaglide— designated FXDB—were built.

Model	Dyna Glide
	Sturgis & Daytona
Code	FXDB
Years	1991 Sturgis,
	1992 Daytona
No. cylinders	V-twin
Valves	ohv
Bore/stroke inch	3½ x 4¼
Capacity cu in	80
Capacity cc	1,310
Ignition	electronic
No of gears	5
Drive system	
Front suspension	teles
Rear suspension	s/a
Wheel type	cast alloy
Wheel size inch	1¾₆
Brakes	discs
Wheelbase inch	65.5
Seat height inch	26.6

introduced the FXDC Dynaglide Custom. Both machines were based around Harley-Davidson's Dynaglide chassis, introduced in the 1991 FXDB Sturgis. The Dynaglide chassis is a steel frame with a single top tube and a rubber engine-isolation mounting system. It also incorporated forgings rather than steel stampings at the frame junctions to ensure smaller discrepancies between frames. The frame was intended to have seventies-inspired rigid custom styling but offer the modern comfort of Low Rider frames by using rear suspension.

The 1992 Dynaglide Custom was styled in a monochromatic black and silver livery that included a silver powder-coated frame. These two Harley-Davidsons as well as the 14 other 80cu in (1,310cc) big twin models were equipped with a new 40mm diameter CV carburetor.

This line up of 16 big twins was divided into:

- the Dynaglide FXD series—FXDB and FXDC.
- the Low Rider FXR series—FXR Super Glide, FXRS Low Rider, FXRS-CONV Low Rider Convertible, FXRS-SP Low Rider Sport Edition, FXRT Sport Glide and FXLR Low Rider Custom.
- the Softail FX/FL series—FXSTS Softail Springer, FXSTC Softail Custom, FLSTC Heritage Softail Classic, FLSTF Fat Boy.
- the Touring FL Series—FLHS Electra Glide Sport, FLHTC Electra Glide Classic, FLHTC Electra Glide Ultra Classic, FLTC Tour Glide Ultra Classic.

The FXR series of big twin Harley-Davidson Evolution models include the FXR Superglide, FXRS-SP Low Rider Sport, FXLR Low Rider Custom, and the FXRS-Convertible.

All the FXR models featured rubber-mounted engines, five-speed transmissions, and belt final drives. The result of this combination is a smooth and vibration free motorcycle. The FXRS-Conv, which was a modern motorcycle with a number of factory custom styling touches, was designed to be a versatile sport touring machine. To make it suitable for the job it was given refinements such as air-adjustable front suspension through a chamber inside the handlebars, a removable Lexan windshield, and removable saddlebags made from nylon and leather. A Harley-Davidson sidecar can also be fitted if required.

The FXD series used the new frame designed for a rubber-mounted engine and the Softail FX/FL series used the Softail frame. This tubular steel component has the lines of an earlier hardtail frame but incorporates rear suspension by hiding the twin rear shock absorbers underneath the frame. The major difference between FX and FL models is that the FX models were designed to look like custom bikes and featured 21in diameter front wheels, while the FL models were more nostalgic in appearance and featured 16in diameter front wheels. All featured rubber-belt final drive. The touring FL

Model	Heritage Softail
	Nostalgia
Code	FLSTN
Years	1993
No. cylinders	V-twin
Valves	ohv
Bore/stroke inch	3½ x 4¼
Capacity cu in	80
Capacity cc	1,310
Ignition	electronic
No of gears	5
Drive system	chain/belt
Front suspension	teles
Rear suspension	s/a
Wheel type	wire
Wheel size inch	1⁹⁄₁₆
Brakes	discs
Wheelbase inch	62.5
Seat height inch	26.5

Model	Dyna Low Rider
Code	FXDL
Years	1993-98
No. cylinders	V-twin
Valves	ohv
Bore/stroke inch	3½ x 4¼
Capacity cu in	80
Capacity cc	1,310
Ignition	electronic
No of gears	5
Drive system	chain/belt
Front suspension	teles
Rear suspension	s/a
Wheel type	cast alloy
Wheel size inch	1⁹⁄₁₆
Brakes	discs
Wheelbase inch	65.4
Seat height inch	27,
	Convertible-30.6

RIGHT: The factory realised quickly that there was a huge demand for bikes with retro styling, and to satisfy the hunger for today's technology with nostalgic overtones created machines like these Springer Softails.

BELOW: For some reason the bikini bike-wash is always popular at rallies and races!

and rear suspension, rubber-mounted engines, and belt final drives.

For 1993 another nostalgic Harley-Davidson was introduced—the FLSTN Softail Heritage Nostalgia (it actually first went on sale in August 1992). It and the Heritage models have stayed in Harley's range ever since. One of the reasons for launching a new model of Heritage Harley-Davidson for 1993 was, of course, that the company celebrated its 90th anniversary in that year.

The FLSTN was actually one of six limited edition anniversary models and

models were the early nineties versions of the Electra Glides and incorporated such technology as air-adjustable front

three new models. The others, brand new for 1993 were the Dyna Wide Glide and the FXDL Dyna Low Rider.

ABOVE & TOP RIGHT: The front wheel size varies across many different models to match the overall styling of the bike—the FXDL Dyna Low Rider, for instance has a 19in diameter wheel, whereas that on the FXDWG Dyna Wide Glide measures 21in.

The Softail chassis has been used to good effect as the basis of many different models. Here are two different model year bikes which have been styled as retro machines—the 1993/1994 Heritage Softail Nostalgia (OPPOSITE BOTTOM LEFT & RIGHT) and a 1996 FLSTW Heritage Softail (RIGHT).

The Wide Glide had originally appeared as a 1980 model and was a Shovelhead-powered factory custom of its day. The new Wide Glide had similar custom styling that included apehanger handlebars, bobbed rear fender, one-piece fatbob fuel tank, a stepped dual seat, and a 21in diameter front wheel positioned in the wideglide telescopic forks. Power for the new

model came from the proven big twin Evolution engine.

The FXDL Dyna Low Rider was based around the Dyna frame that had premiered in the limited edition models over the previous couple of years and combined seventies custom styling with the refinement of a rubber-mounted big twin engine. The new frame had been slightly refined with

redesigned engine mounts. The FLSTN was a very limited edition model as only 2,700 1993 models were built. A novel detail was the use of Dunlop whitewall tires, the first wide whitewalls approved by Harley-Davidson for use on their motorcycles.

Celebrating its birthday Harley-Davidson produced six limited edition 90th anniversary models. These were:

1,200 of the XLH 1,200cc Sportsters, 800 FXLR Low Rider Customs, 1,993 FXDWG Dyna Wide Glides, 1,310 FLHTC Electra Glide Classics, 1,310 FLHTC Electra Glide Ultra Classics, and 200 FLTC Tour Glide Ultra Classics—making a total of 6,873 motorcycles which featured 90th anniversary fuel tank emblems and a two-tone silver and satin custom paint scheme.

The 1995 FXDWG Dyna Wide Glide is another production Harley-Davidson that can be described as a factory custom. The Wide Glide designation refers to the fact that the fork legs are more widely spaced on this model than on other big twin Harley-Davidsons. Its origins are pure chopper, as Harley's designers looked at what modifications were being made to stock

bikes and then produced their interpretation of a modified stock bike. The front end is raked out and fitted with a 21in front wheel, the handlebars are ape-hangers, and it has a small fitted front fender and a bobbed rear one. These were—and still are—popular modifications for building a custom Harley-Davidson, so within certain limits Harley-Davidson offered its own. The

limits are that because the machine is made by a large company it has to comply with various safety restrictions and regulations around the world. Many custom builders, for example, would not fit a front fender, but the factory has to.

In 1995, the FXSTSB Bad Boy became Harley's most nostalgic motorcycle to date. It featured a Softail frame that had an old-fashioned look about it, Springer forks (that until the FXSTS had not been fitted since 1948), and a nostalgic hotrod paint scheme. As well as these old style features it had modern features including the Evolution engine and disc brakes. Its technical specification was similar to the other big twins in the range; a capacity of 80cu in (1,310cc) in the four-stroke OHV V-twin Evolution engine giving a top speed of 120mph and power of 58bhp at 5,000 rpm driving through a five-speed transmission with the whole lot installed in a Softail

ABOVE: The Wide Glide name refers to the wide front ends which the factory fitted in response to their popularity in the custom bike scene.

Model	Dyna Wide Glide
Code	FXDWG
Years	1993-98
No. cylinders	V-twin
Valves	ohv
Bore/stroke inch	3½ × 4¼
Capacity cu in	80
Capacity cc	1,310
Ignition	electronic
No of gears	5
Drive system	chain/belt
Front suspension	teles
Rear suspension	s/a
Wheel type	wire
Wheel size inch	2¹⁄₁₆
Brakes	discs
Wheelbase inch	66.1
Seat height inch	29.7

cradle frame.

The FLSTN of 1996 is another contemporary nostalgic Harley-Davidson based around the Softail frame and Evolution big twin engine. While it features nostalgic items such as partially shrouded telescopic forks and 16in whitewall tires back and front, it is not so much of a nostalgic dresser as the Heritage Softail Classic. Nonetheless it is reminiscent of an early fifties' Hydra Glide—albeit perhaps a slightly customized one. The lines of the FL fenders are unmistakable and the Softail frame gives a rigid appearance—it takes more than a glance to spot the pivot for the rear portion of the frame (it is actually between the exhaust pipes behind the gearbox). The chromed oil tank and other components and two-tone paint job contribute to the custom appearance, as do the staggered dual exhaust pipes. Fender

trim, dash, running lights, turn signals, mirrors, and headlight have all been updated for style or where necessary to conform to highway legislation but remain traditional Harley-Davidson.

By 1996, the FLSTC Heritage Softail Classic was being offered as another of Harley-Davidson's contemporary but nostalgic dresser style motorcycles. Its Hardtail frame styling endowed with the use of the Softail frame in conjunction with hydraulic telescopic front forks is in many ways the fifties Hydra-Glide reincarnated for the nineties. Unlike the Hydra-Glide, though, the Heritage Softail Classic (along with rear suspension) features refinements such as electric start, belt drive, disc brakes front and rear, and the larger capacity Evolution V-twin. Despite such modern components the styling is unmistakably big, old Harley-Davidson; the big valanced

ABOVE: While the size of the front wheel may vary, the rear wheel fitted to big twin Harleys has traditionally had a 16in diameter. This is a solid disc; old-fashioned spoked wheels are also popular.

Model	Fat Boy
Code	FLSTF
Years	1990-99
No. cylinders	V-twin
Valves	ohv
Bore/stroke inch	3½ x 4¼
Capacity cu in	80
Capacity cc	1,310
Ignition	electronic
No of gears	5
Drive system	chain/belt
Front suspension	teles
Rear suspension	s/a
Wheel type	disc
Wheel size inch	1⁵⁄₆
Brakes	discs
Wheelbase inch	62.5
Seat height inch	26.5

FL fenders, the shrouded forks on which the headlights, additional spotlights, and windshield brackets are mounted, the wide dresser bars, timeless fatbob tank that follows into a studded leather seat, and the large studded saddlebags all contribute to this appearance. The end result is the best of both worlds, modern convenience, comfort, and speed and the style of an altogether long gone decade.

The FXRS Conv was still in Harley's range in 1996 as the FXDS Conv Dyna Convertible. The frame used in Dynaglide models was re-engineered for the 1996 models to lower the motorcycle and although it is a traditional looking motorcycle the FXDS Conv is not so nostalgic as several of the other models in the nineties ranges. This is more of a dual purpose bike for cruising and touring. The windshield and panniers are designed to be quickly removable to

allow the motorcycle to change roles and the Evolution engine is rubber mounted to minimize the vibration passed through to rider and pillion.

The Dyna Convertible originated from the Super Glide hence the FX prefix to its model designation. The Super Glide remains in the range as a basic and traditional big twin Harley-Davidson, featuring the Dyna frame and Evolution engine but traditional telescopic forks and spoked wheels. The Dyna Convertible has 13-spoke cast wheels and other touring accessories such as a pillion backrest.

Since the early nineties there have been other models such as the FXDC, a custom Dynaglide, and the FXSTSB. The FXSTSB Bad Boy was almost as close as a major factory could come to building a chopper. It features a Softail frame, springer forks, a bobbed rear fender, and a nostalgic scalloped custom paintjob. The 1996

FXSTSB Bad Boy is Harley's most extreme factory custom to date; in many ways it's more than a factory custom, it is a full "factory chopper." Harley-Davidson admit in some of its advertising that there is a little notoriety in their history. The film, *The Wild One* for example, as has been said before, was based on the incidents in the town of Hollister, California after World War II. Many of the riders in Hollister rode bikes that are reminiscent of the current incarnation. Back then, almost 50 years ago, riders rode bobbers, many of

LEFT & ABOVE: The factory's attitude to listening to its customers requirements has changed beyond all recognition since the bad old days of the seventies. Some riders wanted a semi-tourer with performance, so they got the Sport Glide (ABOVE), whereas others wanted a more conventional bike, so they were offered the FLT (LEFT).

which featured shortened fenders and springer forks all giving a stripped down minimal look. The bikes they

Model	Dyna Super Glide
Code	FXD
Years	1995-98
No. cylinders	V-twin
Valves	ohv
Bore/stroke inch	3½ × 4¼
Capacity cu in	80
Capacity cc	1,310
Ignition	electronic
No of gears	5
Drive system	chain/belt
Front suspension	teles
Rear suspension	s/a
Wheel type	cast alloy
Wheel size inch	1⁹⁄₁₆
Brakes	discs
Wheelbase inch	62.5
Seat height inch	27

LEFT AND THIS PAGE: The Road King is the factory's answer for those who want a middleweight tourer—the 80+ foot-pounds of torque provided by the latest version of the Evolution engine ensures there's plenty of pull for a smooth and easy ride.

rode were based on Knuckleheads and flatheads but Harley-Davidson, ever conscious of its history and heritage, introduced the Bad Boy based around a Softail frame and Evolution engine.

Harley-Davidson has never hesitated to look at what custom builders do to their products and then later offer their own interpretation of any particular style. The look created by the unofficial stylists is of course not as hampered by worldwide legislation as a major motorcycle manufacturer such as Harley-Davidson, however the factory can offer acceptably styled factory customs.

The 1996 FXSTS Softail Custom is such a bike; it unashamedly looks like a neatly customized stock bike rather than a stock bike. It is based around the Softail frame which offers hardtail styling with the benefit of rear suspension. A bobbed rear fender, stepped seat, fatbob tank, raked out

Three police bikes: (RIGHT) is a 1992 FXRP belonging to the Volusia County Sheriff's department, (BELOW RIGHT) is a San Francisco police bike, and (ABOVE) is an ex-police bike that is now in civilian hands.

Model	Bad Boy
Code	FXSTSB
Years	1995-96
No. cylinders	V-twin
Valves	ohv
Bore/stroke inch	3½ × 4¼
Capacity cu in	80
Capacity cc	1,310
Ignition	electronic
No of gears	5
Drive system	chain/belt
Front suspension	leading link
Rear suspension	s/a
Wheel type	wire/disc
Wheel size inch	2¹⁄₁₆
Brakes	discs
Wheelbase inch	64.4
Seat height inch	26.1

front end, forward control pegs and foot pedals, a minimal front fender, and big pullback bars are all the definitive aftermarket parts necessary to build a custom big twin. The solid alloy rear wheel is a more modern custom style part. Harley-Davidson collected these elements and assembled them around a big twin Evolution engine and five-speed transmission and offered the custom bike straight off the dealer's showroom floor.

The Ultra Classic Electra Glide Injection is physically the biggest of Harley-Davidson's current range of motorcycles. It is also one of the most well appointed because, although its frame and engine are similar to other models in the range, it comes with a sound system, cigarette lighter, cruise control, and more instrumentation than other models. Much of this is contained within the fork-mounted fairing. The tank-mounted dash is used

as the cover for the filler cap. The FLHTC in both carburetor and injection forms is also fitted with legshields—called lowers by Harley-Davidson—in which the speakers for the stereo are located. There are also rear speakers and separate controls for the passenger. The hard saddlebags are complemented by the tour pack in which turn signals are incorporated and on which the dual antenna for the radio and CB are mounted. The Ultra Classic Tour Glide is a similar model on which the most visual difference is the use of a differently shaped fairing.

The mighty Electra Glide has been in production since 1965 and has been sequentially updated and is still made in standard form as the FLHT Electra Glide Standard. In its state of the art 1996 form, it is refined and sophisticated but still a big touring motorcycle. In view of its role as a tourer the comfort of rider and pillion has been treated as being of paramount importance, not least in the size and depth of the seats and the fact that footboards are fitted for both people.

The engine is described as isolation-mounted by Harley-Davidson to minimize vibration transmitted from the V-twin to those aboard. A fork-mounted fairing makes distance riding more comfortable as does the air suspension. To enable the occupants of the Electra Glide to travel and carry baggage two

Model	Softail Standard
Code	FXST
Years	1999
No. cylinders	V-twin
Valves	ohv
Bore/stroke inch	3½ x 4¼
Capacity cu in	80
Capacity cc	1,310
Ignition	electronic
No of gears	5
Drive system	chain/belt
Front suspension	teles
Rear suspension	s/a
Wheel type	wire
Wheel size inch	2¹/₁₆
Brakes	discs
Seat height inch	26.2

Model	Night Train
Code	FXSTB
Years	1998–99
No. cylinders	V-twin
Valves	ohv
Bore/stroke inch	3½ x 4¼
Capacity cu in	80
Capacity cc	1,310
Ignition	electronic
No of gears	5
Drive system	chain/belt
Front suspension	teles
Rear suspension	s/a
Wheel type	wire/disc
Wheel size inch	2¹⁄₁₆
Brakes	discs
Seat height inch	25.3

capacious panniers are fitted, one either side of the rear fender and a luggage rack over the same fender is also designed for load carrying, either with a fitted tour pack or simply by strapping bags to the rack.

New for 1997 was the Ol' Boy—another unusually named Harley—and

LEFT & ABOVE: Harleys have a long history of use as police vehicles, and will presumably continue to do so in spite of foreign bikes such as BMWs and Kawasakis being bought by various forces over the years. These (ABOVE) two Volusia County police bikes, and this City of Milwaukee (ABOVE LEFT) police bike on Juneau Avenue are as American as apple pie on Sunday!

yet another nostalgic big twin, the FLSTS Heritage Springer Softail. The line up of touring bikes for 1997 comprised the FLHT Electra Glide Standard, the FLHR and FLHRI Road King Electra Glide Classics, and the FLHTCU and FLHTCUI Ultra Classic Electra Glides. All were available with electronic sequential-port fuel injection (ESPFI) for improved cold starting and running.

The 1997 ESPFI model was smaller and had improved diagnostics over previous models. The touring models' frame had been redesigned to give a lower seat height to enhance the rider's comfort without detracting from ground clearance. A number of

Full-dressers—you either love them or you hate them, there's little common ground! (ABOVE) A 90th Anniversary FLH, and (LEFT & RIGHT) two Electra Glide Ultra Classics.

Model	V2 EVOLUTION ELECTRA GLIDES
	1984-98, FLHTC, Electra Glide Classic;1985-87, FLHT, Electra Glide; 1988-93, FLHS, Electra Glide Sport;1989-94, FLHTC, Ultra Classic Electra Glide; 1995, FLHTCI, Ultra Classic Electra Glide Anniversary; 1995-96, FLHTCU, Ultra Classic Electra Glide;1995-98, FLHT, Electra Glide Standard;1996-98, FLHTCI, Electra Glide Classic (injection); 1996-98, FLHTCUI, Ultra Classic Electra Glide (injection)
No. cylinders	V-twin
Valves	ohv
Bore/stroke inch	3½ × 4¼
Capacity cu in	80
Capacity cc	1,310
Ignition	electronic
No of gears	5
Drive system	chain, 1985-chain/belt
Front suspension	teles
Rear suspension	s/a
Wheel type	cast alloy
Wheel size inch	1⁹⁄₁₆
Brakes	discs
Wheelbase	62.9
Seat height inch	28, Sport 27

Models	V2 EVOLUTION TOUR GLIDES & ROAD KINGS
	1984-91, FLTC, Tour Glide Classic; 1989-93, FLTC, Ultra Classic Tour Glide; 1994-98, FLHR, Electra Glide Road King; 1995, FLTCU, Ultra Classic Tour Glide; 1996-97, FLHRI, Electra Glide Road King (injection) 1998, FLHRCI, Electra Glide Road King Classic (injection)
No. cylinders	V-twin
Valves	ohv
Bore/stroke inch	3½ × 4¼
Capacity cu in	80
Capacity cc	1,310
Ignition	electronic
No of gears	5
Drive system	chain, 1985-chain/belt
Front suspension	teles
Rear suspension	s/a
Wheel type	cast alloy
Wheel size inch	1⁹⁄₁₆
Brakes	discs
Wheelbase	62.9
Seat height inch	29.6

LEFT: The Tour-Glide was made for touring, and that is just what these folks and their friends are doing!

minor upgrades were also made to the electrical system on these big twins, including the use of a new alternator rotor. Dual rate springs replaced electronically controlled anti-dive components in the forks although adjustable air-suspension was retained in both front and rear suspension.

The FLSTS Ol' Boy was a nostalgically-styled Softail that resembled a 1948 FL. This was the one-year only Springer-forked, rigid-framed Panhead-powered big twin. It used Harley-Davidson's modern springer forks, softail frame, and an Evolution big twin engine. Wide handlebars, tasselled seat, spotlights, leather panniers, plus numerous other old-style accessories such as a vintage tail light. All these stylistic elements gave the bike a late-forties' appearance.

The FX range for 1997 comprised the FXD Dyna Super Glide, the FXDL Dyna Low Rider, the FXDS Conv Dyna Convertible, and the FXDWG Dyna Wide Glide. These models ran on from the year before with only minor upgrades. Wheels with aluminium hubs became standard on the Dyna Wide glide for example. The next major upgrade to Harley-Davidson's big twin range would come in the form of the Twin Cam 88, a new larger displacement engine that was designed to supersede the Evolution big twin across the range.

ABOVE & RIGHT: Fuel-injection was fitted to many models in the range in order to improve combustion efficiency and reduce emissions. These Electra Glide Ultra Classics all have this modern replacement for the carburetor.

Model	Heritage Softail Special
Code	FLSTN
Years	1994-96
No. cylinders	V-twin
Valves	ohv
Bore/stroke inch	3½ × 4¼
Capacity cu in	80
Capacity cc	1,310
Ignition	electronic
No of gears	5
Drive system	chain/belt
Front suspension	teles
Rear suspension	s/a
Wheel type	wire
Wheel size inch	1⁹⁄₁₆
Brakes	discs
Wheelbase inch	62.5
Seat height inch	26.5

Model	Electra Glide Standard
Code	FLHT
Years	1999-2002
No. cylinders	V-twin
Valves	ohv
Bore/stroke mm	95.3 × 101.6
Capacity cu in	88
Capacity cc	1,440
Ignition	electronic
No of gears	5
Drive system	chain/belt
Front suspension	teles
Rear suspension	s/a
Wheel type	cast alloy or wire
Wheel size inch	1⁹⁄₁₆ – 1³⁄₁₆
Brakes	discs
Wheelbase inch	63.5
Seat height inch	27.2

Model	Heritage Springer
Code	FLSTS
Years	1997-99
No. cylinders	V-twin
Valves	ohv
Bore/stroke inch	3½ × 4¼
Capacity cu in	80
Capacity cc	1,310
Ignition	electronic
No of gears	5
Drive system	chain/belt
Front suspension	leading link
Rear suspension	s/a
Wheel type	wire
Wheel size inch	1⁹⁄₁₆
Brakes	discs
Seat height inch	26.5

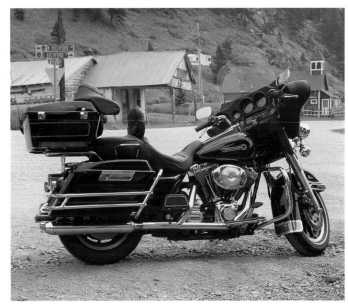

Model	Road King	Model	Road King	Model	Road Glide
Years	1999-2002		Classic (injection)		(injection)
Code	FLHR	Code	FLHRCI	Code	FLTRI
No. cylinders	V-twin	Years	1999-2002	Years	1999-2001
Valves	ohv	No. cylinders	V-twin	No. cylinders	V-twin
Bore/stroke mm	95.3 × 101.6	Valves	ohv	Valves	ohv
Capacity cu in	88	Bore/stroke mm	95.3 × 101.6	Bore/stroke mm	95.3 × 101.6
Capacity cc	1440	Capacity cu in	88	Capacity cu in	88
Ignition	electronic	Capacity cc	1440	Capacity cc	1440
No of gears	5	Ignition	electronic	Ignition	electronic
Drive system	chain/belt	No of gears	5	No of gears	5
Front suspension	teles	Drive system	chain/belt	Drive system	chain/belt
Rear suspension	s/a	Front suspension	teles	Front suspension	teles
Wheel type	cast alloy or	Rear suspension	s/a	Rear suspension	s/a
	wire	Wheel type	wire,	Wheel type	cast alloy
Wheel size inch	1⁹⁄₁₆		2002-cast alloy	Wheel size inch	1⁹⁄₁₆
Brakes	discs	Wheel size inch	1⁹⁄₁₆	Brakes	discs
Wheelbase inch	63.5	Brakes	discs	Wheelbase inch	63.5
Seat height inch	27.2	Wheelbase inch	63.5	Seat height inch	26.9
		Seat height inch	26.9		

LEFT: Compare the engine of this fuel-injection Electra Gllide Classic to the twin-cam Evo at right.

RIGHT & BELOW: The twin-cam version of the Evolution engine was the biggest change to this superb design since it was first introduced in 1985. A close-up of the engine on the twin-cam Night-Train (RIGHT), a Road King Classic FLHRCI 2000 (BELOW LEFT), an FXST Softail (BELOW RIGHT), a 2000 Dynaglide (BOTTOM LEFT) and a 2000 Tour-Glide (BOTTOM RIGHT).

*LEFT, & BELOW LEFT: A Screaming Eagle
Road Glide.*

*RIGHT: The FXSTB Night-Train produced for the
1998 model year was the factory's first all matt
black machine and for many was the coolest bike
the factory ever produced!*

BELOW: A 1998 FXD Dyna Super Glide.

*PAGE 406: The twin-cam engine benefited from a
larger capacity (88cu in1,440cc) as well as an
extra camshaft as een on a 1999 FXDX Dyna
Super Glide.*

*PAGE 407 & PAGES 408–409: Twin-cam Electra-
Glide Ultra Classics.*

Model	Ultra Classic Electra Glide (injection)
Code	FLHTCUI
Years	1999-2002
No. cylinders	V-twin
Valves	ohv
Bore/stroke mm	95.3 x 101.6
Capacity cu in	88
Capacity cc	1440
Ignition	electronic
No of gears	5
Drive system	chain/belt
Front suspension	teles
Rear suspension	s/a
Wheel type	cast alloy
Wheel size inch	16
Brakes	discs
Wheelbase inch	63.5
Seat height inch	27.2

Model	Electra Glide Classic
Code	FLHTC
Years	2002
No. cylinders	V-twin
Valves	ohv
Bore/stroke mm	95.3 x 101.6
Capacity cu in	88
Capacity cc	1440
Ignition	electronic
No of gears	5
Drive system	chain/belt
Front suspension	teles
Rear suspension	s/a
Wheel type	cast alloy
Wheel size inch	16
Brakes	discs
Wheelbase inch	62.7
Seat height inch^	27.3

Model	88ci Dyna Wide Glide
Code	FXDWG
Years	1999-2002
No. cylinders	V-twin
Valves	ohv
Bore/stroke inch	95.3 x 101.6
Capacity cu in	88
Capacity cc	1,440
Ignition	electronic
No of gears	5
Drive system	chain/belt
Front suspension	teles
Rear suspension	s/a
Wheel type	wire
Wheel size inch	2$\frac{1}{16}$
Brakes	discs
Wheelbase inch	66.1
Seat height inch	26.7

Model	88ci Dyna Low Rider
Code	FXDL
Years	1999-2002
No. cylinders	V-twin
Valves	ohv
Bore/stroke inch	95.3 x 101.6
Capacity cu in	88
Capacity cc	1,440
Ignition	electronic
No of gears	5
Drive system	chain/belt
Front suspension	teles
Rear suspension	s/a
Wheel type	wire
Wheel size inch	1⁹⁄₁₆
Brakes	discs
Wheelbase inch	65.5
Seat height inch	26.5

Model	88ci Dyna Super Glide
Code	FXD
Years	1999-2002
No. cylinders	V-twin
Valves	ohv
Bore/stroke inch	95.3 x 101.6
Capacity cu in	88
Capacity cc	1440
Ignition	electronic
No of gears	5
Drive system	chain/belt
Front suspension	teles
Rear suspension	s/a
Wheel type	wire, 2002-wire front, disc rear
Wheel size inch	1⁹⁄₁₆
Brakes	discs
Wheelbase inch	62.5
Seat height inch	26.5

Model	88ci Dyna Super Glide Sport
Code	FXDX
Years	1999-2002
No. cylinders	V-twin
Valves	ohv
Bore/stroke inch	95.3 x 101.6
Capacity cu in	88
Capacity cc	1,440
Ignition	electronic
No of gears	5
Drive system	chain/belt
Front suspension	teles
Rear suspension	s/a
Wheel type	wire, 2000-wire or cast alloy
Wheel size inch	1⁹⁄₁₆
Brakes	discs
Wheelbase inch	63.9
Seat height inch	27

The Sportster

The Evolution-engined Sportster had appeared in 1986 as an 54cu in (883cc) displacement machine. The range was enlarged with the addition of a 67cu in (1,010cc) model which was subsequently increased to 74cu in (1,200cc) displacement. The new engine components were noted for reducing wear and oil consumption in the Sportster models. The transmission was upgraded from four-speed to five-speed to take advantage of the better engine and follow the worldwide trend towards five- and six-speed motorcycles.

The 883 Sportster is the model with the smallest displacement in the Harley-Davidson range—54cu in (883cc)—and the model designation reflects the metric displacement. It is also the smallest model in the range

in terms of weight and length. The 883 model is one of a number of Sportster variants including 74cu in (1,200cc) models. Harley-Davidson market basic, custom, and competition inspired models as well as variations in components—particularly in the types of seats and wheels used to enhance these themes. Overall the Sportster is a traditional

BELOW: Scott Zampach carrying the Number One plate in the 883 Sportster race at Daytona.

RIGHT: A Bartels Harley-Davidson 883 Sportster dirt-track racer.

BELOW RIGHT: Sportster racing is popular the world over—here riders in the French 883 Cup Series are racing at the Montlhéry Circuit, near Paris, France.

motorcycle that has been sequentially upgraded through its long production run.

The 1996 model is powered by the proven OHV Evolution V2 engine with a five speed transmission and belt final drive runs around the rear pulley. The latter feature was newly introduced in 1993. The belt final drive gives a smoother ride especially when coupled with swingarm suspension and rear shock absorbers as they are here. The shock absorber controls the up and down movement of the swingarm in the tubular steel frame over bumps.

The 883 Sportster engine produces 49bhp at 6,000rpm and makes the bike capable of 110mph. The carburetor is a 40mm CV type and the airfilter is an oval racetrack-type, the ignition is electronic, and the exhaust pipes are Staggered duals. The

Sportster's oil tank holds three quarts. The wheels and brakes are traditional; at the front is a 19in spoked wheel and a single disc while at the rear is a 16in spoked wheel with a disc brake. Unlike the larger capacity Harley-Davidson the Sportster has a small and slender 2.25 gallon capacity gas tank which when coupled with buckhorn handlebars and the pair of handlebar mounted clocks—a speedometer and a tachometer—adds up to a unique appearance.

Around the world there are race series for the 883 model Sportsters on both surfaced and unsurfaced tracks. The 883 is used as the basis for dirt-track race bikes in an exclusively Harley-Davidson 883 series that runs

ABOVE: A 1998 74cu in (1,200cc) Evo Sportster.

ABOVE RIGHT: A 1997 Sportster Sport.

alongside the AMA sanctioned 750 class in Grand National events. There are also a series of surfaced track races exclusive to 54cu in (883cc) Sportsters such as US Twinsports.

Based on the success of the various Sportster circuit racing series around the world and the proven dirt- and flat-track heritage of the Sportster a new model appeared for 1996. This was the XL 1200S Sportster 1200 Sport. This nimble new model features a number of performance parts such as the

gas-assisted rear shock absorbers and cartridge-type damper valving on the front forks making the entire machine's suspension adjustable. The front end also features twin floating disc brakes and a disc rear brake. The styling reflects the bike's sporting aspirations; a pair of flat track style handlebars, the redesigned 3.3-gallon gas tank, and a dual sports seat are complemented by the 13-spoke cast wheels.

Both 883 and 1,200 Sportsters are what is described as "unit construction" which means that the engine crankcases and gearbox housing are cast as one large component. The 74cu in (1,200cc) Evolution-engined Sportster has an integral five-speed

transmission. Similar to the 883 the suspension was lowered, and a new emblem and custom style seat were all fitted. Also selected to give a custom appearance were the chromed bullet headlight, low-rise handlebars with stylish controls and hidden wiring, and tall risers. It had a 21in front traditional spoked wheel and 16in tough slotted alloy rear, plus belt drive and disc brakes. The factory offers the 1200 in a variety of finishes.

The racing origins and performance aspect of the machine is underlined by the tank badge, the manufacturer's name Harley-Davidson is prominent, so too is a V logo referring to the legendary V-twin and a panel of race-style chequer completes the design.

By 1997 the Sportster range had received a few relatively minor updates. The range consisted of four

Model	Sportster
Code	XLH883
Years	1986-2002
No. cylinders	V-twin
Valves	ohv
Bore/stroke inch	3 x 3¹³⁄₁₆
Capacity cu in	54
Capacity cc	883
Ignition	electronic
No of gears	4, 1991-5
Drive system	chain, 1993-chain/belt
Front suspension	teles
Rear suspension	s/a
Wheel type	cast alloy, 1993-wire, 1995-cast alloy, 1996-wire
Wheel size inch	1⁹⁄₁₆
Brakes	discs
Wheelbase inch	60.2
Seat height inch	28.5

Model	Sportster
Code	XLH1200
Years	1988-99
No. cylinders	V-twin
Valves	ohv
Bore/stroke inch	3½ x 3¹³⁄₁₆
Capacity cu in	74
Capacity cc	1,200
Ignition	electronic
No of gears	4, 1991-5
Drive system	chain, 1991-chain/belt
Front suspension	teles
Rear suspension	s/a
Wheel type	cast alloy, 1993-wire, 1995-cast alloy, 1998-wire
Wheel size inch	1⁹⁄₁₆
Brakes	discs
Wheelbase inch	60.2
Seat height inch	29

Model	Sportster
Code	XLH1100
Years	1986-87
No. cylinders	V-twin
Valves	ohv
Bore/stroke inch	3.35 × 3$\frac{13}{16}$
Capacity cu in	67.
Capacity cc	1,010
Ignition	electronic
No of gears	4
Drive system	chain
Front suspension	teles
Rear suspension	s/a
Wheel type	cast alloy
Wheel size inch	1$\frac{3}{16}$
Brakes	discs
Wheelbase inch	60.2
Seat height inch	28.5

models—Sportster 883, Sportster 883 Hugger, Sportster 1,200 Sport, and Sportster 1,200 Custom. The latter two models were introduced in 1996 but the biggest update was the restyling of the famous Sportster fuel tank to increase its capacity to 3.3 gallons. Evolution Sportsters remain in production despite the introduction of the Twin-Cam engine in the big twin models.

LEFT & BELOW: Sportster owners like to personalize their bikes, just like the owners of big twins do. For example, compare the machine below with those on page 418. These two Sportsters started out almost the same—they now look very different thanks to a few well chosen accessories.

Model	Sportster Custom
Code	XL1200C
Years	1996-2002
No. cylinders	V-twin
Valves	ohv
Bore/stroke inch	3$\frac{1}{2}$ × 3$\frac{13}{16}$
Capacity cu in	74
Capacity cc	1,200
Ignition	electronic
No of gears	5
Drive system	chain/belt
Front suspension	teles
Rear suspension	s/a
Wheel type	wire/disc
Wheel size inch	2$\frac{1}{16}$
Brakes	discs
Wheelbase inch	59
Seat height inch	27.1

ABOVE: A Sportster custom at Daytona.

LEFT: A close-up of an 883 Sportster engine.

RIGHT: A beautiful 1200 Sportster modified with a Storz XR conversion.

Model	Sportster Sport
Code	XL1200S
Years	1996-2002
No of cylinders	V-twin
Valves	OHV
Bore/stroke inch	3½ x 3¹³⁄₁₆
Capacity cu in	74
Capacity cc	1,200
Ignition	electronic
No of gears	5
Drive system	chain/belt
Front suspension	teles
Rear suspension	s/a
Wheel type	cast alloy
Wheel size inch	1⁹⁄₁₆
Brakes	discs
Wheelbase inch	60.2
Seat height inch	28.9

LEFT & TOP RIGHT: Two XL1200 Sportsters.

BELOW & BOTTOM RIGHT: Two 883 Sportsters; one (BELOW) with a Screamin' Eagle air filter.

VR1000

The VR1000 appeared on a Milwaukee drawing board in 1988 under the direction of Mark Tuttle Vice President of Engineering at Harley-Davidson. The intention was to build a water-cooled, fuel-injected V-twin-engined motorcycle for racing and development purposes. Roush Racing were given a development contract in 1989 and this company developed a working engine. One of the engineers from Roush Racing, Steve Scheibe, later joined Harley-Davidson as the company took the project back under its own roof. The VR1000 appeared on the grid at Daytona in March 1994 with Steve Scheibe as race team manager. The bike's first outing was unsuccessful, its engine broke down while the VR1000 was running well down the pack in the 200 mile race. For the remainder of 1994, French-Canadian racer Miguel Du Hamel rode the VR1000 and although he didn't win the worth of the bike became obvious as development work continued. For 1995 dirt-track racers Doug Chandler and Chris Carr were to ride VR1000s at events around the US. Chris Carr gave the bike its only position start of the year at a race in Pomona, California. Development work continued through 1996 with Carr and Thomas Wilson as riders. Wilson almost won a race on the bike at the AMA Superbike final in Mid-Ohio but a red flag incident elsewhere on the track handed the win to the previous lap leader. Pascal Picotte joined the team for 1997 and 1998 and was later joined by Scott Russell. The latter rider had won the Daytona 200 several times but he brought little success to the VR1000 team. The VR1000 project was closed in August 2001 but was soon followed by the announcement of the VRSCA V-Rod, another liquid-cooled V-twin with a similar model designation.

ABOVE RIGHT: A street-legal VR1000 on display at the 95th Anniversary birthday party in Milwaukee in 1998. Note the addition of lights to this otherwise pure race-bike.

BELOW RIGHT: Chris Carr aboard the factory VR1000 at Daytona.

BELOW: A VR1000 on display as part of a museum exhibition.

Buell

The Buell motorcycle company was created by Erik Buell who had began by working for the Harley factory; while there he spent time doing chassis design, testing, and so on. In 1983 he left and set up his own company, Buell. His first Harley-Davidson powered machine, the RR1000 Battletwin, used an XR1000 engine. This bike continued to be built until Buell ran out of XR engines at which point he turned his attention to the Evolution Sportster powerplant.

In 1993, the Harley-Davidson factory bought 49 percent of the company. They obviously thought this a shrewd investment as they then increased this share to 98 percent a year or so later, leaving Erik Buell as chairman and CTO.

Over the years, Buell have produced a whole range of models, from the single cylinder Blast to the XR1000 and Evolution Sportster engined-sports bikes. These include various forms of the Battletwin, RR1000, RR1200, RSS1200, Thunderbolt, Lightning, Cyclone, and Firebolt.

The Buell S1 Lightning was first produced in 1996, and had a 91hp Evolution Sportster engine that had been heavily "breathed on." This process included Lightning cylinder heads and a lightened crankshaft. The bodywork was styled as a hybrid cross between a dirt tracker and a road racer, and performance was very much the name of the game. This made it very popular with sport riders—especially in Europe where fast bikes have always sold well.

In 1997, Buell produced the M2 Cyclone; this bike was similar in concept

ABOVE RIGHT: Buell RR 1200.

BELOW RIGHT: Buell RR 1000.

BELOW: Buell Blast.

to the Lightning, but was in a slightly softer state tune, with ten horsepower less and a more relaxed riding style. A special edition bike, the White Lightning was built for the 1998 model year. This had a higher output engine called the Thunderstorm, which produced 101hp. Most of these were painted white, but the last models were available in a choice of other colors.

In 1999, the S1 Lightning was discontinued and replaced with the X1 Lightning, which had a fuel injected engine that was still rated at 91hp, as was the original S1.

The chassis design is one of the most notable features of the twin cylinder Buell range, especially the underslung shock absorber arrangement. While there are many design reasons for this layout, the main one is because a V-twin like the Sportster engine leaves little room for more conventional high performance rear suspension.

The Buells are also instantly recognisable due to their unique exhaust system. The short muffler sits under the engine and visually is an "acquired taste"—many bikers have commented that it looks like something off a tractor, but there are aftermarket pipes available for those who can't live with the originals. The air filter too is something that most owners replace very quickly; the S&S component is a popular alternative.

In short, the Buell sports bikes provide the answer for Harley fans who want performance above all else. One advantage of having been more or less taken over by the Harley-Davidson factory is that Buells are now available through the official Harley-Davidson dealer network, along with a full spares back up—all of which has to be good news for Buell owners.

OPPOSITE: *Buell S2 Thunderbolt (LEFT).*
Buell X1 Lightning (BELOW LEFT),
Buell Lightning (BELOW RIGHT),
Buell S2 Thunderbolt (BOTTOM LEFT),
Buell S1 Lightning (BOTTOM RIGHT).

THIS PAGE: *Buell X1 Lightning (RIGHT),*
Buell S1 Lightning (BELOW RIGHT).
Buell with a carbon air filter cover and lightweight
three-spoke cast wheels (CENTER RIGHT), Buell
S1 Lightning (CENTER LEFT),
Buell Thunderbolt (BOTTOM LEFT),
a close-up of the underslung rear shock absorber
on the Buell Thunderbolt
(BOTTOM RIGHT).

PAGE 426: *Buell Lightning.*

PAGE 427 TOP: *Buell RSS 1200.*

PAGE 427 BOTTOM: *Buell S2 Thunderbolt.*

RIGHT: A twin-cam with fat wheels.

The 21st Century

After nearly 100 years of business, Harley entered a new millennium as the most distinctive motorcycling brand in the United States and possibly the world. What could it look forward to and what would motorcycling be like in the 21st century?

There's no doubt that the new century will bring changes. Increasingly strict emission laws are

BELOW: A twin-cam Road King full-dresser.

RIGHT: A closer look at the front end of a twin-cam Heritage Softail.

sounding the death knell for air-cooled motorcycle engines around the world. Many motorcycle manufacturers have been making liquid-cooled engines for a number of years, but until now Harley-Davidson has stayed with the air-cooled V-twin—the staple of the company's

production since 1936. For the new century the company has embraced liquid-cooled engine technology and continues to embrace other forms of new technology in the shape of computer-aided production techniques at its factories. The company's latest motorcycle, the V-Rod (see page 442–443), is powered by the new Revolution engine—a step further than the Evolution—and will be the basis for Harley-Davidson's 21st Century motorcycles and its second century in the business.

In the new world, customer care and and customer relations are increasingly important. Harley has a devoted world-wide audience but needs to ensure that its relationship with its customers never again reaches the lows of the seventies. To do this Harley chose E.piphany Inc. to power its contact center initiatives, enabling proactive service and support for dealers and consumers worldwide.

BELOW RIGHT: A twin-cam police model.

BELOW: A Sportster with XR bodywork and high level Supertrapp exhausts.

OVERLEAF: Two twin-cam police models from Daytona.

The software provided Harley-Davidson with the ability to gain a more complete understanding of its customer base, anticipate the needs of its dealer network, and have the insight to execute the right service action to strengthen relationships. Business intelligence helps reduce response time on a range of issues; a robust service and highly personalized assistance improves response to customer and dealer inquiries

"Because of Harley-Davidson's unequalled product and extraordinary customer loyalty requirements, this was one of the most coveted

opportunities of the year," said Roger Siboni, president and CEO of E.piphany. "We are extremely proud to be chosen by Harley-Davidson as their partner and look forward to helping them further their exceptional reputation."

Paragon Technologies, Inc, a leading deliverer of "smart" material handling solutions, including systems, technologies, products, and services, announced that its SI Systems brand received an order late in March 2002 from the Harley-Davidson Motor Company to design, build, and install a state-of-the-art motorcycle assembly system that will be used for final assembly and testing of an existing model line of Harley-Davidson motorcycles. The system will be installed in a new manufacturing facility currently under construction at the existing York, Pennsylvania, site and will incorporate SI Systems' in-floor

Model	88cu in Dyna Super Glide T-Sport
Code	FXDXT
Years	2001–02
No. cylinders	V-twin
Valves	OHV
Bore/stroke inch	95.3 x 101.6
Capacity cu in	88
Capacity cc	1,440
Ignition	electronic
No of gears	5
Drive system	chain/belt
Front suspension	teles
Rear suspension	s/a
Wheel type	cast alloy
Wheel size inch	21 and 16, 2002 19 and 16
Brakes	discs
Wheelbase inch	63.1, 2002-62.2
Seat height inch	29.7, 2002-27.9

Model	Softail Standard
Code	FXST
Years	2000–02
No. cylinders	V-Twin
Valves	OHV
Bore/stroke mm	95.3 x 101.6
Capacity cu in	88
Capacity cc	1,440
Ignition	electronic
No of gears	5
Drive system	chain/belt
Front suspension	teles
Rear suspension	s/a
Wheel type	wire
Wheel size inch	21 and 16
Brakes	discs
Wheelbase inch	66.8
Seat height inch	25.3, 2001-26.1

Model	Springer Softail
Code	FXSTS
Years	2000–02
No. cylinders	V-Twin
Valves	OHV
Bore/stroke mm	95.3 x 101.6
Capacity cu in	88
Capacity cc	1,440
Ignition	electronic
No of gears	5
Drive system	chain/belt
Front suspension	teles
Rear suspension	s/a
Wheel type	wire
Wheel size inch	21 and 16
Brakes	discs
Wheelbase inch	65.3
Seat height inch	25.7

Model	Fat Boy
Code	FLSTF
Years	2000–02
No. cylinders	V-Twin
Valves	OHV
Bore/stroke mm	95.3 × 101.6
Capacity cu in	88
Capacity cc	1,440
Ignition	electronic
No of gears	5
Drive system	chain/belt
Front suspension	teles
Rear suspension	s/a
Wheel type	disc
Wheel size inch	16
Brakes	discs
Wheelbase inch	64.5
Seat height inch	25.5

Model	Heritage Softail Classic
Code	FLSTC
Years	2000–02
No. cylinders	V-Twin
Valves	OHV
Bore/stroke mm	95.3 × 101.6
Capacity cu in	88
Capacity cc	1,440
Ignition	electronic
No of gears	5
Drive system	chain/belt
Front suspension	teles
Rear suspension	s/a
Wheel type	wire
Wheel size inch	16
Brakes	discs
Wheelbase inch	64.2
Seat height inch	25.3

Model	Heritage Springer
Code	FLSTS
Years	2000–02
No. cylinders	V-Twin
Valves	OHV
Bore/stroke mm	95.3 × 101.6
Capacity cu in	88
Capacity cc	1,440
Ignition	electronic
No of gears	5
Drive system	chain/belt
Front suspension	teles
Rear suspension	s/a
Wheel type	wire
Wheel size inch	16
Brakes	discs
Wheelbase inch	64.2
Seat height inch	25.9

towline technology with innovative proprietary features.

The system will be the fourth such system SI Systems has provided for Harley-Davidson since 1997. Bill Johnson, President and CEO of Paragon Technologies, states:

"We are extremely pleased that Harley-Davidson has selected SI Systems to be their partner in automation for this very important project. Both our organizations have worked closely together for almost a year on this competitively bid project.

We look forward to continuing this relationship with Harley-Davidson by providing an ergonomically friendly system."

Similar towline-based assembly systems have been successfully integrated by SI Systems for vehicle

Model	Softail Deuce
Code	FXSTD
Years	2000-02
No. cylinders	V-Twin
Valves	OHV
Bore/stroke mm	95.3 × 101.6
Capacity cu in	88
Capacity cc	1,440
Ignition	electronic
No of gears	5
Drive system	chain/belt
Front suspension	teles
Rear suspension	s/a
Wheel type	wire/disc
Wheel size inch	21 and 17
Brakes	discs
Wheelbase inch	66.5
Seat height inch	25.9

Model	Softail Deuce (injection)
Code	FXSTDI
Years	2001-02
No. cylinders	V-Twin
Valves	OHV
Bore/stroke mm	95.3 × 101.6
Capacity cu in	88
Capacity cc	1,440
Ignition	electronic
No of gears	5
Drive system	chain/belt
Front suspension	teles
Rear suspension	s/a
Wheel type	wire/disc
Wheel size inch	21 and 17
Brakes	discs
Wheelbase inch	66.5
Seat height inch	28.3

Model	Fat Boy (injection)
Code	FLSTFI
Years	2001-02
No. cylinders	V-Twin
Valves	OHV
Bore/stroke mm	95.3 × 101.6
Capacity cu in	88
Capacity cc	1,440
Ignition	electronic
No of gears	5
Drive system	chain/belt
Front suspension	teles
Rear suspension	s/a
Wheel type	disc
Wheel size inch	16
Brakes	discs
Wheelbase inch	64.4
Seat height inch	26.5

manufacturers, such as Case Tractor, New Holland Tractor, Oshkosh Truck, McNeilus Truck, JLG, and numerous furniture manufacturers as well.

Today Harley-Davidson, Inc. is the parent company for the group of

ABOVE: A British-run Buell racing bike looks lean and mean.

OVERLEAF: "Deuce"—a fuel-injected twin-cam Softail.

companies doing business as Harley-Davidson Motor Company, Buell Motorcycle Company, and Harley-Davidson Financial Services. Harley-Davidson Motor Company, the only major United States-based motorcycle manufacturer, produces

Model	Heritage Softail Classic (injection)
Code	FLSTCI
Years	2001–02
No. cylinders	V-Twin
Valves	OHV
Bore/stroke mm	95.3 × 101.6
Capacity cu in	88
Capacity cc	1,440
Ignition	electronic
No of gears	5
Drive system	chain/belt
Front suspension	teles
Rear suspension	s/a
Wheel type	wire
Wheel size inch	16
Brakes	discs
Wheelbase inch	64.4
Seat height inch	26.5

Model	Sportster Sport
Code	XL1200S
Years	1996-2002
No. cylinders	V-twin
Valves	OHV
Bore/stroke inch	3½ × 3¹³⁄₁₆
Capacity cu in	74
Capacity cc	1,200
Ignition	electronic
No of gears	5
Drive system	chain/belt
Front suspension	teles
Rear suspension	s/a
Wheel type	cast alloy
Wheel size inch	19 and 16
Brakes	discs
Wheelbase inch	60.2
Seat height inch	28.9

Model	Sportster Custom 53
Code	XL53C
Years	1998-2002
No. cylinders	V-twin
Valves	OHV
Bore/stroke inch	3 × 3¹³⁄₁₆
Capacity cu in	55
Capacity cc	883
Ignition	electronic
No of gears	5
Drive system	chain/belt
Front suspension	teles
Rear suspension	s/a
Wheel type	wire/disc
Wheel size inch	21 and 16
Brakes	discs
Wheelbase inch	60
Seat height inch	27.5

heavyweight motorcycles and offers a complete line of motorcycle parts, accessories, apparel and general merchandise. Buell Motorcycle Company produces sport and sport-touring motorcycles. Harley-Davidson Financial Services, Inc. provides wholesale and retail financing and insurance programs to Harley-Davidson dealers and customers.

Harley's Milwaukee neighbor, the Miller Brewing Company has joined the Harley-Davidson Motor Company in celebration of the motorcycle maker's 100th Anniversary. As the oldest of the major breweries in the United States, Miller Brewing Company understands what it takes to succeed over the long haul like Harley-Davidson. And just as important, the company that created Miller Time understands the importance of celebrating such success. So, Miller announced that it will be an exclusive malt beverage

BELOW RIGHT: A 2000 Dyna Super-Glide out for a blast through town.

BELOW: A Heritage Softail

OVERLEAF: Three FLTR Road-Glides at the Sturgis rally in 2000.

sponsor of the Harley-Davidson 100th Anniversary celebration, which begins during the summer of 2002 and continues through August 2003. The partnership will include Miller's involvement in the Harley-Davidson 100th Anniversary Open Road Tour; the Ride Home; and the Celebration and the Party, both in Wisconsin. The two Milwaukee-based icons have partnered on a variety of marketing efforts in the past, including the Harley-Davidson 90th and 95th

anniversaries.

"We are proud to join our friends at Harley-Davidson in celebrating the 100th birthday of the best motorcycles in the world," said John Bowlin, Miller's president and chief executive officer. "Millions of Harley-Davidson aficionados across the world will experience the ultimate Miller Time at the numerous events leading up to the Ride Home. All of us at Miller Brewing Company look forward to raising a Miller Lite in a toast to Harley-Davidson's phenomenal success." Miller is a world-wide sponsor with category exclusivity, joining Ford Motor Company and AOL Time Warner.

Almost 2.5 million people are expected to come together between July 2002 and August 2003 to celebrate the legendary motorcycle manufacturer's 100th Anniversary and kick off the Motor Company's next 100 years. The Open Road Tour,

a 25-acre, 10-city global traveling festival, will kick off in Atlanta. Three major exhibits, the Journey, the Machine, and the Culture, will be featured on the festival grounds during Open Road Tour events. The Journey looks at 100 years of Harley-Davidson; the Machine looks at the motorcycles and the engine; and the Culture looks at Harley-Davidson in the world. The primary food and beverage concession area at the 10 Open Road Tour and Celebration events will be named the Miller Roadside Café.

Then, during August 2003, Harley-Davidson enthusiasts can join the Ride Home, four organized rides throughout the United States to Milwaukee for the August 28–30 Celebration. The 14-month commemoration closes with the Party on August 31, 2003, in Milwaukee. Miller will extend its partnership with the Harley-Davidson 100th Anniversary activities through advertising, promotions, retail merchandising, and public relations. The tagline on Miller's point-of-sale and merchandising supporting the partnership will be, "Miller Celebrates 100 Years of Harley-Davidson."

Legal-drinking-age consumers had an opportunity to win a 2003 Harley-Davidson Fat Boy motorcycle, courtesy of the Miller High Life Motorcycle Sweepstakes promotion.

And so, a hundred years after the company was founded in 1903, Harley-Davidson's future seems more assured than it has for some time. The blend of nostalgia and style, the acceptance and embracing of the individuality of its admirers, the frisson that accompanies the bad boy image all have contributed to the success of the brand. Unlike any other US motorcycle manufacturer Harley was able to withstand the conquest of the United States by the Japanese, and one of the ways it did so was by learning that it did not have to compete in every market, it just needed to produce big American bikes for people who liked the image and the style. Sensible marketing, the brilliant work of Willie G, and the pull of retro styling did the trick. Once Harley got it right, it blew the opposition away. Indeed, in 1998 the opening of a $90 million factory in Kansas City, Missouri, showed that it intended to expand. Production today is nearly 200,000 bikes a year and output had been improved by the new paintshop at the assembly plant in York, Pennsylvania, and will improved further by the methods outlined at the start of this chapter.

Harley-Davidson and its customers are looking forward to a great 100th birthday. Who's to say it won't make 200?

The V-Rod

The VRSCA V-Rod was inspired by the Harley-Davidson VR1000 race-bike program and developed by the company's Powertrain Engineering team. The new engine is the first completely new power unit from Harley-Davidson since the Model K of 1957. The new engine is appropriately described as the Revolution V-twin because the company have moved from 45-degree, air-cooled V-twin engines to 60-degree liquid-cooled V-twin engines. Through a bore and stroke of 3.94in x 2.84in the Revolution displaces 69cu in (1,130cc) and with a compression ratio of 11.3:1 produces 115bhp at 8,250 rpm. The machine is capable of 47 highway or 37 city miles to the gallon. It has a wet sump engine that holds one gallon of oil. The engine features dual overhead camshafts (dohc), a one-piece crankshaft and electronic sequential port fuel injection. It also features ACR—Automatic Compression Release—to ease cold starting. As the engine is the first liquid-cooled Harley-Davidson engine it has numerous engineering features that aren't normally associated with Harley engines. Much of the development was carried out in conjunction with Porsche who have experience of dealing with strict European emission laws. The horizontally-split crankcases house a lightweight "pork chop" crankshaft that has the connecting rods bolted to it. These conrods spin on automotive-type plain bearings that are lubricated by a new oil pump that keeps the oil pressure as high as necessary. At the top of the engine, each cylinder head holds four valves and above these are four chain-driven camshafts and the engine revs to 9,100 rpm. The fuel-injected engine, through a system of rubber mounts and an internal chain driven counter-balancer, vibrates little. It is connected with a new design of five-speed transmission and the whole unit is installed in Harley-Davidson's first perimeter frame. The transmission has spur gears for first and fifth and helical cut second, third and fourth gears. Another spur gear links the transmission to the engine in order to do away with a noisy primary drive chain and a nine-plate clutch is fitted. The external-style frame gives the motorcycle a different appearance to every Harley-Davidson that has gone before but also offers considerable rigidity which enhances the motorcycle's handling.

The V-Rod has a 67.5-inch wheelbase and the frame features a 34-degree rake and 38-degree fork angle. This offset angle enhances the long, low look if the V-Rod. The frame's neck geometry measures 34 degrees and the extra four degrees are built into the fork yokes. This will allow Harley-Davidson to build more sporting models around the same frame in future by reducing the angle incorporated into the yokes. The fork legs are 49mm in diameter and a huge aluminum swinging arm locates the rear wheel and provides suspension in conjunction with a pair of shock absorbers. The four-gallon fuel tank is located under the seat, the sidepanels fenders, chainguard, and upper cowl are all made from aluminium and the

Model	VRSCA
Code	V-Rod
Years	2002
No. cylinders	V-Twin
Valves	dohc, 4 valve
Bore/stroke mm	100 × 72
Capacity cu in	69
Capacity cc	1,130
Ignition	
No of gears	5
Drive system	chain/belt
Front suspension	teles
Rear suspension	s/a
Wheel type	disc
Wheel size inch	19 and 18
Brakes	discs
Wheelbase inch	67.4
Seat height inch	26

headlamp is aerodynamically styled. Solid alloy wheels are fitted front and rear, 19 and 18 inches diameter respectively. Brakes, front and rear, are fully floating disc brakes with four-pot calipers on each. The hydraulic fluid for these is carried in braided steel brakelines. Harley-Davidson believe that the new machine represents "a fusion of traditional Harley-Davidson styling with liquid-cooled contemporary performance to create a new family of power infused custom motorcycles." Willie G. Davidson, grandson of the founders and Vice President of

ABOVE: The start of a whole new generation of Harley-Davidsons—the V-Rod.

Styling believes that, "V-Rod is an extension of our air-cooled V-Twin heritage." The Vice President of Engineering, Earl Werner stated that, "This all-American custom was inspired by Harley-Davidson's drag racing heritage and the VR1000 Superbike race engine. It's really a stunning styling and engineering accomplishment."

Bibliography

Cycle Magazine: "Cycle Road Test: Harley-Davidson 1,200cc Super Glide;" Ziff-Davis Publishing Company, November 1970.

Easyriders Magazine: "Wino' Willie Forkner. All The Old Romance Retold;" Paisano Publications, September 1986.

Easyriders Magazine: "Gary Bang: A Junkie Hooked On Two Wheels;" Paisano Publications, March 1987.

Bacon, Roy (et al): *Harley-Davidson*; Thunder Bay Press, 1999.

Barger, Ralph "Sonny": *Hell's Angel*; Fourth Estate, 2000.

Freedman, J. F.: *Against the Wind*; The Penguin Group, 1991.

Girdler, A.: *Illustrated Harley-Davidson Buyer's Guide*; Motorbooks, 1986.

Girdler, A.: *Harley Racers*; Motorbooks, 1987.

Harris, M.: *Bikers Birth of a Modern Day Outlaw*; Faber and Faber, 1985.

Iron Horse Magazine: *Look Homeward Angel*; J.Q. Adams Productions Inc., December 1994.

Jones, J.: *WWII*; Leo Cooper Ltd, 1975.

Kaye, H. R.: *A Place in Hell*; Holloway House Publishing Co, 1968.

Lavigne, Y.: *Hell's Angels*; Carol Publishing Group, 1987.

MacDonald, W. N.: *Outlaw Motorcycle Gangs*; *Royal Canadian Mounted Police Gazette*, 1994.

Mauldin, Bill: *The Brass Ring*; W. W. Norton & Co Inc, 1971.

Mitchell, D.: *Harley-Davidson Chronicle*; Publications International Inc., 1996.

Reynolds, F. and McClure, M.: *Freewheelin Frank*; Grove Press Inc, 1967.

Scalzo, J.: *The Bart Markel Story*; Bond/Parkhurst Books, 1972.

Steinbeck, J.: *The Grapes of Wrath*; William Heinemann, 1939.

Sucher, H. V.: *Harley-Davidson*; Haynes, 1981.

Thompson, H. S.: *Hell's Angels*; Random House, 1966.

Wethern, G. & Colnett, V.: *A Wayward Angel*; Transworld Publishers Ltd, 1979.

Wolf, D. R.: *The Rebels: a Brotherhood of Outlaw Bikers*; University of Toronto Press, 1991.

Yates, B.: *Outlaw Machine*; Little, Brown and Co, 1999.

Woody Guthrie, "Woody Sez" column in *People's World*, San Francisco, CA, c. 1939–40; reprinted in Marjorie Guthrie et al (eds.): *Woody Sez*; New York, NY, 1975.

Lyrics as recorded by Woody Guthrie, RCA Studios, Camden, NJ, 26 April 1940; released on *Dust Bowl Ballads*, transcribed by Manfred Helfert. © 1960 Hollis Music Inc., New York, NY (as "Going Down the Road")

Website: http://www.harleydavidson.com

Acknowledgements

This book is the result of the work of a number of contributers: Garry Stuart provided the excellent photographs; Roy Bacon supplied the list of types and boxed information; Patrick Hook supplied the captions; John Carroll wrote the text.

Picture Credits

All the photography for this book, including the back cover photography, was provided by kind courtesy of © Garry Stuart. © Jeff Hackett for the photograph on the front cover.

INDEX